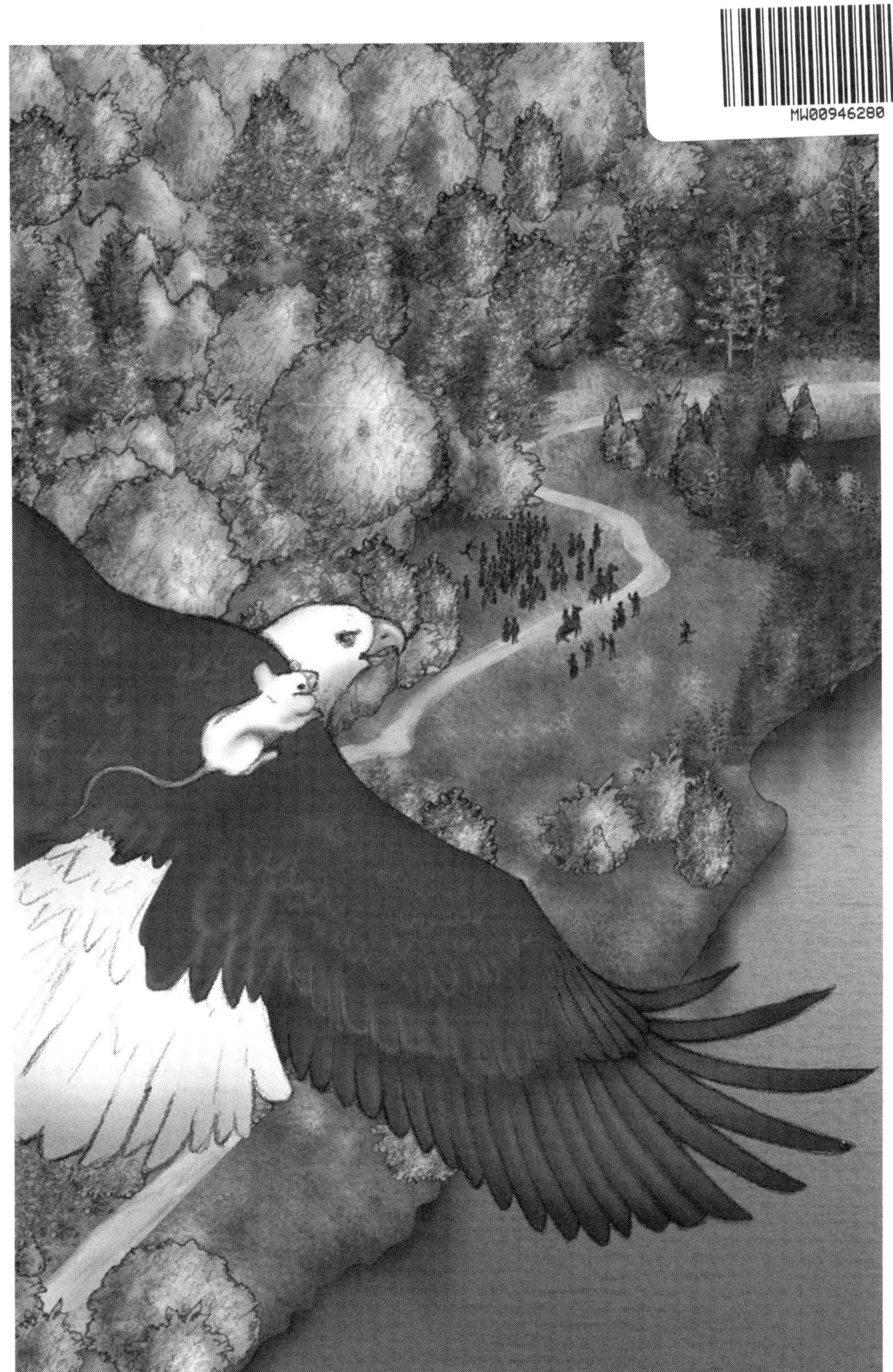

Happy Learning! Claire CR Yattz

VRK STUDY GUIDE

A companion guide for Jenny L. Cote's
The Voice, the Revolution, and the Key

Jenny L. Cote

Epic Order of the Seven®

VRK STUDY GUIDE, A Companion Guide for Jenny L. Cote's The Voice, the Revolution, and the Key, Version 1.0

Published by Jenny L. Cote Publications www.epicorderoftheseven.com

This Study Guide is available at www.epicorderoftheseven.com as a digital download document for printing at home in two formats: condensed and answer ready. (Limited to one download per family with license to print copies for each child within that family.)

Content creation by Claire Roberts Foltz
Cover and internal illustrations by Rob Moffitt, Chicago, Illinois.
Editing by Rich Cairnes, Walworth, Wisconsin.
Proofreading by Nancy Foltz, Milton, Georgia.

What Readers are Saying

The Voice, the Revolution, and the Key brings American history to life. This companion VRK Study Guide is extensive and could easily be utilized for your homeschool history and literature curriculum, spanning at least a semester. The content of each is thoroughly researched and makes learning exciting. We appreciated being able to encompass multiple learning styles by using the print and audio versions of the book along with this Study Guide. I found the format of the final exam to be easy to use, which I appreciate as a homeschool mom. We really cannot say enough good things about this resource! *-Carol R., Homeschool Mom, Mosinee, WI*

I love learning, and this VRK Study Guide is the perfect opportunity to learn even more from this well-researched book. I can't wait for any and all Study Guides that come in the future for these epic books. *-Emma R., 18, Mosinee, WI*

The VRK Study Guide was well done and helped make remembering history facts easier. *-Micah R., 14, Mosinee, WI*

If you enjoyed *The Voice the Revolution and the Key* by Jenny L. Cote, then you will love the VRK Study Guide. The VRK Study Guide helps you dig deeper. Each chapter has its own Study Guide questions at three levels. The questions cause you to discover information that you otherwise would have missed. It's perfect for those who love to learn! *-Elizabeth R., 16, Mosinee, WI*

Jenny L. Cote and Claire Roberts Foltz have done an EPIC job with the VRK Study Guide. It is fun, informative, and user friendly. I especially enjoyed Nigel's Nuggets! *-Edan, 16, CA*

It was an amazing experience and way different than just reading the book. I got to think back on not only the outline of the story, but the history behind the story as well. Sometimes I would go deeper into research because I wanted to learn more on a specific topic. I like how the curriculum is very flexible and I can easily move up or down a level when needed. It was fun and an extraordinary way to show how much HIStory I had learned from the experience. *-Chad Velez, 13, Houston, TX*

The VRK Study Guide is a wonderful companion to the book. I love that my son is getting to dig deeper into the history of our great nation. *-Rosalyn G. -Homeschool Mom Cary, NC*

I really enjoy the Cato's Eagle Eye View and Nigel's Nuggets. I think kids will really enjoy the VRK Study Guide. *-Nathaniel G.,10, Cary, NC*

What a great way to teach U.S. History through great literature. Jenny L. Cote's gift of writing historical fiction coupled with this VRK Study Guide equals a BIG win and opportunity to teach U.S. History in a fun, engaging way. Great to use in a co-op setting and for homeschool families. I like how the different levels allow you to decide the depth you want to go. *-Marlene G., Homeschool mom of two, Mesa, AZ*

We love the Nigel's Nuggets and Cato's Eagle Eye View sections in each chapter. The VRK Study Guide is school in a fun way, just like Jenny L. Cote makes HIStory come alive. It's also a good way to review what you read and pull extra knowledge from the books. We are looking forward to the entire Study Guide series!! *-Madison (16) and Cameron (12), Mesa AZ*

A Word from Jenny L. Cote

After years of requests from parents, grandparents, and educators in the United States and abroad, we are thrilled to offer the first Study Guide to accompany my books. Given the crucial need for the next generation to understand America's true, comprehensive founding history, we decided to begin with the books on the American Revolution but will add Study Guides for the first six Biblical titles as well.

VRK Study Guide Content Creator Claire Roberts Foltz is extremely qualified not only as a certified teacher, but she serves as the Critique Team Leader for my books. She has been part of the writing of these books since page one of book one and was pivotal in the development of the Epic Order of the Seven plotline and brand. She truly is my main muse, and her continual encouragement, support and *eagle eye* for plot and character development has made these books truly EPIC.

It is my hope that through this VRK Study Guide you will learn about America's founding history in a fun way and at a detailed level that we have not seen offered elsewhere. May you fully understand what it took for America to become free and independent and may you fall in love with her to pick up the mantle of greatness in serving our nation. It's up to you as the next generation to know America's story and preserve her solid foundation of a republic while making her the best she's ever been.

Know that you are loved, and you are able!

Jenny L. Cote

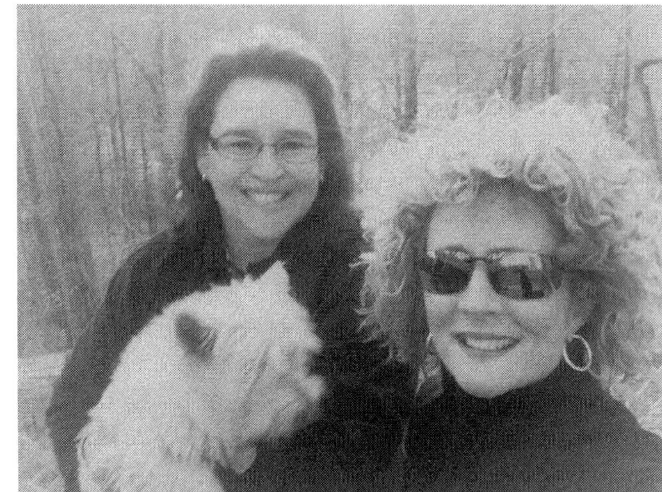

Claire Roberts Foltz

is an author, speaker, and certified teacher in Language Arts, Social Studies, Political Science and Government grades 6-12, all core middle school subjects, and ESOL for all ages. She is also a veteran homeschool teacher for grades K-12. Claire was the first woman student athletic trainer to graduate from the University of Georgia3 and holds a master's degree in Exercise Physiology from the University of Central Florida. Claire was the first Director of Sports Medicine and established the Sports Medicine Program at Children's Healthcare of Atlanta (formerly Scottish Rite Children's Medical Center). She managed her husband's dental practice for many years. Claire and her husband, Jeff, are the proud parents of two grown children, two adorable grandchildren, and one incredible West Highland White Terrier.

. . . He marked out their appointed times in history . . .

— Acts 17:26

INTRODUCTION

The VRK Study Guide is a companion guide for Jenny L. Cote's novel, *The Voice, the Revolution, and the Key.* Although you will find questions in multiple academic content areas, along with imaginative and fun activities related to the novel, it is not designed to be used as a Unit Study.

Three levels of reading content and comprehension questions are included in the VRK Study Guide and are explained below. Parents and students should determine which individual level is most appropriate, but feel free to change levels at any time. As a general guideline, the Eaglet level is intended for upper elementary school students. The Fledgling and Eagle levels are intended for middle and high school students. However, any level may be used by any student. The determination of which level is appropriate is best made by a parent or teacher.

The VRK Study Guide, along with the included testing materials may be used for History or Literature credit on an academic transcript at the middle or high school levels.

There are two printable formats available for this Study Guide in digital form at www.epicorderoftheseven.com. The first contains the questions for each chapter with minimal writing space. The second, answer ready, format has plenty of white space included for writing out answers to questions. The second format is specifically designed for students who require white space, such as students with dyslexia.

As you are working through the VRK Study Guide, you will notice that the questions are in the order that the material appears in the book. Where possible, the exact wording from the book is used to provide context clues. For example, if Nigel said the word "delighted" in the book, the word "delighted" would be likely to appear in the Study Guide question.

There are four Book Part Tests and a Final Examination along with supporting materials and instructions for each and are intended for use by all levels of students.

The Epic Order of the Seven will be referenced continually throughout this Study Guide and will be abbreviated EO7. *The Voice, the Revolution, and the Key* will also be referenced throughout this Study Guide and abbreviated as VRK.

Readers will earn one eagle feather upon completion of each Chapter Guide and one eagle feather upon completion of each Nigel's Nuggets as determined by the reader and their teacher. There are ten content or reading comprehension questions, one Nigel's Nuggets Challenge, and one Cato's Eagle Eye View game activity for each level of each Chapter Guide. Eaglet readers may earn one eagle feather for completion of both portions of Cato's Eagle-Eye View in lieu of Nigel's Nuggets for any given chapter.

Three Levels of the Study Guide

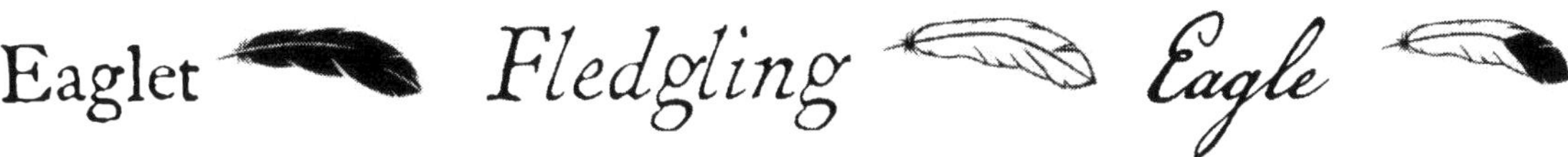

The Eaglet level is intended for families, homeschool co-ops, or classroom teachers who want "one-stop shopping." Eaglet questions, with very few exceptions, are content questions with short answers. The Answer Keys provided for this level include full answers as well as page number references.

The Fledgling level is an expansion of the Eaglet level with additional comprehension, short-answer, and essay questions. The Eagle level is a slight expansion of the Fledgling level. There are more comprehension and thought questions, as well as longer assignments of essay questions on the Eagle level. The Fledgling and Eagle levels will require more involvement on the part of the parent or teacher.

As a general guideline, when The VRK Study Guide is used in a homeschool co-op, or classroom setting, the Eaglet level is recommended. Teachers may choose to pull from Fledgling and/or Eagle level questions during lesson preparation and use them to augment Eaglet level questions.

Bonus Materials with Nigel and Cato

The VRK Study Guide is thematically framed around two beloved character friends from the book: "Nigel" the British mouse and "Cato" the bald eagle. Bonus materials give readers both a detailed and a broad understanding of the material for each chapter in a fun way.

Nigel's Nuggets

These are non-level-specific challenges from Nigel to the reader. They involve hunting down nuggets of research treasure in one of four ways: Books to thumb through, Museums to mosey through, People to talk to, and Grounds to walk through.

A reader's quest for Nigel's Nuggets might naturally lead to an Internet search. Please conduct all Internet searches under the guidance of an adult. Nigel's Nuggets are typically posed in a question-and-answer format. However, it is hoped that all manner of projects may be dreamed up and carried out by the reader's individual creativity.

Jenny L. Cote would love to see pictures of your favorite Nigel's Nuggets creations. They should be sent to jenny@epicorderoftheseven.com and may appear on her website.

Cato's Eagle-Eye View

Readers will look at each chapter from the big picture perspective of Cato the bald eagle as he "mounts up with wings" (Isaiah 40:31). No specific suggestions are given, to allow readers' imaginations to soar with the eagles. Readers will summarize each chapter in two ways: Gliding and Soaring. The Flashcard Game using the Soaring index cards can be played anytime as readers work through the VRK Study Guide.

Gliding: Summarize each chapter in three to five sentences, written or orally.

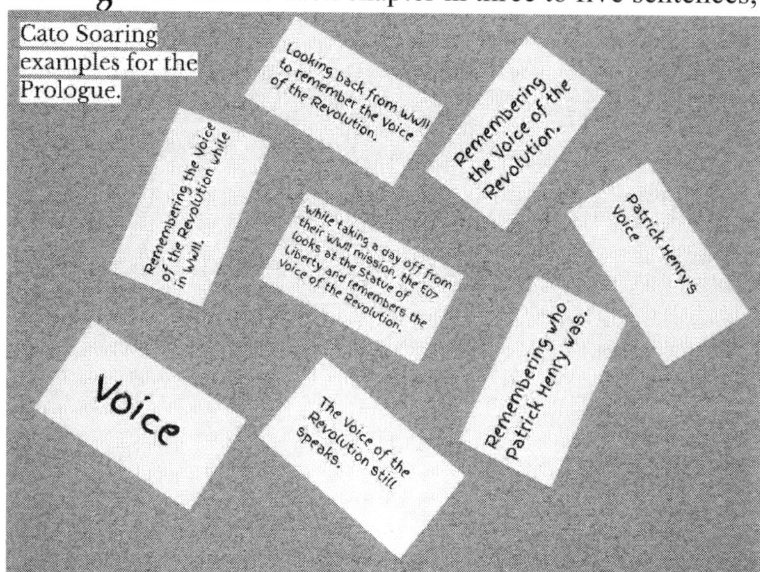
Looking back from WWII to remember the Voice of the Revolution.
Remembering the Voice of the Revolution.
Remembering the Voice of the Revolution while in WWII.
While taking a day off from their WWII mission, the EO7 looks at the Statue of Liberty and remembers the Voice of the Revolution.
Patrick Henry's Voice
Remembering who Patrick Henry was.
Voice
The Voice of the Revolution still Speaks.
Cato Soaring examples for the Prologue.

Soaring: Summarize each chapter in one word, phrase, or sentence, and write it on an index card with the chapter number and title written on the other side.

Soaring Flashcard Game: Shuffle all your Soaring flashcards. Player 1 reads the number and/or title of a chapter on one side of a flashcard. Player 2 answers with the Soaring Summarization on the other side of the flashcard. Reshuffle your flashcards, switch players if desired, and play three times.

Answer Key

An answer key is located in the back of the VRK Study Guide. Page number references are provided where appropriate for all levels. For Fledgling and Eagle levels, references such as "Research" or "The Bible" are provided when answers lie outside the pages of *The Voice, the Revolution, and the Key.*

A Word about the Wording

Some of the questions in the VRK Study Guide may seem oddly worded. This is because we have chosen not to end a sentence with a preposition where possible. This decision was made to reinforce the reader's ongoing grammar instruction, and to use formal grammar, as readers will be exposed to the vernacular of the mid- to late eighteenth century in this series. Readers will note that the practice of not ending a sentence with a preposition was favored by our Founding Fathers.

A Work in Progress

The VRK Study Guide is a work in progress. The feedback we receive from families who have used it will be vital in helping us improve this study guide and all future study guides which will be written to accompany Jenny L. Cote's novels. Feedback may be sent to cbrfoltz@gmail.com and to jenny@epicorderoftheseven.com.

CONTENTS

CHAPTER GUIDES

Getting Started

1) Define the Eaglet, Fledgling, and Eagle (Adult) phases of the life of a bald eagle.

2) How many eagle feathers can you earn if you complete one level of every Chapter Guide and Nigel's Nuggets for the VRK Study Guide, which includes Getting Started and the Prologue Chapter Guide? Approximately how many eagle feathers does an adult bald eagle have, rounded to the nearest thousand?

3) Is it legal to possess an eagle feather in the United States, even if you find it on the ground?

Use the Character Profiles on pages xxv–xxvi to match the Epic Order of the Seven (EO7) team member with their description.

Gillamon — A) A well-fed orange Irish cat, scared of everything, lives to eat and sleep, immortal

Max — B) A White West Highland Terrier, sweet, feisty, and always sticking up for the underdog, immortal

Al — C) A jolly, intellectual British mouse, joined the Team in Egypt, has impeccable manners, loves music, flies by carrier pigeon, immortal

Liz — D) A wise mountain goat, serves as a spiritual being, delivers mission assignments to the EO7, can take any form, immortal

Kate — E) A sweet lamb from Judea, serves as a guide in the IAMISPHERE, can take any shape or form, immortal

Nigel — F) Curly-haired Black Scottish Terrier, faithful leader of the Team, brave, immortal

Clarie — G) Petite, brilliant black cat from Normandy, France, strategic leader of the team, immortal

Nigel's Nuggets

Getting Started

Greetings! Nigel P. Monaco here. I am *terribly* excited that you are going to complete the VRK Study Guide, and use that keen mind of yours to take on my challenges. I am certain you shall create some splendid masterpieces. Therefore, we must have a means to document your progress. Right! You shall need to create something for displaying all the eagle feathers you shall earn whilst completing the Chapter Guides and Nigel's Nuggets.

Please make sure your display identifies the object of our quest:
The Voice, the Revolution, and the Key.

In addition, might I suggest that you keep up with the thrill of the mission by tuning into Season Two of the Epic Order of the Seven, The Podcast, which features *The Voice, the Revolution, and the Key?* I shan't spill the beans, but you'll soon discover that I am off on a brilliant new venture, and I shall be enlisting your help. You can tune in here:
https://www.epicorderoftheseven.com/podcast

Do me the favor of emailing a picture of your creation to jenny@epicorderoftheseven.com.
You might just see your work displayed on Jenny L. Cote's website. That would take the biscuit!

Off I go! I simply cannot *wait* to see your work!

Cato's Eagle-Eye View

Getting Started

Locate video footage of a live Eagle Cam to view a nest of bald eagles with their eaglets. (Ex: https://dukefarms.org/making-an-impact/eagle-cam/)

Eaglet

Prologue: Jewels in Her Crown

1) Name the city in which the Prologue is set.

2) What year is the Prologue set?

3) What is happening all over the world during the time of the Prologue?

4) Who is Liz's "Patrick?"

5) What major thing happened in America during Patrick's life?

6) Match the person to their role in the Revolutionary War as described in the Prologue:

The Voice	Thomas Jefferson
The Pen	Patrick Henry
The Sword	George Washington

7) What are the seven words for which Patrick Henry is most famous?

8) Who or what is Lady Liberty?

9) What event is the EO7 enjoying on their day off?

10) Name all the things Al ate.

Prologue: Jewels in Her Crown

1) Where is the Prologue set? What year? What is going on all over the world at this time?

2) Who were the Voice, the Pen, and the Sword of the Revolution, and why were they given those names?

3) What is the team celebrating, how long had this event been going on, and where was it first held?

4) What is foreshadowing in literature?

5) Is the setting of the Prologue foreshadowing something? If so, what? Do you think that Jenny L. Cote will write about it?

6) Who is the "Patrick" Liz is thinking about, and what are his seven most famous words?

7) SEVEN is an important number in Jenny L. Cote's books. Name three different "sevens" found in the Prologue.

8) Who is Lady Liberty? Have we seen someone like her before in any of Jenny L. Cote's writing(s)? Optional: If so, in which book(s)?

9) Al is not feeling well. Why? Does this happen to him often? What is he wearing to the celebration on his day off?

10) Which members of the EO7 are present in the Prologue and which are not?

Prologue: Jewels in Her Crown

1) Describe the setting of the Prologue. Where and when does it take place? What is going on in the world at the time?

2) This book leads up to the eve of a war—which one? Three major characters and their roles on behalf of the Colonies in the Revolutionary War are foreshadowed in the Prologue. Name them, tell where they were born, and what their roles were.

3) List each EO7 character who appears in the Prologue. Give an example of one of their characteristics from the Character Profiles starting on page xxv. Describe how this characteristic is exhibited in the Prologue.

4) The Prologue foreshadows another EO7 mission. What do you think it will be? Do you think you will be able to read about it in this book, in this series, or in a future series that Jenny L. Cote will write?

5) Who is the main character in this book? For which seven words is he most widely known? What does Liz think about him being known for those seven words?

6) Share at least three other quotations from our main character revealed in the Prologue. Pick one quotation and tell what it means, and why you think this quotation is relevant today.

7) SEVEN is an important number in Jenny L. Cote's books. Why? Give three examples of "sevens" in the Prologue.

8) Where is Al going at the end of the Prologue? Where is it located? Why is he scared? Why might anyone be scared to be on Al's assignment?

9) Nigel is flying to a Battleship at the end of the Prologue. Why did Jenny L. Cote name the ship? Do you think the ship will be important later in history?

10) Read "A WORD FROM THE AUTHOR," on page 607. What triple genre does Jenny L. Cote write? Give at least two examples of different aspects of the genre from the Prologue.

Nigel's Nuggets

Prologue: Jewels in Her Crown

Nigel leaves the celebration to land on the USS Nevada.

A) First, search the Internet for "Judge Chuck Weller, USS Nevada article." Read Judge Weller's article about the Nevada. What did you learn about her? Why would you call a ship a "her?"

B) Now do a separate Internet search for "the USS Nevada." You should see articles from the fall of 2020. What is the latest news about the USS Nevada?

Cato's Eagle-Eye View

Prologue: Jewels in Her Crown

Gliding: Summarize the chapter in three to five sentences, written or orally.

Soaring: Summarize the chapter in one word, phrase, or sentence, and write it on an index card with the chapter number and title written on the other side.

Soaring Flashcard Game: Shuffle all your Soaring flashcards. Player 1 reads the number and/or title of a chapter on one side of a flashcard. Player 2 answers with the Soaring Summarization on the other side of the flashcard. Reshuffle your flashcards, switch players if desired, and play three times.

PART ONE: FIDDLING AROUND (1743-45)

Eaglet

Chapter 1: Down to the Letter

1) Where and when is Chapter 1 set?

2) What performance had the EO7 just attended at the start of Chapter 1?

3) What is Nigel's favorite cheese?

4) What did the King of England do during the *Hallelujah Chorus?*

5) What is the IAMISPHERE?

6) Who is the first boy the EO7 sees in the IAMISPHERE? Who will be assigned "primarily" to him?

7) Which boy does the EO7 see second in the IAMISPHERE? Who will be assigned to him?

8) Which human will be Nigel's mission?

9) The third boy the EO7sees in the IAMISPHERE is an eleven-year-old boy who is crying over the loss of his father. Name him.

10) Kate is assigned to a human who writes a letter to his cousin, John Henry, in America. Who is Kate's human for this mission?

Fledgling

Chapter 1: Down to the Letter

1) Where and when is Chapter 1 set? What premiere had the EO7 just attended? What did the King of England do during the performance?

2) What is the IAMISPHERE? How are the EO7 team members called to the IAMISPHERE in Chapter 1? Who is there to meet them?

3) The EO7 meets three boys in the IAMISPHERE. Who are they? Which one will be Al's human, and which one will be Liz's next human?

4) Who is Kate's human? What do we know about him after reading Chapter 1?

5) What verses is Kate's human reading? What events do they describe? What is his response to what he reads?

6) The EO7 sees a panel with Liz at the desk of her human from a previous mission. Who is he and what was the name of the series of books he wrote?

7) Liz looks at a scene of her human writing. Whom did he just quote?

8) Write a paragraph describing the life of the person Liz's human quoted.

9) Write the quote Liz's human is writing and tell what it means.

10) Who or what is the last character seen in Chapter 1? What do you think about this character? Do you think he or she will be important in the VRK?

Chapter 1: Down to the Letter

1) Where and when is Chapter 1 set? What premiere had the EO7 just attended? How did the King of England respond during this event? Research this work. What was groundbreaking about it?

2) Which of the EO7 Team had attended this event as humans? Are they always humans? What are their roles in the EO7?

3) What is the IAMISPHERE? How does the team access it in Chapter 1? Who is there to meet them and in which form?

4) Who are the three boys we meet in the IAMISPHERE? Which one is assigned to Al and which one to Liz? We have already learned that these boys will have a role in the Revolutionary War. Name the two boys who are from the Colonies and their eventual roles.

5) Who is Kate's human? What do we know about him from Chapter 1? How is he related to the main character of the VRK?

6) Kate's human is reading something. What is it? What event is being described and what is his reaction to what he reads?

7) Write out a portion of what Kate's human is reading. Tell what it means, and why this portion is important to you.

8) The EO7 sees a panel with Liz at the desk of her human. Who is he? What was the name of the series of books he wrote? Whom did Liz's human just quote? Write the quote and explain what it means.

9) The chapter ends with Kate's human writing a letter. To whom is he writing and where does this person live? How do you think this letter foreshadows Liz's mission in the VRK?

10) Who or what is the last character seen in Chapter 1? What do you think about this character? Do you think it will be important in the VRK? Which team do you think it is on?

Nigel's Nuggets

Chapter 1: Down to the Letter

Imagine what it looks like as the Team is being whisked away to the IAMISPHERE in Chapter 1 and what it looks like once they get there.

Create something to show what you just imagined. This would be a great project to capture in pictures and email to Jenny L. Cote at:

jenny@epicorderoftheseven.com

Cato's Eagle-Eye View

Chapter 1: Down to the Letter

Gliding: Summarize the chapter in three to five sentences, written or orally.

Soaring: Summarize the chapter in one word, phrase, or sentence, and write it on an index card with the chapter number and title written on the other side.

Soaring Flashcard Game: Shuffle all your Soaring flashcards. Player 1 reads the number and/or title of a chapter on one side of a flashcard. Player 2 answers with the Soaring Summarization on the other side of the flashcard. Reshuffle your flashcards, switch players if desired, and play three times.

Eaglet

Chapter 2: Conquering Scots and Rising Tides

1) Where and when is Chapter 2 set?

2) Which members of the EO7 are on the ship? How long has their journey been?

3) Name the location in which the Henry family originally lived prior to coming to America. What three kinds of ancestry does Nigel say they possess?

4) Write out Proverbs 22:1.

5) How is Clarie disguised?

6) Name the county and the colony in which the Henrys lived. What was the name of their home?

7) How many classes of people live in Virginia at this time? To which class does the Henry family belong?

8) What is Patrick Henry's father's name? Which military and church positions does he hold?

9) What is stalking the EO7 Team on the ship? What has been his last mission?

10) What is the stalker trying to get from Clarie?

Fledgling

Chapter 2: Conquering Scots and Rising Tides

1) Where is Chapter 2 set and when? Which members of the EO7 are present? What is their mode of transport? How long has their journey taken?

2) Name the three lands the Henrys inhabited before coming to America. Why did they leave the first location for the second? Which city was their third location?

3) What was the name of Patrick's mother? Where did her ancestors live prior to coming to America? Where did they live when they first settled in America?

4) Write out Proverbs 22:1 as well as Proverbs 22:2, which is inferred in Chapter 2. Who infers this? Which Scripture version of Proverbs 22:1–2 did you write?

5) Describe Claire's disguise. What is her mission?

6) Name the county and colony in which the Henrys live. What is the name of their home?

7) How many classes exist in the colony at this time? Describe each class. Which is the Henry's class?

8) What is Patrick's father's name? Where was he educated? What are his primary, his military, and his church professions? Is he successful in his primary profession?

9) What is stalking the EO7 on the ship and why? What does Max do to it?

10) Is the stalker working for The Maker or the enemy? Give two reasons to support your argument.

Chapter 2: Conquering Scots and Rising Tides

1) Where and when is Chapter 2 set? Which members of the EO7 are present? What is their mode of transport and how long has their journey taken? Who is reigning as monarch of England? When was the EO7's destination settled by the English?

2) Name the three lands the Henrys inhabited before coming to America. Why did they leave the first location for the second? Whom did they follow to do so, and in which year? What did this person do? Is what he did still important today? If so, why?

3) What was the family name of Patrick's mother? Where did her ancestors live prior to coming to America? Where did they live when they first settled in America? Briefly describe the people of Wales, the land of their original ancestral home. How are the people of this land different from other English-speaking people? What language did the people originally speak? Is this language still spoken anywhere today?

4) Write out Proverbs 22:1 as well as Proverbs 22:2, which is inferred in Chapter 2. Who infers this? Which Scripture version of Proverbs 22:1–2 did you write? Explain verse 1. Which thing is said to be more important and why? Can you have the most important thing from verse 1 regardless of your status and wealth? Why or why not?

5) Name the colony, county, and home in which the Henrys live. How many classes exist in the colony at this time? Describe each class. Which is the Henrys' class?

6) How did Patrick's father acquire their home? How did he know Sarah, Patrick's mother? How many acres do the Henrys own? What is the main crop they grow?

7) What is Patrick's father's name? Where was he educated? What are his primary, his military, and his church professions? Is he successful in his primary profession? List one reason why Patrick's father might not have been successful in his primary occupation. What occupation might have suited him better?

8) What is stalking the EO7 on the ship and why? What does Max do to the stalker? How is Clarie disguised and what is her mission?

9) What had the stalker done to Nigel earlier? What was the result of this action? What two things did Clarie say about this kind of creature?

10) Is the stalker working for The Maker or the Enemy? Give two reasons to support your argument. What is the first characteristic you notice about the stalker? This creature begs Max not to do what he eventually does. Is the stalker being truthful in his request? Why or why not?

Nigel's Nuggets

Chapter 2: Conquering Scots and Rising Tides

Study the clothing of each class of people in Virginia Colony. Imagine wearing each type of clothing yourself. List one thing you would like and one thing you would dislike if you wore the dress of each class. Create a project to show the dress of any of the three classes of people in Virginia Colony during the time covered in Chapter 2.

Cato's Eagle-Eye View

Chapter 2: Conquering Scots and Rising Tides

Gliding: Summarize the chapter in three to five sentences, written or orally.

Soaring: Summarize the chapter in one word, phrase, or sentence, and write it on an index card with the chapter number and title written on the other side.

Soaring Flashcard Game: Shuffle all your Soaring flashcards. Player 1 reads the number and/or title of a chapter on one side of a flashcard. Player 2 answers with the Soaring Summarization on the other side of the flashcard. Reshuffle your flashcards, switch players if desired, and play three times.

Eaglet

Chapter 3: Forest-Born Demosthenes

1) Where and on what day is Chapter 3 set?

2) Look at a map of Virginia. Is Hanover County closer to Williamsburg or Richmond?

3) Why is Patrick walking into the woods?

4) What type of creatures does he identify by listening to their call?

5) Which EO7 members go with him into the woods?

6) Who is the first member of the EO7 to introduce themselves to Patrick?

7) Liz has a conversation with "Pip." What kind of creature is Pip? Pip tells Liz some of the types of creatures who live in the woods. List at least seven of these types of creatures.

8) Who is the second member of the EO7 to introduce themselves to Patrick?

9) What does Patrick catch?

10) What does Patrick decide to do with his new friends from the EO7?

Fledgling

Chapter 3: Forest-Born Demosthenes

1) In which county is Chapter 3 set? On what day is it set? Why is this date important? Patrick goes to a body of water in the woods. Name the body of water.

2) What does Patrick smell that is sweet? What does he do with it, and for whom?

3) Look at a map of Virginia and find Patrick's county. Name the county and tell whether it is closer to Richmond or Williamsburg. Name at least two counties that border this county.

4) Describe Patrick's physical appearance.

5) What is Patrick heading into the woods to do? Which members of the EO7 go with him? Whom does he meet first and second?

6) What does Patrick catch?

7) Name seven kinds of birds Patrick identifies. Name seven other kinds of creatures listed in Chapter 3 that also live in the area.

8) Patrick identifies birds by their call. What type of bird will be important in this book? Why do you think so?

9) Liz strikes up a conversation with a creature to gain Patrick's attention. What is its name? What specific type of creature is it? What sound does it make?

10) What does Patrick decide to do with the EO7 members he meets? Do you think he will be successful?

Chapter 3: Forest-Born Demosthenes

1) In which county is Chapter 3 set? On which date, and why is this date important? Patrick goes to a body of water in the woods. Name the body of water. Look at a map of Virginia and find Patrick's county. Name the county and tell whether it is closer to Richmond or Williamsburg. Name all the counties that border this county.

2) What does Patrick smell that is sweet? What does he do with it and for whom? Who do you think these people might be in relation to Patrick?

3) Describe Patrick's physical appearance including his attire. Is Patrick wearing shoes? Was this a common practice? Do you like going barefoot? Why or why not?

4) Why is Patrick going into the woods? Is he successful? What does he catch?

5) Which members of the EO7 go with Patrick? Whom does he meet first and second and how does he meet each one?

6) Liz strikes up a conversation with a creature to gain Patrick's attention. What is its name? What specific type of creature is it? What sound does it make? How tall is it and what is its coloring?

7) Name seven kinds of birds Patrick identifies. Name seven other kinds of creatures listed in Chapter 3 that also live in the area.

8) Patrick identifies birds by their call. What type of bird will be important in this book? Why do you think so?

9) What does Patrick decide to do with the EO7 members he meets? Do you think he will be successful? Why or why not?

10) Which EO7 member will be waiting for Patrick at home and in which form?

Nigel's Nuggets

Chapter 3: Forest-Born Demosthenes

OPTION 1: Create something describing the different birds found in Chapter 3. Only one bird is mentioned by name in Chapter 3. Come up with names for the other types of birds in Chapter 3.

OPTION 2: Create something describing the other types of creatures living in Patrick's woods.

Listen to Season Two of the Epic Order of the Seven, The Podcast, for this episode from *The Voice, the Revolution, and the Key*. Tune in here: https://www.epicorderoftheseven.com/podcast

Cato's Eagle-Eye View

Chapter 3: Forest-Born Demosthenes

Gliding: Summarize the chapter in three to five sentences, written or orally.

Soaring: Summarize the chapter in one word, phrase, or sentence and write it on an index card with the chapter number and title written on the other side.

Soaring Flashcard Game: Shuffle all your Soaring flashcards. Player 1 reads the number and/or title of a chapter on one side of a flashcard. Player 2 answers with the Soaring Summarization on the other side of the flashcard. Reshuffle your flashcards, switch players if desired, and play three times.

Eaglet

Chapter 4: Settled at Studley

1) What is the common name of the type of trees that lined the walk to Studley Plantation?

2) Patrick has little sisters. Name them.

3) Who is visiting the Henrys?

4) Where does Patrick take Max and Liz to hide them?

5) What does Patrick feed Max and Liz?

6) Patrick also has brothers. Name them.

7) What is Patrick's nickname?

8) What does Patrick call Liz before explaining to his mother that she is really a black cat?

9) Whom does Patrick meet on his way to see his father and uncle? How is he/she disguised?

10) What names are first suggested for Max and Liz? What does Patrick wind up deciding to call them?

Chapter 4: Settled at Studley

1) What is the setting of Chapter 4? What is the common name of the type of trees that lined the walk to Studley Plantation?

2) Who is the first person Patrick meets as he nears his home? What does he give her?

3) Name all of Patrick's brothers and sisters.

4) Who is visiting the Henrys? What is his relationship to Patrick? Why does Patrick think he is visiting?

5) Where does Patrick take Max and Liz before he introduces them to his parents? What does he feed the two animals?

6) What argument does Patrick use to convince his mother to let him keep Max and Liz? What does he call Liz before he tells his mother she is really a cat?

7) Whom does Patrick meet on his way to take Max and Liz to meet his family? What is his/her disguise? What is the reason for this EO7 member's presence?

8) Who suggests names for Max and Liz? What names are suggested? What kind of variation of those names does Patrick suggest? Patrick has one of these name variations himself. What is it?

9) What does Max say about his and Liz's names for this assignment?

10) What EO7 member scurries out of the sight of the humans, and why?

Chapter 4: Settled at Studley

1) What is the setting of Chapter 4? What is the common name of the type of trees that line the walk to Studley Plantation?

2) Look at the second word in the scientific name of the trees that line the walk to Studley Plantation.. See if you can break it apart into two separate words. What is the botanical meaning of the first half of the word? What does the whole word mean?

3) Find pictures of both kinds of trees. Name one similarity and one difference between the two.

4) Who is the first person Patrick meets? What does he give her? How are they related? Name all the other children who are similarly related to Patrick.

5) Who is visiting the Henrys? What is his relationship to Patrick, and why does Patrick think he is visiting? What is he discussing with Patrick's father? Why do they stop their discussion?

6) Where does Patrick take Max and Liz before he introduces them to his parents? What does he feed the two animals? Why does Patrick hide Max and Liz at first?

7) What argument does Patrick use to convince his mother to let him keep Max and Liz? What does he call Liz before he tells his mother Liz is really a cat? What concern does Mrs. Henry express about a creature that might be in the woods? Who has seen this creature and when?

8) Patrick runs to the barn to yell for Max and Liz. What does Liz "saunter around" to get to Patrick? What is its scientific name?

9) Whom does Patrick meet on his way to take Max and Liz to meet his family? What is his/her disguise? What is the reason for this EO7 member's presence? Who suggests names for Max and Liz? What names are suggested? What kind of variation of those names does Patrick suggest? Patrick has one of these name variations himself. What is it?

10) What does Max say about his and Liz's names for this assignment? Which EO7 member scurries out of the sight of the humans? Why?

Nigel's Nuggets

Chapter 4: Settled at Studley

Where is or was Studley Plantation located? Is it still there today? If not, what is in the location now?

Create pictures of a Black Locust tree and a Boxwood hedge.

Cato's Eagle-Eye View

Chapter 4: Settled at Studley

Gliding: Summarize the chapter in three to five sentences, written or orally.

Soaring: Summarize the chapter in one word, phrase, or sentence and write it on an index card with the chapter number and title written on the other side.

Soaring Flashcard Game: Shuffle all your Soaring flashcards. Player 1 reads the number and/or title of a chapter on one side of a flashcard. Player 2 answers with the Soaring Summarization on the other side of the flashcard. Reshuffle your flashcards, switch players if desired, and play three times.

Eaglet

Chapter 5: Great Awakenings

1) For whom is Patrick named? What is his profession?

2) What was the first colony founded in America? What was the year of its founding?

3) What did the Separatists who settled in Plymouth Colony call themselves? Which ship carried them to America? Which year did this voyage take place?

4) Name five Protestant Dissenting faiths listed in Chapter 5.

5) Who is Reverend Williams? Whom will he send to Virginia?

6) What faith do John Henry and Uncle Patrick Henry follow? What faith do Sarah Henry and her father, Isaac Winston, follow?

7) At the end of Cousin David Henry's letter, what does he say that one voice might do?

8) What gift does Uncle Patrick give to Patrick?

9) Read "A WORD FROM THE AUTHOR" found on pages 607–9. Where did the use of birthday candles originate?

10) What date is Patrick's birthday?

Fledgling

Chapter 5: Great Awakenings

1) For whom is Patrick named? What is his profession? What date is Patrick's birthday? Which birthday is he celebrating? What year would he have been born?

2) What was the first colony founded in America? Why was it founded and when? How was its name chosen? What was its official religion?

3) When did England become a Protestant country? What did it mean for a person to "dissent?" Which group wanted to reform the Anglican Church, but not leave it? Which group wanted to leave the Anglican Church altogether?

4) List the thirteen original colonies. State the reason for the founding of each as listed in Chapter 5.

5) Name two of the Great Awakening preachers mentioned in Chapter 5. Why does Liz say that the Great Awakening is a good thing?

6) Why do John Henry and Uncle Patrick Henry like Max the moment they see him?

7) Which of Patrick Henry's family members are Anglican? Which are Dissenters?

8) Name the non-Protestant faith that dissented against England turning into a Protestant country. Name five Protestant dissenting faiths listed in Chapter 5.

9) Patrick Henry's role in the Revolutionary War is foreshadowed in Chapter 5. What is said to foreshadow this role, and who says it?

10) What gift does Uncle Patrick give to Patrick? Read "A WORD FROM THE AUTHOR" found on pages 607–9. Where did the use of birthday candles originate?

Chapter 5: Great Awakenings

1) For whom is Patrick named and what is his profession? What date is Patrick's birthday? Which birthday is he celebrating? What year would he have been born? Read "A WORD FROM THE AUTHOR" found on pages 607–9. Where did the use of birthday candles originate?

2) What was the first colony founded in America? Why was it founded and when? How was its name chosen? What was its official religion? List the thirteen original colonies. State the reason for the founding of each as listed in Chapter 5.

3) When did England become a Protestant country? What did it mean for a person to "dissent?" Which group wanted to reform the Anglican Church, but not leave it? Which group wanted to leave the Anglican Church altogether? What was the non-religious reason for England leaving the Catholic Church? Was there a religious reason for England leaving the Catholic Church?

4) In his lifetime, did King Henry VIII of England get the one thing he wanted because England left the Catholic Church? After Henry VIII died, three of his children succeeded him. Who became King of England after Henry VIII's last child died?

5) Name two of the Great Awakening preachers mentioned in Chapter 5. Why does Liz say that the Great Awakening is a good thing? Chapter 5 lists several positive outcomes for Dissenters and one negative outcome. What is "the catch" for Dissenters?

6) Which of Patrick Henry's family members are Anglican? Which are Dissenters? Name the non-Protestant faith that dissented against England turning into a Protestant country. Name five Protestant dissenting faiths listed in Chapter 5.

7) Patrick Henry's role in the Revolutionary War is foreshadowed in Chapter 5. What is said to foreshadow this role and who says it? What event that David Henry attended did he describe in his letter? What memento from this event did he send to his Henry cousins in Virginia?

8) Which EO7 members did David Henry meet when he attended *Messiah?* In which forms were they disguised when they met him? Why was *Messiah* not well received when it premiered?

9) How does Sarah Henry sum up *Messiah's* reception?

10) What does Patrick do with his birthday gift from Uncle Henry? How does Uncle Henry respond, and what does he say? How do Patrick's mother and father respond?

Nigel's Nuggets

Chapter 5: Great Awakenings

Research and present something about the Great Awakening that is appropriate for the level of the Chapter Guide you just completed.

Cato's Eagle-Eye View

Chapter 5: Great Awakenings

Gliding: Summarize the chapter in three to five sentences, written or orally.

Soaring: Summarize the chapter in one word, phrase, or sentence and write it on an index card with the chapter number and title written on the other side.

Soaring Flashcard Game: Shuffle all your Soaring flashcards. Player 1 reads the number and/or title of a chapter on one side of a flashcard. Player 2 answers with the Soaring Summarization on the other side of the flashcard. Reshuffle your flashcards, switch players if desired, and play three times.

Eaglet

Chapter 6: Back in St. Andrew's Day

1) Which EO7 members are in the IAMISPHERE in Chapter 6?

2) What are their natural forms?

3) Who is in the first panel that Gillamon shows Clarie?

4) Whom do the people in the first panel meet? What does John the Baptist say about him?

5) Who were John the Baptist's followers? Whom do they start following instead? Whom do they bring with them?

6) What famous miracle takes place with Al's help? Do you think Al will get his share of the leftovers? What will be his favorite part if he does?

7) How was Andrew crucified?

8) What human and EO7 member are in the next panel that Gillamon shows Clarie?

9) In what way does Clarie think that Andrew and Patrick are similar?

10) Where do Clarie and Gillamon go once they leave the IAMISPHERE?

Chapter 6: Back in St. Andrew's Day

1) Which EO7 members are in the IAMISPHERE in Chapter 6? What are their natural forms?

2) Who is in the first panel that Gillamon shows Clarie? Whom do they meet, and what does John the Baptist say about him?

3) Who were John the Baptist's followers? Whom do they start following instead? Whom do they bring with them? Where is Andrew's original home? Where does he say he lives now? What is Andrew and John's profession?

4) Is John satisfied with his profession? What does he say about it in Chapter 6? What does John ask Jesus, and how does Jesus respond?

5) Where does Jesus take his new followers? Which EO7 members do they meet?

6) Whom does Andrew go awaken? What does he tell him? What does Jesus say about Andrew in the next panel, which Gillamon shows Clarie?

7) How did the quality that Jesus used to describe Andrew help with the famous miracle in the next panel? Which EO7 member is also observant? What is the thing for which he is always searching?

8) How was Andrew crucified? What human and what EO7 member are in the next panel that Gillamon shows Clarie?

9) In what way does Clarie think Andrew and Patrick are similar? Name something that Patrick notices and imitates from Chapter 1.

10) When they leave the IAMISPHERE, where do Clarie and Gillamon go? What is being celebrated? Create a picture of a St. Andrew's cross.

Chapter 6: Back in St. Andrew's Day

1) Which EO7 members are in the IAMISPHERE in Chapter 6? What are their natural forms?

2) Who is in the first panel that Gillamon shows Clarie? Whom do they meet and what does John the Baptist say about him? Who were John the Baptist's followers? Whom do they start following instead? Whom do they bring with them? Where is Andrew's original home? Where does he say he lives now? What is Andrew and John's profession?

3) Research Capernaum. How is it important in Jesus' earthly ministry? Who lives there? Name at least one event that happened in Capernaum and is recorded in the Bible.

4) Is John satisfied with his profession? What does he say about it in Chapter 6? What does John ask Jesus, and how does Jesus respond? What famous quote from the Bible did Jesus say referencing the men's new profession after they heeded the call to follow him?

5) Where does Jesus take his new followers? Which EO7 members do they meet? Have all seven members of the EO7 been together at once in the VRK? Why do you think they are all together at this moment in time?

6) Whom does Andrew go awaken? What does he tell him? What does Jesus say about Andrew in the next panel that Gillamon shows Clarie? How did this quality help with the famous miracle in the next panel? Which EO7 member is also observant? What is the thing for which he is always searching?

7) Jesus changes Andrew's brother's name. Why does Jesus do this? What is his new name? What does Jesus say about him as He gives Andrew's brother his new name?

8) "Pat" is Patrick's nickname. What nickname is the disciple John known by today? In Chapter 6, the first time Jesus met John, he asked him about his "job." What was the topic of the last words Jesus uttered specifically to John right before he died on the cross as recorded in the Bible? Write out what Jesus said to John. How was Andrew crucified? What human and what EO7 members are in the next panel that Gillamon shows Clarie? In what way does Clarie think that Andrew and Patrick are similar? Name something that Patrick notices and imitates from Chapter 1.

9) When they leave the IAMISPHERE, where do Clarie and Gillamon go? What is being celebrated? What is the significance of this celebration to Scotland? Create a picture of a St. Andrew's cross.

10) As Liz puts everything together at the end of Chapter 6, what comment does she make about history? Explain how the events Gillamon reviewed with Clarie in the IAMISPHERE in Chapter 6 connect to the St. Andrew's Day Festival in Virginia.

Nigel's Nuggets

Chapter 6: Back in St. Andrew's Day

Learn about St. Andrew's Day from its beginnings in Scotland until its celebration in Hanover County, Virginia Colony, in 1743. Create a project to demonstrate the celebration.

Listen to Season Two of the Epic Order of the Seven, The Podcast, for this episode from *The Voice, the Revolution, and the Key.* Tune in here: https://www.epicorderoftheseven.com/podcast

Cato's Eagle-Eye View

Chapter 6: Back in St. Andrew's Day

Gliding: Summarize the chapter in three to five sentences, written or orally.

Soaring: Summarize the chapter in one word, phrase, or sentence and write it on an index card with the chapter number and title written on the other side.

Soaring Flashcard Game: Shuffle all your Soaring flashcards. Player 1 reads the number and/or title of a chapter on one side of a flashcard. Player 2 answers with the Soaring Summarization on the other side of the flashcard. Reshuffle your flashcards, switch players if desired, and play three times.

Eaglet

Chapter 7: Magical Meetings

1) Name three foods that are brought to the St. Andrew's Day festival.

2) Name three drinks that are brought to the St. Andrew's Day festival.

3) What would Al have done with all that food if he had been there? What would probably have happened to Al as a result?

4) What does Gillamon have with him that holds a clue to his natural identity?

5) What myth have humans made up about the St. Andrew's Day festival?

6) Name two of the contests held that day and their prizes.

7) What does Clarie pull out of her silk handbag and give to Nigel?

8) Where does Gillamon put Nigel when the humans walk up?

9) Who are John Henry's three sons? Which contest does Patrick enter?

10) Who is Patrick's best friend?

Fledgling

Chapter 7: Magical Meetings

1) Name seven main courses or side dishes, seven desserts, and three drinks brought to the St. Andrew's Day festival.

2) To whom did Liz refer as the "founder of the feast?" Why? List four separate passages in which this event is found in the Bible, including book, chapter, and verses.

3) How are Gillamon and Clarie dressed? Describe their outfits. What does Gillamon have with him that holds a clue as to his natural identity?

4) What is the myth that Gillamon says the humans invented? What does Gillamon say may happen regarding the myth? What does he say may "lie ahead today?" Gillamon says this will affect Patrick. Could it also affect others? If so, how do you know?

5) List five contests and their prizes.

6) Liz is concerned she has not yet done much in her mission. How does Gillamon reassure her?

7) What three things does John Henry remind his sons that Scots always need to remember?

8) Where does Gillamon put Nigel when the humans walk up? Who are John Henry's three sons? Which contest does Patrick enter? How does Gillamon introduce himself and Clarie?

9) What does Patrick put together about Gillamon and Clarie and how?

10) What does Clarie say to almost destroy their cover? How does she cover her tracks? Who notices that something does not add up? What physical clue about Clarie does he notice?

Chapter 7: Magical Meetings

1) Name seven main courses or side dishes, seven desserts, and three drinks at the St. Andrew's Day festival. To whom did Liz refer as the "founder of the feast?" Why? List four separate passages in which this event is found in the Bible, including book, chapter, and verses.

2) How are Gillamon and Clarie disguised? Describe their outfits. Describe the outfits the common folk and Indians might have worn. What is the clue that gives away Gillamon's natural identity?

3) What is the myth the humans made up? What does Gillamon say may happen regarding the myth? What does he say may "lie ahead today?" Will it affect Patrick? Could it affect others? If so, how do you know? Give an example of how this passage might be both fiction and fantasy, two of Jenny L. Cote's writing genres.

4) List five contests and their prizes. Which contest will Gillamon judge? Who will assist him? Describe in detail the prize for this contest. Why do you think Jenny L. Cote described this prize in such specific detail?

5) Why is Gillamon's assisting judge qualified for the position? How do you know this?

6) Is Liz concerned about the progress of her Patrick Henry mission? How do you know this? What does Gillamon say to Liz after she comments about the mission?

7) What three things does John Henry remind his sons that Scots need to remember? Which humans walk up to Gillamon and Clarie? What does Gillamon do with Nigel when they do? How does Gillamon introduce himself and Clarie? What does Patrick put together about Gillamon and Clarie? What item causes Patrick to put things together?

8) What does Clarie say to almost ruin their cover? How does she recover? Who notices that something does not add up? What physical clue about Clarie does he notice? Which characteristic of Patrick's does this demonstrate?

9) Who is Patrick's best friend? Why does Jenny L. Cote tell us this? What do you think his importance in Patrick's life might be?

10) Read the last sentence in Chapter 7. What do you think this might be? Do you think that whatever it is will be revealed? Do you think that it is a good or bad character? Why?

Nigel's Nuggets

Chapter 7: Magical Meetings

OPTION 1: The St. Andrew's Day festival would be Al's kind of festival. Imagine he had attended. Create something to show what might have happened if he had.

OPTION 2: Wassail is mentioned as well as other items with which you might be unfamiliar. What is wassail? Describe three other dishes which are unfamiliar to you. Find a recipe for all four items you described. Make at least one of them or go all out and make a St. Andrew's Day feast to enjoy with your family and/or friends.

Cato's Eagle-Eye View

Chapter 7: Magical Meetings

Gliding: Summarize the chapter in three to five sentences, written or orally.

Soaring: Summarize the chapter in one word, phrase, or sentence and write it on an index card with the chapter number and title written on the other side.

Soaring Flashcard Game: Shuffle all your Soaring flashcards. Player 1 reads the number and/or title of a chapter on one side of a flashcard. Player 2 answers with the Soaring Summarization on the other side of the flashcard. Reshuffle your flashcards, switch players if desired, and play three times.

Eaglet

Chapter 8: Life Lessons and Fiery Fiddling

1) Where does Patrick ask Max and Liz to be during his race?
2) What does Patrick ask Jane to hold?
3) Who is Jane's friend? What is her nickname?
4) Who is the thin boy in the race? Why might he have been thin?
5) What happens to Jimmy at the start of the race?
6) Why is it important for Jimmy to win?
7) Who is declared the winner of the race? Why does Patrick say, "He's no winner?"
8) What does Sallie give Patrick?
9) Who wins the fiddle contest? What does he do with his prize?
10) Why does Uncle Langloo say that a man needs a fiddle and a gun?

Fledgling

Chapter 8: Life Lessons and Fiery Fiddling

1) Where are Max, Liz, Nigel, and Gillamon during Patrick's race? Who is making their way to join Max and Liz? Who is Jane's friend? What is her nickname?

2) Sallie and Jimmy are human characters. Do you think they are fictional, or real people who lived? What clues do you have to back up your answer for each character?

3) Explain what happens in the race. Is the outcome fair? Find a verse in the Bible that tells about times when evil people win.

4) What is Sallie's response to the outcome of the race? Do you think the judge had all the facts when he declared the winner? Why or why not?

5) What happens with Sam and William? What does Sam do with his prize? Where have they gathered and why?

6) What are the rules of the fiddle contest?

7) What happens after the nineteenth fiddler plays? Describe the mystery fiddler.

8) Describe each character's reaction to the mystery fiddler: Nigel, Max, Liz, and Patrick.

9) Who wins the fiddle contest? What does he play for the crowd next? What does he do with his prize? What is his relationship to the Henry family?

10) What does Uncle Langloo promise to do with Patrick? What does he say are the two things a man needs and why does he say a man needs each of them?

Chapter 8: Life Lessons and Fiery Fiddling

1) Where does Patrick ask Max and Liz to be during the race? Describe Sallie and her family. What is their relationship to the Henry family? Do you think she will be an important character in the VRK? Why?

2) Sallie and Jimmy are human characters. Do you think they are fictional, or real people who lived? What clues do you have to back up your answer for each character? Which genre is this chapter?

3) Explain what happens in the race. Why is it important for Jimmy to win? Is the outcome fair? Find a verse in the Bible that tells about times when evil people win.

4) What is Sallie's response to the outcome of the race? Do you think the judge had all the facts when he declared the winner? Why or why not? Why do you think this scene with Sallie is included? What could it foreshadow? What new thing do we learn about the shadowy figure?

5) What happens with Sam and William? What does Sam do with his prize? Where have they gathered and why? Why do you think there were only nineteen fiddlers?

6) What are the rules of the fiddling contest? What do Patrick, Max, Liz, Gillamon, Clarie, and Nigel each do during the contest?

7) What is the material of the mystery fiddler's bow? What happens to it as he plays?

8) Describe each character's reaction to the mystery fiddler: Nigel, Max, Liz, and Patrick. Who wins the fiddle contest? What does he play for the crowd next? What does he do with his prize? What is his relationship to the Henry family?

9) What does Uncle Langloo promise to do with Patrick? What does he say are the two things a man needs and why does he say a man needs each of them? Liz mentions another prize Patrick wins. What is it? What do you think this might foreshadow?

10) Lay out all the clues from this chapter that Liz put together.

Nigel's Nuggets

Chapter 8: Life Lessons and Fiery Fiddling

Read the entry about Patrick's fiddle on page 608, "A WORD FROM THE AUTHOR." Where is this fiddle now? Do an Internet search about Red Hill. What new news about the fiddle belonging to the Henry Family has become available since the VRK was published? Plan a one-day trip to see Red Hill and the fiddle. Share your itinerary. What is the one thing you are most looking forward to on your trip? What new thing did you learn while you were planning your trip?

Cato's Eagle-Eye View

Chapter 8: Life Lessons and Fiery Fiddling

Gliding: Summarize the chapter in three to five sentences, written or orally.

Soaring: Summarize the chapter in one word, phrase, or sentence and write it on an index card with the chapter number and title written on the other side.

Soaring Flashcard Game: Shuffle all your Soaring flashcards. Player 1 reads the number and/or title of a chapter on one side of a flashcard. Player 2 answers with the Soaring Summarization on the other side of the flashcard. Reshuffle your flashcards, switch players if desired, and play three times.

Eaglet

Chapter 9: Fiddle a Riddle

1. Where is Patrick's fiddle at the start of Chapter 9?
2. What determines whether you call an instrument a violin or a fiddle?
3. What does Max think Nigel's head looks like?
4. What happens to Max when he tries to save Nigel? Does he like the experience?
5. What becomes physical black musical notes that float in the air with words inside them?
6. What does the EO7 have to use to produce the musical messages? Whose do they decide to use?
7. List seven of the voices in the riddle. *PARENTS: Please help your reader make a poster including all nine voices of the Fiddle's Riddle so they may fill in the answer for each riddle as it is solved in the VRK. They should list the chapter as well as the answer.*
8. Write out the word "HONESTY" one letter per line and fill in the words from the New England Primer for each letter.
9. Write out the sum of all the Ten Commandments.
10. Liz thinks she has solved the "Voice in the Wilderness" riddle. What is her solution to the riddle?

Chapter 9: Fiddle a Riddle

1. Where and when is Chapter 9 set? Where are the Henry family? Where are the EO7 team members? Where is Patrick's fiddle? What determines whether you would call an instrument a fiddle or a violin?

2. Describe what happens when Max remarks that "the lad is gettin' the hang of playin' his fiddle."

3. Who is speaking to Max, Liz, and Nigel, and how? What are the first four things said to them?

4. Make a poster of the Fiddle's Riddle. When each voice riddle is answered in the VRK, fill in on your poster the answer to the riddle including the chapter number.

5. How and where does Liz plan to begin solving the riddle?

6. How does the schoolmaster primarily teach? Does Liz think this will work for Patrick? What does she think he needs?

7. Write the New England Primer examples for each letter in the word "HONESTY." How many letters are in the word? Find a Bible reference for three of the letters from the word "HONESTY."

8. Liz thinks Plutarch is the key to one of the first two riddles. What does she recall Gillamon saying about Plutarch? How does she think this will help Patrick?

9. Which of the two voices involves Plutarch? Liz thinks she has solved the "Voice in the Wilderness" riddle. What is her solution?

10. What does Liz propose to do to make it possible for Patrick to study Plutarch, and how would this work?

Chapter 9: Fiddle a Riddle

1. Where and when is Chapter 9 set? Where is the Henry family? Where are the EO7 team members? Where is Patrick's fiddle? What determines whether you would call an instrument a fiddle or a violin?

2. Describe what happens when Max remarks that "the lad is gettin' the hang of playin' his fiddle." Who is speaking to Max, Liz, and Nigel and how? What are the first four things said to them?

3. Make a poster of the Fiddle's Riddle. When each voice riddle is answered in the VRK, fill in the answer to the riddle, including the chapter number, on your poster.

4. How and where does Liz plan to begin solving the riddle? How does the schoolmaster primarily teach? Does Liz think this will work for Patrick? What does she think he needs?

5. Write the New England Primer examples for each letter in the word "HONESTY." How many letters are in the word? Find a Bible reference for three of the letters from the word "HONESTY". Make a 3-letter and a 5-letter word that is biblical, or virtuous, using only letters found in the New England Primer.

6. Write out the Golden Rule. Where is it found in the Bible? What is the sum of the Ten Commandments? Write out "Learn these four lines." What does it mean to you? Why is it a good way to live your life?

7. Write memory helps from the Bible for the word "virtues" using biblical examples such as the helps found in the alphabetical listing in the New England Primer, but different from the examples it uses.

8. Liz thinks Plutarch is the key to one of the first two riddles. What does she recall Gillamon saying about Plutarch? How does she think this will help Patrick?

9. Liz thinks the schoolmaster offers excellent lessons and prayers. Name seven additional things she would like to see Patrick being taught.

10. Which of the two voices involves Plutarch? Liz thinks she has solved the "Voice in the Wilderness" riddle. What is her solution to the riddle? What does Liz propose to do to make it possible for Patrick to study Plutarch, and how would this work?

Nigel's Nuggets

Chapter 9: Fiddle a Riddle

I say, this is one of my favorite chapters in the VRK, because I helped my friend, Max, take flight. I cannot be sure, but I think the electric moment inspired my new venture. Pop over to the VRK Podcast to hear all about it. www.epicorderoftheseven.com/podcast

Then you simply *must* create something utterly astounding to demonstrate my and Max's great violin flying escapade!

Cato's Eagle-Eye View

Chapter 9: Fiddle a Riddle

Gliding: Summarize the chapter in three to five sentences, written or orally.

Soaring: Summarize the chapter in one word, phrase, or sentence and write it on an index card with the chapter number and title written on the other side.

Soaring Flashcard Game: Shuffle all your Soaring flashcards. Player 1 reads the number and/or title of a chapter on one side of a flashcard. Player 2 answers with the Soaring Summarization on the other side of the flashcard. Reshuffle your flashcards, switch players if desired, and play three times.

Eaglet

Chapter 10: A Voice in the Wilderness

1) What does Uncle Langloo tell Patrick about his gun?
2) What does it mean when the crow "belts out a staccato of caws?"
3) What do deer tracks look like?
4) What are the paw pad tracks missing that Max's prints have?
5) What kind of paw prints are they?
6) Why don't the crows eat Nigel?
7) What bit Paul?
8) What did Gillamon wear to the St. Andrew's Day festival that Patrick really liked?
9) How many eagle feathers can be earned at a time?
10) Uncle Langloo tells Patrick to project his voice to grab the attention of his listeners. What does he tell Patrick next?

Chapter 10: A Voice in the Wilderness

1) What does it mean when the crow "belts out a staccato of caws?"

2) Name and describe three kinds of tracks, besides Max's, that Uncle Langloo and Patrick discuss.

3) What does Uncle Langloo say when Patrick asks if they should hunt down the predator? What was his reason for saying this?

4) What kind of creature sounded the alarm? What was its name? Which EO7 member was with it?

5) What creature does Uncle Langloo say it was "alright to kill"? What creature have they not seen? Why?

6) What does Uncle Langloo think of the rich Tidewater types? What does he say is more important than the clothes you wear?

7) Summarize the conflict in the Henry family over religion. Who believed what? How does Uncle Langloo say you find out what you believe?

8) What does Uncle Langloo say the Indians revere above all creatures and why?

9) What does Uncle Langloo say an eagle feather meant to the Indians? Why is possessing one such a big deal?

10) What does Uncle Langloo think is most important about speaking? Write out his thoughts as they appear in Chapter 10.

Chapter 10: A Voice in the Wilderness

1) What does Uncle Langloo tell Patrick about his gun? Why does Uncle Langloo take notice when the cries of the crow change? What does it mean? Does Max notice as well? What alerts him?

2) Describe and draw pictures of Max's paw prints plus those of the three other creatures Uncle Langloo and Patrick discover.

3) What does Uncle Langloo say when Patrick asks if they should hunt down the predator? What reason does he give? Write a paragraph about the predator.

4) What kind of creature raises the alarm? How many sounds can it make? What is its coloring and height? What does it eat? What is its name?

5) Which EO7 member is with the creature? Is he in danger? Why or why not? Is this normal? What is the reaction of the EO7 member to this bit of information? What does he say?

6) Describe the firepit that Patrick digs and the fire he, Max, and Uncle Langloo build.

7) What kind of creature does Uncle Langloo say it was "alright to kill"? Research this creature. Why might it be a bad thing to be bitten by one? If this creature became a character in one of Jenny L. Cote's books, which side do you think it would be on and why?

8) Summarize the conflict in the Henry family over religion. Who believed what? How does Uncle Langloo say you find out what you believe?

9) What did Uncle Langloo say the Indians revered above all creatures and why? What does Uncle Langloo say an eagle feather means to the Indians? Why is possessing one such a big deal?

10) Max tells Nigel, "Crows may be smart, but they're obnoxious." What reason does Nigel give for perhaps needing to stop using them for transportation? What does Max suggest instead? Why would this be a good idea for Nigel's upcoming mission? Where is this mission?

Nigel's Nuggets

Chapter 10: A Voice in the Wilderness

Find out about the different types of eagle feathers. Make a presentation about at least two different kinds. After you finish this Nigel's Nuggets challenge, how many eagle feathers do you have if you have completed each Chapter Guide and each Nigel's Nuggets so far?

Cato's Eagle-Eye View

Chapter 10: A Voice in the Wilderness

Gliding: Summarize the chapter in three to five sentences, written or orally.

Soaring: Summarize the chapter in one word, phrase, or sentence and write it on an index card with the chapter number and title written on the other side.

Soaring Flashcard Game: Shuffle all your Soaring flashcards. Player 1 reads the number and/or title of a chapter on one side of a flashcard. Player 2 answers with the Soaring Summarization on the other side of the flashcard. Reshuffle your flashcards, switch players if desired, and play three times.

Eaglet

Chapter 11: Plutarch's Nine Lives

1) Who was Julius Caesar's worst enemy?

2) Gillamon says that Cato had two choices. What were they?

3) What is the name of the statue on Plutarch's desk?

4) What genre of writing did Plutarch originate?

5) What was Plutarch's credo?

6) What does Liz accidently break off the statue?

7) What was Plutarch's ninth life?

8) In what points does Cato feel he has conquered Caesar?

9) Liz misses something when Plutarch starts to write about Cato the Younger. What is it?

10) Liz wakes up from her dreams and goes looking for John Henry's copy of *Plutarch's Lives*. What is there, and what is missing?

Fledgling

Chapter 11: Plutarch's Nine Lives

1) Who was Nero? Describe him as a leader.

2) Write a paragraph about Cato the Younger based on Chapter 11.

3) Who was Plutarch? Why was he important to the current mission?

4) Who was Nike? Is there a real statue of her?

5) What new genre of writing did Plutarch start? What was his credo?

6) What did Plutarch want to show, inspire, and urge men to do?

7) From Chapter 11, list seven of the "Lives" Plutarch wrote.

8) What does Plutarch say to Liz in response to "Winged Victory" being broken?

9) What do you think is watching Liz and Plutarch? Do you think the urn was broken by accident? Why or why not?

10) Can Liz find a copy of the portion of *Plutarch's Lives* that contains Cato the Younger? Where does she look? What falls onto the floor and what does it say?

Chapter 11: Plutarch's Nine Lives

1) Who was Nero? Describe his character as a leader. Tell the story of Nero and his "fiddling."

2) Write a paragraph about Cato the Younger based on Chapter 11. Write a paragraph explaining how Julius Caesar became the dictator of the Roman Empire.

3) Who was Plutarch? Why was he important to this current mission? What does Liz remember that Gillamon said at the start of this mission about connections?

4) Who was Nike? Is there a real statue of her? If so, write a paragraph about it, including its current location.

5) What new genre of writing did Plutarch start? What did Plutarch state was his purpose in doing so? What was his credo?

6) What did Plutarch want to show, inspire, and urge men to do? About what did he caution them?

7) From Chapter 11, list seven of the "Lives" Plutarch wrote. Aside from Cato and Caesar, write a paragraph about one of the other lives from your list of seven.

8) What does Plutarch say to Liz in response to "Winged Victory" being broken? How does this apply to you?

9) What do you think is watching Liz and Plutarch? Do you think the urn was broken by accident? Why or why not? Do you think it is a coincidence the urn fell amongst oleander plants?

10) Can Liz find a copy of the portion of Plutarch's Lives that contains Cato the Younger? Where does she look? What falls on the floor and what does it say? Why is Liz so excited by this summons?

Nigel's Nuggets

Chapter 11: Plutarch's Nine Lives

My pet, Liz, is going to see her true love, Al, in the next chapter. My friend, Max, is always calling Al a "daft kitty." That Max can certainly come up with a clever quip! Did you hear him in the Chapter 11 VRK Podcast? www.epicorderoftheseven.com/podcast

If not, after you give it a listen, come back here, and describe your favorite scene from Chapter 11 in words or with any other type of creation.

Cato's Eagle-Eye View

Chapter 11: Plutarch's Nine Lives

Gliding: Summarize the chapter in three to five sentences, written or orally.

Soaring: Summarize the chapter in one word, phrase, or sentence and write it on an index card with the chapter number and title written on the other side.

Soaring Flashcard Game: Shuffle all your Soaring flashcards. Player 1 reads the number and/or title of a chapter on one side of a flashcard. Player 2 answers with the Soaring Summarization on the other side of the flashcard. Reshuffle your flashcards, switch players if desired, and play three times.

Eaglet

Chapter 12: A Tragedy in London

1) What is the setting for Chapter 12 including the date, the city, and the exact location?

2) Liz tells us the former name of this city. What was it? What had this city become in Chapter 12?

3) Who lives at the White House? Where is it located?

4) What is Al doing when Liz spots him?

5) What is the name of Al's friend?

6) What is printed on Molly's collar?

7) What does Al tell Liz about why she has been called to London?

8) What does Liz say she also needs to do while she is in London? Is she able to accomplish her task?

9) What is the name of the event the EO7 members will attend while Liz is in London?

10) At the very end of Chapter 12, Liz says, "There is one thing I know for certain." What is the one thing?

Chapter 12: A Tragedy in London

1) Where and when is Chapter 12 set? What was the first name of the city? Tell of two other times Liz had stood along this riverbank.

2) Who lives where: King George and Queen Caroline; their daughters Anne, Caroline, and Amelia; and Prince Frederick and his wife, Augusta, along with their many children, including George?

3) What is Al doing, and with whom, when Liz spots him? What kind of creature is with Al and what does her collar say?

4) What does Al tell Liz about why she has been called to London? Which other EO7 member does he tell Liz she will see? What does Liz say she also needs to do while she is in London? Name the article she wishes to obtain and its creator.

5) As Al and Liz set off that night, what is their destination including the street? Which EO7 members will attend in human form? With whom will they sit? Which other VIP humans are present?

6) What is being performed? Who wrote it and when? When was it first performed?

7) Is *Cato* popular in America? Why or why not? What does Gillamon suggest?

8) Write out the portion of the opening that Liz quotes to herself. What is a "tragic muse?"

9) Write out Cato's words. Which portions of these words do you think will be important to Patrick?

10) What event from Liz's dream the night before caused her to put the Fiddle's Riddle together? Is she right? How do you know?

Chapter 12: A Tragedy in London

1) Where and when is Chapter 12 set? What was the first name of the city? Tell of two other times Liz had stood along this riverbank. Who was Liz with the first time she stood on the banks of this river? To whom did he report? Which of these two people you just mentioned was a real historical person?

2) Who lives where: King George and Queen Caroline; their daughters Anne, Caroline, and Amelia; and Prince Frederick and his wife, Augusta, along with their many children, including George? Why do Prince Frederick and his family choose not to live with his parents? What will young George become one day?

3) What is Al doing, and with whom, when Liz spots him? What kind of creature is with Al and what does her collar say? Describe this creature including explaining what its purpose in life is. Find the entry about this creature in "A WORD FROM THE AUTHOR." Was it real or fictional?

4) What does Al tell Liz about why she has been called to London. What does he tell her? Which other EO7 member does he tell Liz she will see? What does Liz say she also needs to do while she is in London? Name the article she wishes to obtain and its creator. Does Liz accomplish her mission?

5) As Al and Liz set off that night, what is their destination including the street? Which EO7 members will attend in human form? With whom will they sit? Which other VIP humans are present?

6) What is being performed? Who wrote it and when? When was it first performed? Who wrote the Foreword? What publication did this writer found? Who is the current editor?

7) Is *Cato* popular in America? Why or why not? What does Gillamon suggest? What does Clarie suggest? Do you think that either of their suggestions will work?

8) Write out the portion of the opening that Liz quotes to herself and tell what it means.

9) Write out Cato's words. Which portions of these words do you think will be important to Patrick? What did this passage mean to Liz?

10) What comes "rushing back" to Liz's mind? What does this cause her to do? What are her conclusions, and what does she know for certain? Do you think she is correct? If so, what clue backs up your argument?

Nigel's Nuggets

Chapter 12: A Tragedy in London
Voice One Riddle

Turn to the Bibliography, beginning on page 621. You will be going on a Bibliography Quest using entries from the Bibliography to answer the first two parts of the Fiddle's Riddle.

Riddle 1: Write the first four words in the blank below.

1) From the Mayer, Henry entry, write the 1st word in the title cited.
2) From the Kukla, Amy and Jon Kukla entry, write the 3rd word in the title cited.
3) From the Henry, Patrick, and James M. Elson entry, write the 3rd word in the title cited.
4) From the Bluford, Robert entry, write the 7th word in the title cited.

____

From the title cited in the Adams John Quincy, Daniel Fenton, Moore Baker, and C.W. Felton entry, counting both the initial "M" and the prefix "de" as words, fill in the blank below to spell out the 5th word of the riddle:

Write the 1st letter of the 34th word.
Write the 2nd letter of the 8th word.
Write the 1st letter of the 4th word.
Write the 9th letter of the 12th word.
Write the 5th letter of the 18th word.
Write the 4th letter of the 32nd word.
Write the 7th letter of the 1st word.
Write the 5th letter of the 18th word.
Write the 6th letter of the 25th word.
Write the 6th letter of the 15th word.

____

Nigel's Nuggets

Chapter 12: A Tragedy in London
Voice One Answer

Riddle 1, Answer 1: Write out the letters in the blank below.
For the first word:

Find the entry with the title: "Tobacco: Colonial Cultivation Methods."
Write the 1st letter of the first author's last name.
Write the 5th letter of the 2nd word of the title cited.
Write the 6th letter of the 1st word of the title cited.
Write the 3rd letter of the 3rd word of the title cited.
Write the 2nd letter of the 4th word of the title cited.

____

For the second word:

Find the entry with the title: *Memoirs of General Lafayette.*
Write the 1st letter of the author's last name.
From the Hannings, Bud entry, write the 7th letter of the 4th word of the title cited.
From the Hannings, Bud entry, write the 6th letter of the 9th word of the title cited.
From the Hannings, Bud entry, write the 9th letter of the 1st word of the title cited.
From the Hannings, Bud entry, write the 3rd letter of the 6th word of the title cited.
From the Hannings, Bud entry, write the 2nd letter of the 8th word of the title cited.
From the Hannings, Bud entry, write the 4th letter of the 5th word of the title cited.

____

Now write Riddle 1 and its answer:

____

____

____

Nigel's Nuggets

Chapter 12: A Tragedy in London

Voice Two Riddle and Answer

Riddle 2: Write the words in the blank below.
1) From the Weitzman, David M entry, write the 6th word in the title cited.
2) From the Sabin, Lewis, and Bill Ternary entry, write the 3rd word in the title cited.
3) From the Morrow, George A entry, write the 17th word in the title cited.
4) From the Kelly, C. Brian, and Ingrid Smyer-Kelly entry, write the 5th word in the title cited.

From the Morgan, Edmund Sears, and Helen M Morgan entry, fill in the blank below to spell out the 5th word of the riddle.

Write the 1st letter of the 5th word of the title cited.
Write the 1st letter of the 3rd word of the title cited.
Write the 1st letter of the 2nd word of the title cited.
Write the 1st letter of the 1st word of the title cited.

Riddle 2, answer 2: Write out the letters in the space below.

Find the entry with the title: *Marquis de Lafayette: French Hero of the American Revolution* and write the first letter of the last name of the author's last name.
From the Davies, Samuel entry, ignoring numbers and initials of names in the title cited,
Write the 3rd letter of the 9th word of the title cited.
From the Davies, Samuel entry, ignoring numbers and initials of names in the title cited,
Write the 4th letter of the 19th word of the title cited.
From the Davies, Samuel entry, ignoring numbers and initials of names in the title cited,
Write the 11th letter of the 16th word of the title cited.
From the Davies, Samuel entry, ignoring numbers and initials of names in the title cited,
Write the 5th letter of the 14th word of the title cited.
From the Davies, Samuel entry, ignoring numbers and initials of names in the title cited,
Write the 8th letter of the 29th word of the title cited.
From the Davies, Samuel entry, ignoring numbers and initials of names in the title cited,
Write the 5th letter of the 12th word of the title cited.
From the Davies, Samuel entry, ignoring numbers and initials of names in the title cited,
Write the 2nd letter of the 33rd word of the title cited.

Now write Riddle 2 and its answer:____

____

Cato's Eagle-Eye View

Chapter 12: A Tragedy in London

Gliding: Summarize the chapter in three to five sentences, written or orally.

Soaring: Summarize the chapter in one word, phrase, or sentence and write it on an index card with the chapter number and title written on the other side.

Soaring Flashcard Game: Shuffle all your Soaring flashcards. Player 1 reads the number and/or title of a chapter on one side of a flashcard. Player 2 answers with the Soaring Summarization on the other side of the flashcard. Reshuffle your flashcards, switch players if desired, and play three times.

Eaglet

Chapter 13: Another Cato: Another Tragedy

1) Why does Gillamon tell Al, Liz, and Kate to hide under his coat?

2) What year did Addison start writing *Cato*?

3) Where are the EO7 team members going? Who built this place and when?

4) What word does Kate use to describe what they will find at their destination?

5) What is the purpose of the side trip?

6) What kind of creature is involved in the side mission and where will it go?

7) Who opens the door of the carriage? What has she been doing? How is she dressed?

8) Where will Liz go when the side trip is finished? Who will her escort be?

9) What does Liz set free? What is its name?

10) At the end of Chapter 13, Liz and Gillamon leave with something in a bag. What is crying inside the bag and what name does Liz give it?

Chapter 13: Another Cato: Another Tragedy

1) Where does Kate think Al and Liz are going after the play? What do they do instead? With whom?

2) Where is the EO7 going on their side trip? How does Al feel about this and why? What does Liz say to reassure Al?

3) Kate explains to Liz what happens to the dogs and cats. What does she reveal to Liz?

4) Find the entry for the menagerie in "A WORD FROM THE AUTHOR." Read the entry and write a paragraph about what you have learned.

5) What is the purpose of the side trip? Why are they not able to do more?

6) What specific animal is Liz there for? What will she do with it and why?

7) Who opens the door of the carriage? What has she been doing? How is she dressed? Where will Liz go when the side trip is finished? Who will escort her?

8) How is Gillamon able to get Liz inside the tower? What does Gillamon open a cage to "give liberty to?"

9) What creature does Liz notice? What is its name? What does she do with it and where does she tell it to go?

10) Where do Gillamon and Liz go after their side trip? What do they bring with them? How will *Plutarch's Lives* get to the Henrys in America? What does Liz name the creature she and Gillamon rescued?

Chapter 13: Another Cato: Another Tragedy

1) What does Liz think of the play? Why did Gillamon want her to see it?

2) Where is the EO7 going on their side trip? How does Al feel about this and why? What does Liz say to reassure Al?

3) Find the entry for the menagerie in "A WORD FROM THE AUTHOR." Read the entry and write a paragraph about what you have learned. Name seven kinds of animals housed in the menagerie. Where were these animals' original homes?

4) What is the purpose of the side trip? Why are the EO7 unable to do more? What is the name of the owl? What are the names of the lions?

5) What specific animal is Liz there for? What will she do with it and why? How will she get it to its final destination? Why is its intermediate stop not a problem?

6) Who opens the door of the carriage? What has she been doing? How is she dressed? Where will Liz go when the side trip is finished? Who will escort her? Where will Al and Kate go? Who will take them?

7) How was Gillamon able to get Liz inside the tower? What does Gillamon open a cage to "give liberty to?" Where did they tell this creature they were taking him? What was his response?

8) What creature does Liz notice? What is its name? What does she do with it and where does she tell it to go?

9) What is the last thing this creature says to Liz? What do you think it reveals about her character? Do you think Liz did a good thing by releasing this creature? Why or why not?

10) Where do Gillamon and Liz go after their side trip? What do they bring with them? How will *Plutarch's Lives* get to the Henrys in America? What does Liz name the creature she and Gillamon rescued?

Nigel's Nuggets

Chapter 13: Another Cato: Another Tragedy

Well, that Biblioquest in Chapter 12 took the biscuit! Just brilliant (if I do say so myself). This challenge will be quite the respite. We're going to use this time to make sure everyone is up to speed.

Right. Have you figured out any parts of the Fiddle's Riddle? If so, have you updated your poster yet? If not, please do. Make sure to include the answer to the riddle, and the chapter(s) in which you discovered it.

Cato's Eagle-Eye View

Chapter 13: Another Cato: Another Tragedy

Gliding: Summarize the chapter in three to five sentences, written or orally.

Soaring: Summarize the chapter in one word, phrase, or sentence and write it on an index card with the chapter number and title written on the other side.

Soaring Flashcard Game: Shuffle all your Soaring flashcards. Player 1 reads the number and/or title of a chapter on one side of a flashcard. Player 2 answers with the Soaring Summarization on the other side of the flashcard. Reshuffle your flashcards, switch players if desired, and play three times.

Eaglet

Chapter 14: Willing to Soar

1) How old is Cato? What two things does Liz tell him he needs to learn to do?

2) What is Patrick taking Uncle Langloo to see?

3) How does Uncle Langloo think Cato wound up on the ground?

4) How does Uncle Langloo say that Cato will have to learn to fly?

5) What does Uncle Langloo say Patrick can to do help Cato?

6) What does Patrick feed Cato? Does Cato eat it?

7) What does Patrick order Max to do? What news does Liz share with Max and Nigel?

8) What does Max say that Patrick has "his heart set on" and how will he accomplish this?

9) A pigeon flies Nigel up to meet the bald eagle in Patrick's woods. How does Nigel get back down to the ground? Does he enjoy the experience?

10) Does Liz think the bald eagle helped Cato?

Fledgling

Chapter 14: Willing to Soar

1) What two things does Liz tell Cato he needs to learn to do? How did Cato get captured by the humans? Does Cato trust humans? Who does Liz ask him to trust? Why should Cato trust this person?

2) What bird call does Patrick make? What does it sound like? What is Patrick taking Uncle Langloo to see? Where is it located?

3) How does Patrick suggest Cato get back to his tree? Why does Uncle Langloo say this will not work?

4) How does Uncle Langloo say that Cato will have to learn to fly? What does Uncle Langloo say Patrick can do to help Cato?

5) Do you think Cato trusts Patrick at first? What does Patrick do to try to earn Cato's trust? Do you think he is successful?

6) What news does Liz share with Max and Nigel? How does Nigel arrive? What does Nigel tell Cato about himself?

7) What does Nigel fly up to meet? Describe its nest. What two things does Nigel think about the appearance of this creature?

8) How does Nigel get back down to the ground? How does the eagle prepare to land? Does it flap its wings? Does Nigel enjoy his experience?

9) What two things does the eagle ask Cato? What three things does he tell Cato?

10) Who thinks the eagle did not help Cato and why? Who thinks the eagle did help Cato and why?

Chapter 14: Willing to Soar

1) What two things does Liz tell Cato he needs to learn to do? How did Cato get captured by the humans? Does he trust humans? Whom does Liz ask him to trust? Why should Cato trust this person? Is Liz able to feed Cato? Who does she think could do the job?

2) What bird call does Patrick make? What does it sound like? What is Patrick taking Uncle Langloo to see? Where is it located? What kind of bird does Patrick think is next to Liz? What reason does Uncle Langloo give to show Patrick he is wrong?

3) How does Patrick suggest Cato get back to his tree? Why does Uncle Langloo say this will not work? How do eagles encourage their young to fly?

4) How does Uncle Langloo say that Cato will have to learn to fly? What does Uncle Langloo say Patrick can do to help Cato? What is Patrick's main concern? Why does Uncle Langloo say that Cato may be left alone?

5) Do you think Cato trusts Patrick at first? What does Patrick do to try to earn Cato's trust? Do you think he is successful? Do you think Cato believes in himself? Do you think it is important that he does? Why or why not?

6) What news does Liz share with Max and Nigel? How does Nigel arrive? What does Nigel tell Cato about himself? Do you think Nigel was wise to do so? Why?

7) What does Nigel fly up to meet? Describe its nest. What two things does Nigel think about the appearance of this creature? What was this nest used for recently? How do you know?

8) How does Nigel get back down to the ground? How does the eagle prepare to land? Does it flap its wings? How does Nigel describe his flight?

9) What two things did the eagle ask Cato? What three things did he tell Cato?

10) Who thinks the eagle did not help Cato and why? Who thinks the eagle *did* help Cato and why? What do *you* think and why?

Nigel's Nuggets

Chapter 14: Willing to Soar

Ah, maps! Maps and mapmaking, or cartography, are two of my favorite pleasures in life. You simply must try your hand at the task. Find the original location of Studley Plantation and Totopotomoy Creek on a map. Make a simple map with those two features. Make sure to include cardinal direction points of reference.

Cato's Eagle-Eye View

Chapter 14: Willing to Soar

Gliding: Summarize the chapter in three to five sentences, written or orally.

Soaring: Summarize the chapter in one word, phrase, or sentence and write it on an index card with the chapter number and title written on the other side.

Soaring Flashcard Game: Shuffle all your Soaring flashcards. Player 1 reads the number and/or title of a chapter on one side of a flashcard. Player 2 answers with the Soaring Summarization on the other side of the flashcard. Reshuffle your flashcards, switch players if desired, and play three times.

Eaglet

Chapter 15: Teaching Cato

1) How does Liz tell Max and Nigel that the gruff eagle could "push" Cato?

2) Copy the verse from Deuteronomy 32. What can God do that a parent eagle cannot?

3) Why does Patrick say that God makes a better parent than does an eagle?

4) Patrick tells Cato he cannot start learning to fly in a nest. What does he propose instead?

5) Liz asks Clarie to carry Cato to the eagle's nest. Does Clarie think this will truly help Cato?

6) The Henry family is discussing the play *Cato.* Has it been performed in America?

7) Whose letter to the Henrys arrives the same day as Cousin David Henry's letter?

8) Whom does Patrick use to demonstrate flying to Cato?

9) What does Cato say when the eagle flies above him?

10) What does the eagle say to Cato when he falls to the ground? Is Cato able to do so?

Chapter 15: Teaching Cato

1) Where do Max and Nigel stay? Why are they upset? What does Liz help them realize?

2) Copy the verse from Deuteronomy 32. Find the verse numbers for the Isaiah 40 quotation. What are pinions?

3) Why does Liz not go with Patrick into the woods to check on Cato?

4) What happens while Patrick is trying to catch a fish for Cato? What does Max come to realize about the eagle?

5) Who shows up at Studley in disguise? What does Liz ask Clarie to do? What is her reasoning behind the request? Does Clarie think it is a good idea? Why or why not?

6) What event does the letter from David Henry tell the Henrys about? Where do they learn that *Cato* has been performed? Who has printed copies of the play?

7) Summarize the contents of Gillamon's letter, including what it inspires John Henry to suggest.

8) How does Patrick demonstrate flying to Cato? What is Nigel's reaction? What is Cato's?

9) Why does Patrick put his shirt around Cato? What does he do with Cato next?

10) Describe what happens after Cato falls to the ground.

Chapter 15: Teaching Cato

1) Where do Max and Nigel stay? Why are they upset? What does Liz help them realize? Why does Cato need to be "pushed?"

2) Copy the verses from Isaiah 40 and Deuteronomy 32 with full references including verse numbers. Explain what each verse means.

3) Why does Liz not go with Patrick into the woods to check on Cato? Who is "Little Cato?" Who is "Patrick's Cato?"

4) How does Patrick propose to teach Cato to fly? What does he do? How does Max describe the eagle? What does he think the eagle's intentions are? What does the eagle actually do? What does Max realize about the eagle as a result?

5) Who shows up at Studley in disguise? What does Liz ask Clarie to do? What is her reasoning behind the request? Does Clarie think it is a good idea? Why or why not? What does Clarie tell Liz about Cato's future?

6) What event does the letter from David Henry tell the Henrys about? Where do they learn that *Cato* has been performed? Who has printed copies of the play? This information interests Liz. Who might also be interested to learn who printed the copies of the play and why?

7) Summarize the contents of Gillamon's letter, including what it inspires John Henry to suggest. What does Sarah Henry say about John's proposal? What else does she say about the boys' future as farmers?

8) How does Patrick demonstrate flying to Cato? What is Nigel's reaction? What is Cato's? What does Patrick tell Cato he has to let him do?

9) Why does Patrick put his shirt around Cato? What does he do with Cato next? Once Cato is on the branch, what does Nigel encourage him to do? Is Cato able to do so?

10) Describe what happens after Cato falls to the ground. How does Cato feel physically and emotionally as he stands on the boulder?

Nigel's Nuggets

Chapter 15: Teaching Cato

Describe one funny scene and one inspiring scene from Chapter 15. Create something to demonstrate one or both.

Cato's Eagle-Eye View

Chapter 15: Teaching Cato

Gliding: Summarize the chapter in three to five sentences, written or orally.

Soaring: Summarize the chapter in one word, phrase, or sentence and write it on an index card with the chapter number and title written on the other side.

Soaring Flashcard Game: Shuffle all your Soaring flashcards. Player 1 reads the number and/or title of a chapter on one side of a flashcard. Player 2 answers with the Soaring Summarization on the other side of the flashcard. Reshuffle your flashcards, switch players if desired, and play three times.

Eaglet

Chapter 16: Cato Teaching

1) What animals can Patrick hear calling to one another? What does he wish to be doing?

2) What does Patrick say that the past will do?

3) What does John Henry say that Cato's tree will become when he learns to fly?

4) What does John Henry say, "We tend to care more about?"

5) What does Patrick's father challenge him to compare with the account of Cato in *Plutarch*?

6) Finish the thought Liz expresses about Cato: "He has chosen to be an eagle . . ."

7) What does Patrick notice when he looks down at the squishy mud between his toes?

8) What did Cato do just before the panther got to him? What did Liz say about it?

9) What does the Latin phrase *ab initio* mean in English?

10) What does Patrick say that "Cato devoted himself to the study, above everything, of?"

Chapter 16: Cato Teaching

1) Look up the translation for the Latin phrase on page 126 in the glossary. Does John Henry translate it word for word?

2) What kind of lessons does Patrick say he remembers most? What example does he give?

3) What will Patrick and William present in a month? What arrives from Williamsburg?

4) What does Patrick's father challenge him to compare with the account of Cato in *Plutarch*? What does John Henry say to Patrick and William as Patrick begins to look at the play?

5) What has Cato been able to accomplish one month later?

6) What does Liz say about the old eagle? What did Cato do right after Patrick showed up?

7) What does Patrick do to try to save Cato? Does he do what he aimed to do?

8) What does Cato do just before the panther gets to him? What does Liz say about it? What does Patrick say to Cato in Latin and in English?

9) What does *ab initio* mean in English? Has Nigel missed anything? What will William review? What will Patrick review?

10) Read the passage that Patrick quotes about Cato from *Plutarch.* What one thing stands out to you about Cato and why?

Chapter 16: Cato Teaching

1) Look up the translation for the Latin phrase on page 126 in the glossary. Does John Henry translate it word for word? Why did John Henry say it was important to study ancient languages?

2) What kind of lessons does Patrick say he remembers most? What example does he give? What Latin phrase does John Henry say with a raised finger and what does it mean?

3) Patrick asks if he and William will "get to read the book Mr. Gillamon sent?" Look up the entry on *Plutarch's Parallel Lives* in "A WORD FROM THE AUTHOR." This work is typically published in either ___________ or _________ volumes. How did Jenny L. Cote choose which number of volumes to include as the number in the Henry library in the VRK?

4) What does Patrick's father challenge him to compare with the account of Cato in *Plutarch*? What does John Henry say to Patrick and William as Patrick begins to look at the play?

5) What has Cato been able to accomplish one month later? Finish the thought Liz expresses about Cato: "He has chosen to be an eagle . . ."

6) What does Liz say about the old eagle? What does Cato do right after Patrick shows up? What does Patrick discover next? How does Patrick discover the animal?

7) What does Patrick do to try to save Cato? Does he accomplish what he aimed to do? What had Patrick's father told him about pointing a gun?

8) What does Cato do just before the panther gets to him? What does Liz say about it? What does Patrick say to Cato in Latin and in English? How does Max respond?

9) What does *Ab initio* mean in English? Has Nigel missed anything? What will William review? What will Patrick review? Why is it significant that the boys are reviewing the two lives that they are reviewing? What happened between the two men?

10) Read the passage Patrick quotes about Cato from *Plutarch.* What two things stand out to you about Cato and why? What does Patrick say he has learned "most" about Cato? Do you think this is still true today? Why or why not?

Nigel's Nuggets

Chapter 16: Cato Teaching

I shudder just remembering that day. Such a close call our young Cato had! I say that Denny Brownlee chap does a bang-up job of telling the tale. Have you listened in to the VRK Podcast lately? Do, do! www.epicorderoftheseven.com/podcast

And then, describe or create a picture of your favorite moment from Chapter 16. When you finish your masterpiece, you've finished Part One of the VRK and the VRK Study Guide. Jolly good show! Please make sure to submit all your best works to:

jenny@epicorderoftheseven.com

Cato's Eagle-Eye View

Chapter 16: Cato Teaching

Gliding: Summarize the chapter in three to five sentences, written or orally.

Soaring: Summarize the chapter in one word, phrase, or sentence and write it on an index card with the chapter number and title written on the other side.

Soaring Flashcard Game: Shuffle all your Soaring flashcards. Player 1 reads the number and/or title of a chapter on one side of a flashcard. Player 2 answers with the Soaring Summarization on the other side of the flashcard. Reshuffle your flashcards, switch players if desired, and play three times.

PART TWO: RUMORS OF WARS
(1745-59)

Eaglet

Chapter 17: Peace, Peace, When There Is No Peace

1) Which Great Awakening preacher has come to preach at St. Paul's Parish?

2) What did George Whitefield do when the Anglican Church in England did not assign him a pulpit? What was unique about his voice?

3) What is Patrick doing when he hears his father and John Henry discussing George Whitefield's preaching?

4) Look up the entry for George Whitefield in "A WORD FROM THE AUTHOR." Did he preach at St. Paul's Parish in Hanover in 1745?

5) Copy the Scripture George Whitefield used as the basis of his sermon.

6) What does Patrick say as he walks away after Uncle Patrick leaves?

7) Which EO7 members were present with Jeremiah when he wrote those words? What was his warning to Jerusalem?

8) Max comments that the Henry and Winston families are on the *same side.* What does he say about their fighting?

9) What is the next part of the Fiddle's Riddle? What is its answer? Liz thinks she has solved it. Has she?

10) Whom will Gillamon and Clarie escort to Williamsburg? How does Gillamon say he will influence Patrick?

Chapter 17: Peace, Peace, When There Is No Peace

1) Which Great Awakening preacher has come to preach at St. Paul's Parish? Look in "A WORD FROM THE AUTHOR." Did this event really happen? What did George Whitefield do when the Anglican Church of England did not assign him a pulpit? What was unique about his voice?

2) What was George Whitefield's effect on Benjamin Franklin? How does Sarah Henry describe George Whitefield's effect on people? What is his effect on Patrick?

3) Write out the text for the day. Summarize the first part of George Whitefield's sermon in three to five sentences.

4) How does John Henry describe George Whitefield's "Historical Faith" comment and why? Summarize this part of George Whitefield's sermon.

5) What is Uncle Patrick's reaction to the sermon? Why does Sarah Henry say the Great Awakening is good?

6) What does Patrick say as he walks away after Uncle Patrick leaves? Which EO7 members were with Jeremiah when he wrote those words? What was his warning to Jerusalem?

7) What does Max say after he comments that the Henry and Winston families are on the *same side?* How does Nigel respond? What is the next part of the Fiddle's Riddle? What is its answer? Liz thinks she has solved it. Has she?

8) What does the team use to contact Gillamon? Does Gillamon confirm Liz's supposition about the answer to the next part of the riddle?

9) Whom will Gillamon and Clarie escort to Williamsburg? How does Gillamon say he will influence Patrick? How does Max say that his getting a license will benefit the humans?

10) What does Gillamon say about the warring between believers? What happens next? What is Liz's comment about the time when she trades in her daisy stem for a quill?

Chapter 17: Peace, Peace, When There Is No Peace

1) Which Great Awakening preacher has come to preach at St. Paul's Parish? Look in "A WORD FROM THE AUTHOR." Did this event happen? What did George Whitefield do when the Anglican Church of England did not assign him a pulpit? What was unique about his voice?

2) What was George Whitefield's effect on Benjamin Franklin? How does Sarah Henry describe George Whitefield's effect on people? What is his effect on Patrick? How old is George Whitefield? How does he "hold the people captive?"

3) Copy the text for the day. Summarize the first part of Whitefield's sermon.

4) How does John Henry describe George Whitefield's "Historical Faith" comment? Summarize this part of George Whitefield's sermon and tell what it means to you.

5) What is Uncle Patrick's reaction to the sermon? Why does Sarah Henry say the Great Awakening is good? What do you think Uncle Patrick means by his threat?

6) What does Patrick say as he walks away after Uncle Patrick leaves? Which EO7 members were with Jeremiah when he wrote those words? What was his warning to Jerusalem? Did Jeremiah's prophecy come to pass? What does Liz say about the result? What does Nigel say?

7) What does Max say after he comments that the Henry and Winston families are on the *same side*. How does Nigel respond? What is the next part of the Fiddle's Riddle? What is its answer? Liz thinks she has solved it. Has she? How does Liz sum things up as Patrick walks away?

8) What does the team use to contact Gillamon? Does Gillamon confirm Liz's supposition about the answer to the next part of the riddle? What does Gillamon say after he answers Liz?

9) Whom will Gillamon and Clarie escort to Williamsburg? How does Gillamon say he will influence Patrick? How does Max say that his getting a license will benefit the humans?

10) What is Liz's comment about the time when she trades in her daisy stem for a pen? What does she mean by this comment?

Nigel's Nuggets

Chapter 17: Peace, Peace, When There Is No Peace
Third Riddle

Hello, readers! Nigel here on current assignment. Very hush, hush. I say, the most amazing thing has happened. Liz was explaining the scientific meaning of something to Max, who did not understand it, the poor lad. Fortunately, Al saved the day. You see, his human has a smartphone, and apparently Al knows how to work it. That little device absolutely takes the biscuit! You can use one, or perhaps a laptop, to solve the third installment of the Fiddle's Riddle. You'll need to go to a website that Al uses frequently to help him understand Liz. It's called *Google Translate*. Al has this all set up for you. Have fun!

The Third Riddle:

From Spanish, translate "una" to English:

From Scottish Gaelic, translate "guth" to English:

From Czech, translate "v" to English:

From Afrikaans, translate "die" to English:

From Western Frisian, translate "oanwezich" to English:

From Danish, translate "vagne" to English:

Oh, dear, dear. That won't do. You'll need to add an "s" to the end of the English word you got.

From Luxembourgish, translate "eiwegkeet" to English:

Now he's just being cheeky.

From German, translate "viel" to Danish:

Jolly good show! You have translated the third part of the Fiddle's Riddle. Please write it below:

____

Let's move on to the answer!

From Catalan, translate "el" to English:

From Irish, translate "iontach" to English:

From Welsh, translate "deffroad" to English:

Dare I say that Welsh is the best language the Maker created? Yes, I think I must dare.

Now that you have the answer to the third riddle, please write it below:

Cato's Eagle-Eye View

Chapter 17: Peace, Peace, When There Is No Peace

Gliding: Summarize the chapter in three to five sentences, written or orally.

Soaring: Summarize the chapter in one word, phrase, or sentence and write it on an index card with the chapter number and title written on the other side.

Soaring Flashcard Game: Shuffle all your Soaring flashcards. Player 1 reads the number and/or title of a chapter on one side of a flashcard. Player 2 answers with the Soaring Summarization on the other side of the flashcard. Reshuffle your flashcards, switch players if desired, and play three times.

Eaglet

Chapter 18: A Voice in the Present

1) How much money does Sarah Henry's father have to pay as his punishment? What is not a part of his penalty?
2) What is Samuel Davies granted in Williamsburg? What is the name of his new posting?
3) How many people are at Polegreen on Sunday?
4) Who is with Sallie Shelton?
5) How does Nigel arrive?
6) Patrick states the main point of the sermon. What does he say? Which Scripture reference does he use?
7) What does John Henry say about Patrick's memory?
8) Who shows up during the discussion? Are all the adults expecting him?
9) What Bible verse does Samuel Davies quote to Patrick about his future?
10) How does Patrick respond to Uncle Patrick's caution never to preach outside?

Chapter 18: A Voice in the Present

1) About whom is Sarah Henry awaiting word? What has he done? What is his punishment? What is not part of the penalty?

2) What is Samuel Davies granted in Williamsburg? What is the name of his new posting? What does he do when he learns about the case against Isaac Winston?

3) How many people are at Polegreen on Sunday? How do they arrive? What is the service time and why? How many people can the church hold?

4) Who calls the service to attention? What is the Scripture verse of the day? Who is hiding in the burlap sack?

5) What are Patrick's first two reactions to the sermon? How does he summarize it? What does Patrick say about his listening and remembering skills?

6) Summarize in one paragraph Patrick's recital of the sermon.

7) How does Sarah Henry describe the recital of the sermon? How does John Henry respond?

8) Who arrives at the Henrys' home during the discussion? What is Sarah Henry's reaction? What does Uncle Patrick say to John Henry?

9) What does Samuel Davies say about his purpose among the people of Hanover? What does Uncle Patrick say to challenge him? How does Samuel Davies respond to Uncle Patrick?

10) How does Uncle Patrick respond to Samuel Davies' comments? How does Patrick respond to Uncle Patrick's caution not to preach outdoors?

Chapter 18: A Voice in the Present

1) About whom is Sarah Henry awaiting word? What has he done? What is his punishment? What is not part of the penalty? Approximately what would be the equivalent of the fine in current U.S. dollars?

2) What is Samuel Davies granted in Williamsburg? What is the name of his new posting? What does he do when he learns about the case against Isaac Winston? What does Samuel Davies learn about the situation in the Henry and Winston families?

3) How many people are at Polegreen on Sunday? How do they arrive? What is the service time and why? How many people can the church hold? Where does Samuel Davies preach? What is Sarah Henry's reaction to this news?

4) Who calls the service to attention? What is the Scripture verse of the day? Who is hiding in the burlap sack? Describe Samuel Davies physically. How old is he? Why does he not look healthy?

5) What are Patrick's first two reactions to the sermon? How does he summarize it? What does Patrick say about his listening and remembering skills? What does Sarah Henry challenge Patrick to do?

6) Summarize in two or three paragraphs Patrick's recital of the sermon.

7) How does Sarah Henry describe the recital of the sermon? How does John Henry respond?

8) Who arrives at the Henry home during the discussion? What is Sarah Henry's reaction? What does Uncle Patrick say to John Henry? Why do you think Uncle Patrick reacts as he does? Do you think he would have come to the Henry home if he had known Samuel Davies would be there as well? Why or why not?

9) What does Samuel Davies say about his purpose among the people of Hanover? What does Uncle Patrick say to challenge him? How does Samuel Davies respond to Uncle Patrick? What is John Henry's reaction to Samuel Davies' offer of his hand of friendship? What is Uncle Patrick's reaction?

10) How does Uncle Patrick respond to Samuel Davies' comments? How does Patrick respond to Uncle Patrick's caution not to preach outdoors?

Nigel's Nuggets

Chapter 18: A Voice in the Present

Nigel here. Just popping over from the Podcast. Have you visited recently? It's jolly good stuff! www.epicorderoftheseven.com/podcast

For your challenge, please pick a scene from Chapter 18, and create something in words or artwork to demonstrate the scene you have chosen.

Cato's Eagle-Eye View

Chapter 18: A Voice in the Present

Gliding: Summarize the chapter in three to five sentences, written or orally.

Soaring: Summarize the chapter in one word, phrase, or sentence and write it on an index card with the chapter number and title written on the other side.

Soaring Flashcard Game: Shuffle all your Soaring flashcards. Player 1 reads the number and/or title of a chapter on one side of a flashcard. Player 2 answers with the Soaring Summarization on the other side of the flashcard. Reshuffle your flashcards, switch players if desired, and play three times.

Eaglet

Chapter 19: High and Mighty

1) In what year is Chapter 19 set? How old is Patrick? What season of the year is it?

2) Which humans are with Patrick?

3) What did Al bring Liz from the Alps?

4) Samuel challenges Patrick about having an eagle feather. Does Patrick have one?

5) What does Patrick do because of Samuel's challenge?

6) Cato sees the real threat to Patrick. What is it?

7) What does Patrick do when he sees the panther?

8) What does Patrick say to William and Samuel about his arm as they surround him?

9) Max thanks Cato for sounding the alarm about the panther. What does he say next?

10) Nigel summons Max back to Studley. What has happened to Patrick?

Chapter 19: High and Mighty

1) In what year is Chapter 19 set? How old is Patrick? What season of the year is it? Which humans are with Patrick? What do the boys have with them?

2) What does Patrick do when Sallie looks up and smiles? What does Nigel have to say about this? Which habit does Liz hope Patrick does not acquire?

3) What kind of bird does Jane think she has spotted? What does this give Patrick the opportunity to do next? How does Samuel challenge Patrick?

4) What does Patrick do because of Samuel's challenge? How does each of the following react: the girls, William, Liz, Max, and Nigel?

5) Who flies by? What does he see when a gust of wind blows? What does he do next to try to keep Patrick safe? What makes Samuel's face fall?

6) What does Patrick do when he notices the panther? What do Samuel and William do? Why are they not able to do what they try to do? What does Cato tell Patrick he should do?

7) Describe what happens from the time Max urges Patrick to jump until the panther lunges at Patrick.

8) What happens to Patrick when he jumps? What does he think he has injured? What does he tell William and Samuel that he thinks has happened?

9) What does Max do next? What does he say to Cato to thank him? What does he realize about the panther?

10) Nigel summons Max back to Studley. What has happened to Patrick? Max has sensed a creature watching Patrick for three years. Who or what do you think this might be? What is Cato's reaction to Patrick's injury? What does Cato tell Max about the panther?

Chapter 19: High and Mighty

1) In what year is Chapter 19 set? How old is Patrick? What season of the year is it? Which humans are with Patrick? What do the boys have with them? What are they telling the girls about? What do they mean by "points?"

2) What does Patrick do when Sallie smiles? What does Nigel have to say about this? Which habit does Liz hope Patrick does not acquire? Do you think Patrick is showing off for Sallie? Why? Do you think Jane or Elizabeth would have caused the same reaction?

3) What kind of bird does Jane think she has spotted? What does this give Patrick the opportunity to do next? How does Samuel challenge Patrick? Why do you think Samuel challenged Patrick?

4) What does Patrick do because of Samuel's challenge? How does each of the following react: the girls, William, Liz, Max, and Nigel? What is foreshadowed?

5) Who flies by? What does he see when a gust of wind blows? What does he do next to try to keep Patrick safe? What makes Samuel's face fall? What has Patrick done to leave himself unprotected? Have we seen this creature before? How do you know?

6) What does Patrick do when he notices the panther? What do Samuel and William do? Why are they not able to do what they try to do? What does Cato tell Patrick he should do? Does Patrick understand Cato? What does Cato think to himself?

7) Describe what happens from the time Max urges Patrick to jump until the panther lunges at Patrick. What happens to the panther?

8) What happens to Patrick when he jumps? What does he think he has injured? What does he tell William and Samuel he thinks has happened? What does William instruct Samuel to do? Why?

9) What does Max do next? What does he say to Cato to thank him? What does he realize about the panther? Why does Max growl? What does he say? What does his statement mean?

10) Nigel summons Max back to Studley. What has happened to Patrick? Max has sensed a creature watching Patrick for three years. Who or what do you think this might be? What is Cato's reaction to Patrick's injury? What does Cato tell Max about the panther? What does the creature do to the panther? How do you think this is accomplished?

Nigel's Nuggets

Chapter 19: High and Mighty

I hope you are enjoying my new venture on the VRK Podcast. Broadcasting is quite the thrilling endeavor! Create a video of you presenting a newscast from the field following the events in the woods. Be sure to include a follow-up with an update on the outcome for Patrick and the panther. This would be a perfect time for you to send your Nigel's Nuggets to Jenny L. Cote. You might see your newscast on her website!

jenny@epicorderoftheseven.com

Cato's Eagle-Eye View

Chapter 19: High and Mighty

Gliding: Summarize the chapter in three to five sentences, written or orally.

Soaring: Summarize the chapter in one word, phrase, or sentence and write it on an index card with the chapter number and title written on the other side.

Soaring Flashcard Game: Shuffle all your Soaring flashcards. Player 1 reads the number and/or title of a chapter on one side of a flashcard. Player 2 answers with the Soaring Summarization on the other side of the flashcard. Reshuffle your flashcards, switch players if desired, and play three times.

Eaglet

Chapter 20: Honey to the Bones

1) Who is missing at the start of Chapter 20?

2) To whom is Patrick referring when he exclaims, "He's alright. Oh, he's alright?"

3) Who comes to check on Patrick?

4) Samuel Davies tells Patrick's parents that the panther has been found. How did it die?

5) What does Patrick tell Samuel Davies about Liz?

6) What does Patrick confess to Samuel Davies about his reason for climbing the tree?

7) Samuel Davies tells Patrick there is something healing to the bones. What is it?

8) To what does Patrick say he gives his first allegiance?

9) What is the thing that has caused the colonies to come together for the first time?

10) What does Samuel Davies give Patrick as a get-well gift?

Fledgling

Chapter 20: Honey to the Bones

1) Why is Patrick upset at the start of Chapter 20? Liz says something to Patrick in French. Translate it to English. Where is the translation located in the VRK? Include the name of the section, and the starting page number.

2) Summarize the conversation Max and Nigel have under the window by Patrick's room once he is asleep.

3) Who comes to check on Patrick? What great loss has he recently suffered? Samuel Davies tells Patrick's parents the panther has died. How did it die?

4) What does Patrick tell Samuel Davies about Liz? What does Samuel Davies say about friends? How does Patrick assume the panther was killed? What are Patrick's and Liz's reactions to the news about the way the panther died?

5) Describe the conversation Patrick and Samuel Davies have about showing off. Patrick says he has learned his lesson. What lesson has he learned? What does Samuel Davies say about the eagle feather?

6) Samuel Davies comforts Patrick with words from Scripture. Which book and verse?

7) Patrick asks Samuel Davies how he handles men saying mean words about him and his Dissenter preaching. Summarize Samuel Davies' response.

8) Patrick asks Samuel Davies, "Which is right? What the government says or what God says?" How does Samuel Davies reply? Patrick wonders about the situation in his own family. What advice does Samuel Davies give Patrick? What does Samuel Davies say the Great Awakening has done for the first time?

9) Patrick tells Samuel Davies he is unable to play the fiddle. What gift, which he is unable to use, does Samuel Davies give him? Why is he unable to use it?

10) What reassurance does Samuel Davies give Patrick about Patrick's confession regarding his accident? What does this say about Samuel Davies' character?

Chapter 20: Honey to the Bones

1) Why is Patrick upset at the start of Chapter 20? Liz says something to Patrick in French. Translate it to English. Where is the translation located in the VRK? Include the name of the section, and the starting page number.

2) Summarize the conversation Max and Nigel have under the window by Patrick's room once he is asleep. What does Max mean when he says, "Even earlier than that?"

3) Who comes to check on Patrick? What great loss has he recently suffered? Samuel Davies tells Patrick's parents the panther has died. How did it die? Was this type of death alluded to in the last chapter? What do you think all of this means?

4) What does Patrick tell Samuel Davies about Liz? What does Samuel Davies say about friends? How does Patrick assume the panther was killed? What is Patrick's and Liz's reaction to the news about the way the panther died? In question 3, you made a guess about what the poisoning means. Does Liz's comment support your conclusion? If not, what do you conclude now?

5) Describe the conversation Patrick and Samuel Davies have about showing off. Patrick says that he has learned his lesson. What lesson has he learned? What does Samuel Davies say about the eagle feather?

6) Samuel Davies comforts Patrick with words from Scripture. Which book and verse? What do you think this verse meant to Patrick?

7) Patrick asks Samuel Davies how he handles men saying mean words about him and his Dissenter preaching. Summarize Samuel Davies' response.

8) Patrick asks Samuel Davies, "Which is right? What the government says or what God says?" How does Samuel Davies reply? Patrick wonders about the situation in his own family. What advice does Samuel Davies give Patrick? What does Samuel Davies say the Great Awakening has done for the first time? Do you think that this was a coincidence?

9) Patrick tells Samuel Davies he is unable to play the fiddle. What gift, which he is unable to use, does Samuel Davies give him? Why is Patrick unable to use it? Write a paragraph about tuberculosis. What name would Samuel Davies and Patrick have used for tuberculosis?

10) What reassurance does Samuel Davies give Patrick about Patrick's confession regarding his accident? What does this say about Samuel Davies' character? How does Liz say Samuel Davies has sweetened the riddle?

Nigel's Nuggets

Chapter 20: Honey to the Bones

Check out the entry on Samuel Davies from Part Two of A WORD FROM THE AUTHOR. Present a research project about Samuel Davies and his life. Be sure to describe some of the many struggles he endured in his life, and how he overcame them.

Cato's Eagle-Eye View

Chapter 20: Honey to the Bones

Gliding: Summarize the chapter in three to five sentences, written or orally.

Soaring: Summarize the chapter in one word, phrase, or sentence and write it on an index card with the chapter number and title written on the other side.

Soaring Flashcard Game: Shuffle all your Soaring flashcards. Player 1 reads the number and/or title of a chapter on one side of a flashcard. Player 2 answers with the Soaring Summarization on the other side of the flashcard. Reshuffle your flashcards, switch players if desired, and play three times.

Eaglet

Chapter 21: God's Riddle

1) Where is Chapter 21 set? In which building and what is the date?

2) Whom do we meet at the beginning of Chapter 21? How old is he? Is he interested in organized religion?

3) What books become numbered among Benjamin Franklin's favorite books at his age eleven?

4) With whom does Benjamin Franklin apprentice? What does he long to do? Is he allowed to do so? What does he do to get around this?

5) Whom does Gillamon introduce to Benjamin Franklin? For whom do they both work?

6) What does Benjamin Franklin purchase and take over the printing of in 1729? What does he begin publishing in 1732?

7) Who is the person Gillamon cannot wait for Benjamin Franklin to meet next?

8) What chapter of Scripture is "today's Holy Writ?" Who reads it?

9) Gillamon poses a question at the bottom of page 172. What question is it in which Benjamin Franklin finds *an intriguing thought?*

10) Benjamin Franklin surmises that lightning seems to strike something *of choice.* What is it?

Fledgling

Chapter 21: God's Riddle

1) Where is Chapter 21 set? In which building and what is the date? Whom do we meet at the beginning of Chapter 21? How old is he? Is he interested in organized religion?

2) What books become numbered among Benjamin Franklin's favorite books at his age eleven? With whom does Benjamin Franklin apprentice? What does he long to do? Is he allowed to do so? What does he do to get around this?

3) Whom does Gillamon introduce to Benjamin Franklin? For whom do they both work? What does Benjamin Franklin purchase and take over printing in 1729? What does he begin publishing in 1732?

4) Benjamin Franklin is moving on from the printing business. What is the plan for his next venture? For what purpose is he soliciting investors?

5) What does Benjamin start doing when the church bell begins ringing? What year had it arrived, and from where? How much does it weigh?

6) Who is the special guest at church? What has he done for the church recently? What does he leave in the pew? What chapter of Scripture does he read?

7) Research the events that led to the 38th chapter of Job. Why was the Lord telling Job to brace himself?

8) What does Benjamin Franklin mentally pause to do after each question and why?

9) What does Benjamin Franklin say he *knew the extent of*? What does he wonder next?

10) Gillamon poses a question at the bottom of page 172. What question is it in which Benjamin Franklin finds *an intriguing thought?* What is it? Benjamin Franklin surmises that lightning seems to strike something *of choice.* What is it?

Chapter 21: God's Riddle

1) Where is Chapter 21 set? In which building and what is the date? Whom do we meet at the beginning of Chapter 21? How old is he? Is he interested in organized religion? What does Benjamin Franklin do as he studies the flickering candles?

2) What books become numbered among Benjamin Franklin's favorite books at his age eleven? With whom does Benjamin Franklin apprentice? What does he long to do? Is he allowed to do so? What does he do to get around this? Benjamin Franklin is duped into doing something. What is it?

3) Whom does Gillamon introduce to Benjamin Franklin? For whom do they both work? What does Benjamin Franklin purchase and take over the printing of in 1729? What does he begin publishing in 1732? What does Benjamin Franklin believe about God?

4) Benjamin Franklin is moving on from the printing business. What is the plan for his next venture? For what purpose is he soliciting investors? Is he successful in securing them? What is the resulting entity? Is it still in existence today?

5) What does Benjamin start doing when the church bell begins ringing? What year had it arrived, and from where? How much does it weigh? How does Benjamin Franklin make his calculations? What is his answer?

6) Who is the special guest at church? What has he done for the church recently? What does he leave in the pew? What chapter of Scripture does he read? What is the weather outside? Why do you think it causes Gillamon to smile?

7) Research the events that led to the 38th chapter of Job. Why was the Lord telling Job to brace himself? What was the main point Job's friends made to him throughout the book of Job? Do you think they were helpful? Why or why not?

8) What does Benjamin Franklin mentally pause to do after each question and why? Write his thought about *seas.* Why would this analogy be helpful in studying electricity?

9) What does Benjamin Franklin say he *knew the extent of?* What does he wonder next? Please do an Internet search for "message in a bottle." Using the *Wikipedia* search result, describe Benjamin Franklin's contribution that may have arisen from this question.

10) Gillamon poses a question at the bottom of page 172. What is it? Benjamin Franklin surmises that lightning seems to strike something *of choice.* What is it? Why have churches been ringing their bells during storms for centuries?

Nigel's Nuggets

Chapter 21: God's Riddle

As you know, I have a high regard for inventors, and Benjamin Franklin is one of my favorites. It was quite the honor to be assigned to his mission. Make a presentation about Benjamin Franklin. There is too much material from which to choose if you look at his whole life. Limit this challenge to any time in his life from childhood up through and including the time period covered in Chapter 21.

Cato's Eagle-Eye View

Chapter 21: God's Riddle

Gliding: Summarize the chapter in three to five sentences, written or orally.

Soaring: Summarize the chapter in one word, phrase, or sentence and write it on an index card with the chapter number and title written on the other side.

Soaring Flashcard Game: Shuffle all your Soaring flashcards. Player 1 reads the number and/or title of a chapter on one side of a flashcard. Player 2 answers with the Soaring Summarization on the other side of the flashcard. Reshuffle your flashcards, switch players if desired, and play three times.

Eaglet

Chapter 22: A Brilliant Move

1) Clarie shows up in Chapter 22. How is she disguised? Why are the Henrys moving? What will Max and Liz's assignments be?

2) What does Clarie say that Patrick cannot know? What must Max and Liz do to prevent this? To whom will Max go?

3) What does Clarie tell the EO7 about Samuel Davies? What will Nigel be doing? Who will be with him on his mission?

4) Clarie tells Liz she will help John Henry 'come up with' the name of the new Henry home. What is the name Liz chooses?

5) Cato flies Nigel to Philadelphia. How long does it take them to arrive? How many miles does Cato fly?

6) How long does Nigel tell Cato they will be in Philadelphia? What does he suggest Cato do during that time?

7) Nigel's eyes widen as he discovers what Benjamin Franklin intends to do with a turkey. What does the inventor intend to do?

8) Who are Charles and George Dabney?

9) What does Patrick do for the *third* time? What is the result each time?

10) At the end of Chapter 22, Patrick is telling his father the most important thing he has learned about the Declaration of Arbroath. What does he say about the document after he puts his hand on the book?

Chapter 22: A Brilliant Move

1) Where is Chapter 22 set and when? What is being built and in which style? How many acres are there on the new Henry property? Describe the land.

2) Clarie shows up in Chapter 22. How is she disguised? Why are the Henrys moving? What will Max and Liz's assignments be? What does Clarie say that Patrick cannot know? What must Max and Liz do to prevent this? Where will Max and Nigel be going? What does Clarie tell the EO7 about Samuel Davies? Who will be with Nigel on his mission?

3) Explain Nigel's mission including the way Benjamin Franklin, David Henry, Peter Collinson, and Handel's lives intersect due to Gillamon and Clarie's intervention.

4) Liz asks, "Will any of this help my Henry and America?" How does Clarie respond? What privilege does she give Liz next? What does Liz come up with?

5) Cato flies Nigel to Philadelphia. How long does it take them to arrive? How many miles does Cato fly? Specifically, where do they land? How long does Nigel tell Cato they will be in Philadelphia? What does he suggest for Cato to do during that time?

6) Describe Benjamin Franklin's study. Describe the inventor's appearance. What is he doing? What famous Benjamin Franklin quotation is the last thing he says as he blows out his oil lamps?

7) Describe Benjamin Franklin's proposed turkey experiment.

8) Who are Charles and George Dabney? What do they decide to do together with Patrick? Where will they go to do so? What is the condition of this location?

9) Describe the boys' outing. What does Patrick do for the *third* time? What is the result each time?

10) How long had England and Scotland been at war? What battle ended it? Who were the Kings of England and Scotland? Describe the Declaration of Arbroath. What is the most important thing Patrick says he has learned about it? What does Patrick say about the document after he puts his hand on the book?

Chapter 22: A Brilliant Move

1) Where is Chapter 22 set and when? What is being built and in which style? How many acres are there on the new Henry property? Describe the land. Why are the Henrys moving?

2) Clarie shows up in Chapter 22. How is she disguised? What will Max and Liz's assignments be? What does Clarie say that Patrick cannot know? What must Max and Liz do to prevent this? Where will Max and Nigel be going? What does Clarie tell the EO7 about Samuel Davies? Who will be with Nigel on his mission?

3) Explain Nigel's mission including the way Benjamin Franklin, David Henry, Peter Collinson, and Handel's lives intersect due to Gillamon and Clarie's intervention. Who suggests that *Messiah* be performed as a benefit concert? Clarie mentions the concert in relation to two keys. What are these two keys?

4) Liz asks, "Will any of this help my Henry and America?" How does Clarie respond? What privilege does she give Liz next? What does Liz come up with?

5) Cato flies Nigel to Philadelphia. How long does it take them to arrive? How many miles does Cato fly? Specifically, where do they land? Why does Jenny L. Cote mention the building by name? What does it foreshadow? How long does Nigel tell Cato they will be in Philadelphia? What does he suggest Cato do during that time?

6) Describe Benjamin Franklin's study. Describe the inventor's appearance. What is he doing? What famous Benjamin Franklin quotation is the last thing he says as he blows out his oil lamps? List at least three other of Benjamin Franklin's famous quotations from Chapter 22.

7) Describe Benjamin Franklin's proposed turkey experiment. How does Nigel sum it up?

8) Who are Charles and George Dabney? What do they decide to do together with Patrick? Where will they go to do so? What is the condition of this location?

9) Describe the boys' outing. What does Patrick do for the *third* time? What is the result each time? What would you do to "get him back somehow?"

10) How long had England and Scotland been at war? What battle ended the fighting? Who were the Kings of England and Scotland? Describe the Declaration of Arbroath. What is the most important thing that Patrick says he has learned about it? What does Patrick say about the document after he puts his hand on the book? What does this foreshadow?

Nigel's Nuggets

Chapter 22: A Brilliant Move

OPTION 1: Create a cartoon of your favorite scene from Chapter 22.

OPTION 2: Make a presentation about the Henry home, Mount Brilliant.

Cato's Eagle-Eye View

Chapter 22: A Brilliant Move

Gliding: Summarize the chapter in three to five sentences, written or orally.

Soaring: Summarize the chapter in one word, phrase, or sentence and write it on an index card with the chapter number and title written on the other side.

Soaring Flashcard Game: Shuffle all your Soaring flashcards. Player 1 reads the number and/or title of a chapter on one side of a flashcard. Player 2 answers with the Soaring Summarization on the other side of the flashcard. Reshuffle your flashcards, switch players if desired, and play three times.

Eaglet

Chapter 23: Keys to the Future

1) What thought does Clarie have as she watches Benjamin Franklin and Nigel work?

2) How is Clarie disguised?

3) What *brilliant* idea does Benjamin Franklin share with Collinson?

4) What does Clarie say is the key to opening new doors for the future?

5) Who is with Kate at the *Messiah* benefit concert? What does he do when he realizes he might have put the letters in the wrong place?

6) How does Gillamon describe the evening to Peter Collinson?

7) To whom is Benjamin Franklin's proposed experiment presented on February 4, 1752?

8) What does the King of France say should be done with Benjamin Franklin's proposed experiment?

9) Is the experiment in France successful?

10) Why does Gillamon tell Clarie not to let Nigel know of the results of the experiment?

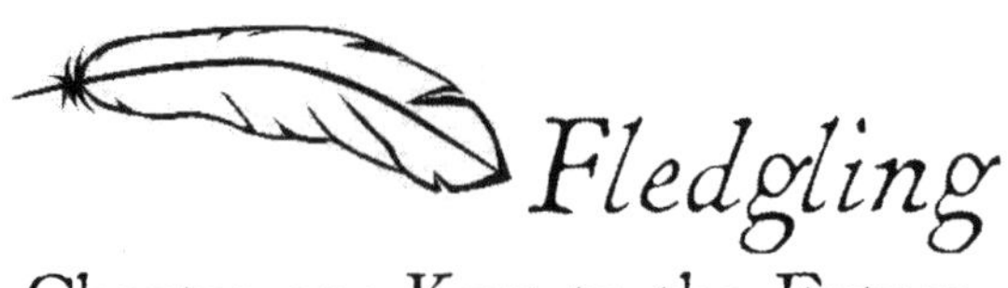

Chapter 23: Keys to the Future

1) Draw a picture of Benjamin Franklin and Nigel working together. What thought does Clarie have as she watches them work?

2) What does Benjamin Franklin read aloud? What is he encouraging Collinson to do with his idea?

3) How is Clarie disguised? What *brilliant* idea does Benjamin Franklin share with Collinson? What does Clarie say is the key to opening new doors for the future? What does Clarie mean by this? To which person(s) might she be referring?

4) What assignment does Clarie give Nigel? What is Nigel's concern? How does Clarie respond to this?

5) Which EO7 members are at the *Messiah* benefit concert? Which humans? Who is with Kate? What does he do when he realizes he might have put the letters in the wrong place?

6) Describe the events between the humans, and the events' outcomes. How does Gillamon describe the evening to Peter Collinson?

7) Describe the setting of the Palace of Versailles, including the Hall of Mirrors.

8) What does the King of France say about Benjamin Franklin? How does Comte de Buffon answer him?

9) When is the experiment first carried out? Where? How does the experiment unfold? What is the result?

10) How does Clarie react to the experiment? What caution does Gillamon give her and why?

Chapter 23: Keys to the Future

1) Draw a picture of Benjamin Franklin and Nigel working together. What thought does Clarie have as she watches them work?

2) What does Benjamin Franklin read aloud? What is he encouraging Collinson to do with his idea? What does it say about Benjamin Franklin's character that he shared his ideas?

3) How is Clarie disguised? What *brilliant* idea does Benjamin Franklin share with Collinson? What does Clarie say is the key to opening new doors for the future? What does she mean by this? To which person(s) might she be referring?

4) What assignment does Clarie give Nigel? What is Nigel's concern? How does Clarie respond to this? What does Nigel think about Clarie's advice?

5) Which EO7 members are at the *Messiah* benefit concert? Which humans? Who is with Kate? What does he do when he realizes he might have put the letters in the wrong place?

6) Describe the events between the humans, and the events' outcomes. How does Gillamon describe the evening to Peter Collinson?

7) Describe the setting of the Palace of Versailles, including the Hall of Mirrors.

8) What does the King of France say about Benjamin Franklin? How does Comte de Buffon answer him? Describe the proposed experiment. What is the response of the King?

9) When is the experiment first carried out? Where? How does the experiment unfold? What is the result? Describe the King of France's response to the experiment.

10) How does Clarie react to the experiment? What caution does Gillamon give her and why? What does Gillamon say about the key?

Nigel's Nuggets

Chapter 23: Keys to the Future

Propose a trip to the Palace of Versailles. Give a brief presentation to win support for your trip. Plan and present an itinerary of your visit. Your visit should be at least one day.

Cato's Eagle-Eye View

Chapter 23: Keys to the Future

Gliding: Summarize the chapter in three to five sentences, written or orally.

Soaring: Summarize the chapter in one word, phrase, or sentence and write it on an index card with the chapter number and title written on the other side.

Soaring Flashcard Game: Shuffle all your Soaring flashcards. Player 1 reads the number and/or title of a chapter on one side of a flashcard. Player 2 answers with the Soaring Summarization on the other side of the flashcard. Reshuffle your flashcards, switch players if desired, and play three times.

Eaglet

Chapter 24: The Key to Our Shuccshessh

1) Where is Chapter 24 set and when?

2) What is Benjamin Franklin doing? What is his new elected office? What has he been given?

3) What goes running by Nigel and Cato? What barrels into them next?

4) What is the name of the creature who barreled into them? What does he tell Nigel and Cato to call him?

5) What is the name of the lizard?

6) What are the squirrel and the lizard playing? What are they using to play with?

7) Where is William Franklin June 6, 1752?

8) What does Nigel tell Cato he can do once Benjamin and Will Franklin enter the shed?

9) What does Benjamin Franklin tell William Franklin to do once the kite is in the air?

10) What does Benjamin Franklin discover about lightning?

Chapter 24: The Key to Our Shuccshessh

1) Where is Chapter 24 set and when? What is Benjamin Franklin doing? What is his new elected office? What has he been given?

2) What goes running by Nigel and Cato? What barrels into them next? What is the name of the creature who barrels into them? What does he tell Nigel and Cato to call him?

3) What is the name of the lizard? What are the squirrel and the lizard playing?

4) What are they using to play with? What does it go to? What idea does this give Nigel?

5) Where is William Franklin on June 6, 1752? How old is he? What is the weather? What does he have with him?

6) What two reasons does Benjamin Franklin give William for being out in the middle of nowhere?

7) Benjamin Franklin has the experiment set up in his hands. Describe it.

8) Why does Nigel say Benjamin Franklin has to be inside the shed? What does Nigel tell Cato he can do once Benjamin and William Franklin enter the shed? What does Benjamin Franklin tell William to do once the kite is in the air?

9) What happens to Nigel when it begins to rain? What does Cato do to help? What do they do next?

10) What happens after Benjamin Franklin says a quick prayer?

Chapter 24: The Key to Our Shuccshessh

1) Where is Chapter 24 set and when? What is Benjamin Franklin doing? What is his new elected office? What has he been given? Where does Nigel land? Who is transporting him?

2) What goes running by Nigel and Cato? What barrels into them next? What is the name of the creature who barrels into them? What does he tell Nigel and Cato to call him? What is this creature's concern about Cato?

3) What is the name of the lizard? What are the squirrel and the lizard playing?

4) What are they using to play with? What does it go to? What idea does this give Nigel?

5) Where is William Franklin on June 6, 1752? How old is he? What is the weather? What does William have with him? What is the purpose of the Leyden jar?

6) What two reasons does Benjamin Franklin give William for being out in the middle of nowhere?

7) Benjamin Franklin has the experiment set up in his hands. Describe it. How does Cato know the storm is intensifying?

8) Why does Nigel say Benjamin Franklin has to be inside the shed? What does Nigel tell Cato he can do once Benjamin and William Franklin enter the shed? What does Benjamin Franklin tell William to do once the kite is in the air?

9) What happens to Nigel when it begins to rain? What does Cato do to help? What do they do next? What does Benjamin Franklin think after quite a bit of time has passed with nothing happening?

10) What happens after Benjamin Franklin says a quick prayer? What does Nigel say to the Maker at the end of the experiment?

Nigel's Nuggets

Chapter 24: The Key to Our Shuccshessh

Imagine your favorite scene from Chapter 24. Present it in comedic form. Let your imagination shhhoar!

Cato's Eagle-Eye View

Chapter 24: The Key to Our Shuccshessh

Gliding: Summarize the chapter in three to five sentences, written or orally.

Soaring: Summarize the chapter in one word, phrase, or sentence and write it on an index card with the chapter number and title written on the other side.

Soaring Flashcard Game: Shuffle all your Soaring flashcards. Player 1 reads the number and/or title of a chapter on one side of a flashcard. Player 2 answers with the Soaring Summarization on the other side of the flashcard. Reshuffle your flashcards, switch players if desired, and play three times.

Eaglet

Chapter 25: The Art of Persuasion

1) Where and when is Chapter 25 set? How old is Patrick?

2) What has John Henry rented for his sons, Patrick and William? Where is it? What will their profession be?

3) What can customers ask to do if they do not have money or goods with which to trade? What is the main crop in Virginia?

4) Where do Patrick and William live and with whom? Whom do they get to hear preach?

5) Who comes into Patrick's store? How does he tell Patrick he is doing today?

6) What does Patrick's customer purchase for his horse, May? May is about to have her foal. What is Mr. Poindexter hoping for? Why?

7) What concern about the way Patrick operates his store does Liz share with Nigel?

8) What tragedy is George Washington about to experience? What tragedy had Al's George experienced?

9) Who is with Sarah Shelton at Polegreen? How old is Sarah? Whom is she hoping to see?

10) What does Liz tell Nigel about Patrick's invitation to the Shelton's barbeque?

Fledgling

Chapter 25: The Art of Persuasion

1) Where and when is Chapter 25 set? How old is Patrick? What has John Henry rented for his sons, Patrick and William? Where is it? What will their profession be?

2) How do customers pay for goods? What if they have nothing with which to pay? What is the main crop in Virginia? When do farmers know if they can settle their debts?

3) What words of wisdom has John Henry shared with Patrick before he opens the store?

4) Who comes into Patrick's store? How does he tell Patrick he is doing today? Give a brief history of the Poindexter family. Flip through the first pages of the VRK. Where have you seen the name Poindexter?

5) What does Patrick's customer purchase for his horse, May? May is about to have her foal. What is Mr. Poindexter hoping for? Why? What magazine does Patrick show Mr. Poindexter? Who is the editor? Summarize the article Patrick and Mr. Poindexter discuss.

6) Who is Patrick's next customer? Describe his appearance and their conversation. What does Patrick wind up doing for his customer?

7) What tragedy is George Washington about to experience? What tragedy had Al's George experienced? What does Liz say the humans discuss in the store? How does Patrick "tip" conversations?

8) What does Nigel say about the store? How does Liz reply? What does she mean by saying "the art of persuasion is being tried on Patrick?"

9) Describe what happens when Sarah Shelton and Mrs. Shelton visit Patrick's store—one paragraph will do the trick. What is the result of the visit?

10) What does Liz tell Nigel about Patrick's invitation to the Shelton's barbeque? What does Liz realize about Patrick's invitation that Nigel does not?

Chapter 25: The Art of Persuasion

1) Where and when is Chapter 25 set? What has John Henry rented for his sons, Patrick and William? Where is it? What will their profession be? What other option might John Henry have rather been able to provide for his sons? Where do Patrick and William live?

2) How do customers pay for goods? What if they have nothing with which to pay? What is the main crop in Virginia? When do farmers know if they can settle their debts? What event happens as Patrick and William set up shop? How might this affect their success?

3) What words of wisdom has John Henry shared with Patrick before he opens the store? What is the meaning of John's advice?

4) Who comes into Patrick's store? How does he tell Patrick he is doing today? Give a brief history of the Poindexter family. Flip through the first pages of the VRK. Where have you seen the name Poindexter? Why do you think Jenny L. Cote chose this name for this character?

5) What does Patrick's customer purchase for his horse, May? May is about to have her foal. What is Mr. Poindexter hoping for? Why? What magazine does Patrick show Mr. Poindexter? Who is the editor? Summarize the article Patrick and Mr. Poindexter discuss. What does Patrick ask Mr. Poindexter about the article? How does Mr. Poindexter respond?

6) Who is Patrick's next customer? Describe his appearance and their conversation. What does Patrick wind up doing for his customer? Do you think Patrick's customer will be able to pay him back? Why or why not?

7) What tragedy is George Washington about to experience? What tragedy had Al's George experienced? What does Liz say the humans discuss in the store? How does Patrick "tip" conversations?

8) What does Nigel say about the store? How does Liz reply? What does she mean by saying "the art of persuasion is being tried on Patrick?"

9) Describe what happens when Sarah Shelton and Mrs. Shelton visit Patrick's store. What is the result of the visit?

10) What does Liz tell Nigel about Patrick's invitation to the Shelton's barbeque? What does Liz realize about Patrick's invitation that Nigel does not? What does this foreshadow?

Nigel's Nuggets

Chapter 25: The Art of Persuasion

Imagine that you are Jenny L. Cote, and you have intended to create a new character of a horn worm but have not had time to do so. Create the character, name it, and describe its appearance. Present your research about the horn worm and make a picture of it. Write or dictate a brief, one-to-five-paragraph story about your character including any EO7 team members and any characters from the VRK.

Cato's Eagle-Eye View

Chapter 12: A Tragedy in London

Gliding: Summarize the chapter in three to five sentences, written or orally.

Soaring: Summarize the chapter in one word, phrase, or sentence and write it on an index card with the chapter number and title written on the other side.

Soaring Flashcard Game: Shuffle all your Soaring flashcards. Player 1 reads the number and/or title of a chapter on one side of a flashcard. Player 2 answers with the Soaring Summarization on the other side of the flashcard. Reshuffle your flashcards, switch players if desired, and play three times.

Eaglet

Chapter 26: Puppy Love

1) Where is Chapter 26 set and when? How long has the Shelton family lived there? When had the family originally acquired the land and from whom?

2) What does Sarah "Sallie" Shelton have for Patrick after he fiddles? What does Patrick say as he is given his reward?

3) What interrupts Patrick and Sallie's conversation? What is its name?

4) Patrick explains what has happened to Max. What does he say? What has happened to Liz?

5) What does Liz tell Nigel and Clarie about Patrick's store? Clarie says Patrick's store is two things. What are they?

6) What does Benjamin Franklin say about thunder and lightning? Write out Benjamin Franklin's second quotation in this passage.

7) Write out Benjamin Franklin's quotation about ears.

8) What gifts does Patrick bring Sallie for Christmas? From which location did he have them sent?

9) What does Sallie give Patrick for Christmas?

10) What is the condition upon which Patrick can take the gift? How does he respond?

Chapter 26: Puppy Love

1) Where is Chapter 26 set and when? How long has the Shelton family lived there? When did the family originally acquire the land and from whom? What entertainment is Patrick providing for the barbeque? What does Sarah "Sallie" Shelton have for Patrick after he fiddles? What does Patrick say as he is given his reward?

2) What interrupts Patrick and Sallie's conversation? What is its name? Describe its appearance.

3) Patrick explains what has happened to Max. What does he say? What has happened to Liz? As Sallie watches Patrick and Nelson, what does she realize?

4) Sum up Clarie, Liz, and Nigel's conversation under the floorboards of Patrick's store.

5) What does Patrick's customer remark about Benjamin Franklin? Summarize the article in the *Pennsylvania Gazette*.

6) What does Benjamin Franklin say about thunder and lightning? Write out Benjamin Franklin's second quotation in the passage. Explain what it means.

7) Describe the Christmas decorations of the Sheltons' home.

8) What gifts does Patrick bring Sallie for Christmas? From which location did he have them sent? What was in the bow?

9) What does Sallie give Patrick for Christmas? What have we learned about Nelson prior to Christmas?

10) What is the condition upon which Patrick can take the gift? How does he respond? Read "A WORD FROM THE AUTHOR." Is Nelson a real or fictional character?

Chapter 26: Puppy Love

1) Where is Chapter 26 set and when? How long has the Shelton family lived there? When did the family originally acquire the land and from whom? What entertainment is Patrick providing for the barbeque? What does Sarah "Sallie" Shelton have for Patrick after he fiddles? What does Patrick say as he is given his reward?

2) What interrupts Patrick and Sallie's conversation? What is its name? Describe its appearance.

3) Patrick explains what has happened to Max. What does he say? What has happened to Liz? As Sallie watches Patrick and Nelson, what does she realize? What does that expression mean? How does it apply to Patrick and Sallie?

4) Sum up Clarie, Liz, and Nigel's conversation under the floorboards of Patrick's store. Where will Liz be during the next part of the mission?

5) What does Patrick's customer remark about Benjamin Franklin? Summarize the article in the *Pennsylvania Gazette*.

6) What does Benjamin Franklin say about thunder and lightning? Write out Benjamin Franklin's second quotation in the passage. Explain what it means. What does it foreshadow?

7) Describe the Christmas decorations of the Sheltons' home. Many of the items came from Patrick's store. Why do you think the Sheltons chose to patronize Patrick's store?

8) What gifts does Patrick bring Sallie for Christmas? From which location did he have them sent? What was in the bow?

9) What did Sallie give Patrick for Christmas? What have we learned about Nelson prior to Christmas?

10) What is the condition upon which Patrick can take the gift? How does he respond? Read "A WORD FROM THE AUTHOR." Is Nelson a historical or fictional character?

Nigel's Nuggets

Chapter 26: Puppy Love

Hello readers, Nigel here. Ah, puppies, Christmas, and love! So many delicious morsels for researching, so little time. I am going to present a documentary about Christmas in the mid-eighteenth century in Colonial Virginia on my Nigel's News Nuggets for the VRK Podcast. However, I simply cannot do it all myself. I say, it would be jolly good of you to help me out. I don't have an email address, but you can always reach me at: jenny@epicorderoftheseven.com

Please do mark your submission, "Attention: Nigel P. Monaco." Happy creating—cheerio!

Cato's Eagle-Eye View

Chapter 26: Puppy Love

Gliding: Summarize the chapter in three to five sentences, written or orally.

Soaring: Summarize the chapter in one word, phrase, or sentence and write it on an index card with the chapter number and title written on the other side.

Soaring Flashcard Game: Shuffle all your Soaring flashcards. Player 1 reads the number and/or title of a chapter on one side of a flashcard. Player 2 answers with the Soaring Summarization on the other side of the flashcard. Reshuffle your flashcards, switch players if desired, and play three times.

Eaglet

Chapter 27: Baptism by Ice

1) Where is Chapter 27 set and when? Who is the governor of Virginia?

2) Which two brothers were the principal founders of the Ohio Company?

3) Which three countries controlled most of North America?

4) Governor Dinwiddie is watching a young man walk toward the governor's palace. Who is he? How old is he? What is the purpose of his visit?

5) Gillamon sends word for Kate and Al to join Max. Who Is Max's current human? Where do they join Max?

6) What does the French Commander's letter say in reply to Governor Dinwiddie's letter? Where does Gillamon tell Al to go for his part of the assignment? How does Al react?

7) How does Al wind up saving George Washington and Gist?

8) What do George Washington and Gist need to build to cross the Allegheny? Whom do Max and Kate enlist to help?

9) Who pushes against George Washington's foot and helps him back to the raft when he falls in the river?

10) What does George Washington say he wants to have with him if he ever has to "cross an icy river at night again"?

Fledgling

Chapter 27: Baptism by Ice

1) Where is chapter 27 set and when? Who is the governor of Virginia? Which two brothers were the principal founders of the Ohio Company? Which two rivers bordered the land grant? What was the most prized area of the grant?

2) Which portions of North America were controlled by Britain, France, and Spain?

3) What had King George II of England instructed Governor Dinwiddie to do and why? Was Governor Dinwiddie's first attempt successful? Governor Dinwiddie is watching a young man walk toward the governor's palace. Who is he? How old is he? What is the purpose of his visit?

4) Gillamon sends word for Kate and Al to join Max. Who is Max's current human? Where do they join Max? What does Al say about the place he has left, and how he feels about having to do so?

5) Describe George Washington, Gillamon, and Max's trip so far. What does the French Commander's letter say in reply to Governor Dinwiddie? Where does Gillamon tell Al to go for his part of the assignment? How does Al react?

6) Describe the events of December 26–27, 1753, in two to three paragraphs.

7) What do George Washington and Gist find when they reach the Allegheny on December 29?

8) What do George Washington and Gist need to build to cross the Allegheny? Whom do Max and Kate enlist to help? Describe Max and Kate's conversation with Howard.

9) What time of day do George Washington and Gist finish their raft? What does Gist want to do? What does George Washington want to do? What do they do? What does Max do in response? Describe Washington's Crossing in a few sentences.

10) Where do George Washington and Gist wind up for the night? How do Max and Kate help them? How do the men finish their crossing? What does George Washington say he wants to have with him if he ever has to "cross an icy river at night again"?

Chapter 27: Baptism by Ice

1) Where is chapter 27 set and when? Who was the governor of Virginia? Which two brothers were the principal founders of the Ohio Company? Which two rivers bordered the land grant? What was the most prized area of the grant? What is its modern-day location?

2) Which portions of North America were controlled by Britain, France, and Spain? Based on the way the British colonists were expanding into North America, with which country would they most likely have a conflict, and over which area?

3) What had King George II of England instructed Governor Dinwiddie to do and why? Was Governor Dinwiddie's first attempt successful? Governor Dinwiddie is watching a young man walk toward the governor's palace. Who is he? What is the purpose of his visit? Is George Washington related to the of the Ohio Company? If so, how?

4) Gillamon sends word for Kate and Al to join Max. Who is Max's current human? Where do they join Max? What does Al say about the place he has left, and how he feels about having to do so?

5) Describe George Washington, Gillamon, and Max's trip so far. What does the French Commander's letter say in reply to Governor Dinwiddie? Where does Gillamon tell Al to go for his part of the assignment? How does Al react?

6) Describe the events of December 26–27, 1753, in three to five paragraphs.

7) What do George Washington and Gist find when they reach the Allegheny on December 29? Why is this the worst possible river condition?

8) What do George Washington and Gist need to build to cross the Allegheny? Whom do Max and Kate enlist to help? Describe Max and Kate's conversation with Howard.

9) What time of day do George Washington and Gist finish their raft? What does Gist want to do? What does George Washington want to do? What do they do? What does Max do in response? Describe Washington's Crossing in one to three paragraphs.

10) Where do George Washington and Gist wind up for the night? How do Max and Kate help them? How do the men finish their crossing? What does George Washington say he wants to have with him if he ever has to "cross an icy river at night again"? Which EO7 members does he mean?

Nigel's Nuggets

Chapter 27: Baptism by Ice

I hope you are enjoying your training as a broadcaster. This episode needs an update from the front. Present a newscast about Washington and Gist's crossing of the Allegheny.

Cato's Eagle-Eye View

Chapter 12: A Tragedy in London

Gliding: Summarize the chapter in three to five sentences, written or orally.

Soaring: Summarize the chapter in one word, phrase, or sentence and write it on an index card with the chapter number and title written on the other side.

Soaring Flashcard Game: Shuffle all your Soaring flashcards. Player 1 reads the number and/or title of a chapter on one side of a flashcard. Player 2 answers with the Soaring Summarization on the other side of the flashcard. Reshuffle your flashcards, switch players if desired, and play three times.

Eaglet

Chapter 28: Starting a War

1) What does George Washington inform Governor Dinwiddie about the absolute decision of the French?

2) What does Governor Dinwiddie want from George Washington in two days' time?

3) What do George Washington's men start building in May, 1754?

4) Gillamon tells Max that more than fighting words are coming. What else is coming?

5) What does Chief Half-King do to the French Commander with no warning? What do other warriors do after that? Which command does George Washington issue? How many of the wounded French soldiers survive?

6) The French claim they are on a diplomatic mission. Does George Washington believe them?

7) What happens when Colonel Joshua Fry dies?

8) After the battle with the French of July 3, 1754, George Washington signs a paper which he misunderstands. What does he admit to? What does Gillamon say the document will do? Name the event Gillamon referenced.

9) What does Benjamin Franklin's July, 1754, cartoon say? Which colony is left off?

10) What does Benjamin Franklin's plan of union suggest for the colonies?

Chapter 28: Starting a War

1) What does George Washington inform Governor Dinwiddie about the absolute decision of the French? What does Governor Dinwiddie say about the French response to his letter? Who is keeping Governor Dinwiddie from getting the funds he needs? What does he vow to do?

2) Where have George Washington, Gillamon, and Max gone after receiving instructions from Governor Dinwiddie? How is Gillamon disguised? What do George Washington's men start building in May, 1754?

3) Where and how had George Washington become famous?

4) What plan "now that George be here" does Gillamon explain to Max? Gillamon also tells Max that more than fighting words are coming. What else is coming?

5) How does the May 28, 1754, battle start? How long does it last? Why is it so short? What happens for the first time under George Washington's command?

6) Describe the events that took place after the battle, including those started by Chief Half-King. What do the captured French claim? Does George Washington believe them? Why or why not?

7) What is reported to George Washington on July 3, 1754, at 8 pm? Does he trust the French message? Why or why not?

8) What happens when Colonel Joshua Fry dies? The French terms of surrender are translated for George Washington. What is he told? What does he think of the terms?

9) What does George Washington "admit" to in error when he signs the French terms? What does Gillamon say that the terms actually mean? What does he explain that George Washington signing the terms will mean, and what event will start?

10) What does Benjamin Franklin's July, 1754, cartoon say? Which colony is left off? What does Benjamin Franklin's plan of union suggest for the colonies?

Chapter 28: Starting a War

1) What does George Washington inform Governor Dinwiddie about the absolute decision of the French? What does Governor Dinwiddie say about the French response to his letter? Who is keeping Governor Dinwiddie from getting the funds he needs? What does the Governor vow to do? What does he request from George Washington in order to achieve his purpose?

2) Where have George Washington, Gillamon, and Max gone after receiving instructions from Governor Dinwiddie? How is Gillamon disguised? What did George Washington's men start building in May, 1754?

3) Where and how had George Washington become famous?

4) What plan "now that George be here" does Gillamon explain to Max? Gillamon also tells Max that more than fighting words are coming. What else is coming? Sometimes, one small event can trigger a world war. How did this happen in World War I?

5) How does the May 28, 1754, battle start? How long does it last? Why is it so short? What happens for the first time under George Washington's command?

6) Describe the events that took place after the battle, including those started by Chief Half-King. What do the captured French claim? Does George Washington believe them? Why or why not? What does Gillamon witness? What do you think this man will do?

7) What is reported to George Washington on July 3, 1754, at 8 pm? Does he trust the French message? Why or why not? Under the circumstances, would you trust the request?

8) What happens when Colonel Joshua Fry dies? The French terms of surrender are translated for George Washington. What is he told? What does he think of the terms? Do you agree with George Washington's assessment of the terms? Why or why not?

9) What does George Washington "admit" to in error when he signs the French terms? What does Gillamon say that the terms actually mean? What does he explain that George Washington signing the terms will mean, and what event will start? Will this war become a worldwide war?

10) What does Benjamin Franklin's July, 1754, cartoon say? Which colony is left off? What does Benjamin Franklin's plan of union suggest for the colonies?

Nigel's Nuggets

Chapter 28: Starting a War

In Chapter 28, George Washington assumes command of all the Virginia forces. It is one of the hardest duties of a commanding officer to write letters of condolence to the families of those serving under him who have been killed in battle. Research this practice and read some of the famous letters in American history written to families of the fallen by their commanding officers. Note what kind of information the commander conveys to the family. Create a fictitious character in your mind who dies in battle and whose circumstances would plausibly fit with the events of Chapter 28. Now imagine that you are George Washington, and write or dictate a letter to the deceased's family.

Cato's Eagle-Eye View

Chapter 12: A Tragedy in London

Gliding: Summarize the chapter in three to five sentences, written or orally.

Soaring: Summarize the chapter in one word, phrase, or sentence and write it on an index card with the chapter number and title written on the other side.

Soaring Flashcard Game: Shuffle all your Soaring flashcards. Player 1 reads the number and/or title of a chapter on one side of a flashcard. Player 2 answers with the Soaring Summarization on the other side of the flashcard. Reshuffle your flashcards, switch players if desired, and play three times.

Eaglet

Chapter 29: Love and War

1) Which colleges give Benjamin Franklin honorary degrees? What does he have installed on the top of the Pennsylvania State House tower?

2) What does Governor Dinwiddie offer George Washington after the general starts a world war? What does George Washington decide to do instead?

3) What will Patrick Henry become?

4) Clarie tells the team that George Washington was intentionally exposed to smallpox. What does Max think of this?

5) Clarie explains that all three of the EO7's humans will have hard times in the coming years and tells them why this is necessary. To whom does Liz say, "Again, as we saw . . .?" Where did this happen?

6) Liz changes the subject. What does she wish to talk about and why? Who are the couple she wishes to discuss? How old are they? Where will they live?

7) Which uncle performs the ceremony? Which uncle surprises Patrick by attending? Who does the second uncle bring with him?

8) How far away from the Sheltons will Patrick and Sallie be living? What reason does Mr. Shelton offer for choosing to give them Pine Slash?

9) What does Nelson ask Liz as the ceremony starts? How does Liz reply?

10) Whom does Cupid's arrow strike during the ceremony? With whom is he smitten?

Chapter 29: Love and War

1) Which colleges give Benjamin Franklin honorary degrees? What does he have installed on the top of the Pennsylvania State House tower? What does Governor Dinwiddie offer George Washington after the general starts a world war? What does George Washington decide to do instead? What will Patrick Henry become?

2) Clarie tells the team that George Washington was intentionally exposed to smallpox. What does Max think of this? How will this benefit George Washington?

3) Clarie explains that all three of the EO7's humans will have hard times in the coming years and tells them why this is necessary. Write out Clarie's words.

4) To whom does Liz say, "Again, as we saw . . .?" Where did this happen? Tell Joseph's story in one to three paragraphs.

5) Recap the EO7's conversation, from just after Liz mentions Joseph until she changes the subject. Write the Scripture Max quotes and give its reference.

6) Was it common in the mid-eighteenth century for people to marry at the ages Patrick and Sallie did?

7) Where will Max, Nelson, Clarie, Kate, Nigel, and Liz be on the next part of their missions?

8) Who is with Sallie as she gets ready for the wedding? Who will marry Jane someday? What does Sallie say her friends' future husbands might do?

9) Which uncle performs the ceremony? Which uncle surprises Patrick by attending? Who does the second uncle bring with him? How far away from the Sheltons will Patrick and Sallie be living? What reason does Mr. Shelton offer for choosing to give them Pine Slash?

10) What does Nelson ask Liz as the ceremony starts? How does Liz reply? Whom does Cupid's arrow strike during the ceremony? With whom is he smitten? Is the wedding ceremony similar to the wedding ceremony still used in most Protestant churches today? Look at A WORD FROM THE AUTHOR. Are Sallie and Elizabeth historical or fictional characters? Do you think the wedding scene in chapter 20 is historical or fictional, or both, and why?

Chapter 29: Love and War

1) Which colleges give Benjamin Franklin honorary degrees? What does he have installed on the top of the Pennsylvania State House tower? What does Governor Dinwiddie offer George Washington after the general starts a world war? What does George Washington decide to do instead? What will Patrick Henry become?

2) Clarie tells the team that George Washington was intentionally exposed to smallpox. What does Max think of this? How will this benefit George Washington? What kind of creature is capable of doing this?

3) Clarie explains that all three humans will have hard times in the coming years and tells them why this is necessary. Write out Clarie's words. What do they mean?

4) To whom does Liz say, "Again, as we saw . . . ?" Where did this happen? Tell Joseph's story in three to five paragraphs.

5) Recap the EO7's conversation, from just after Liz mentions Joseph until she changes the subject. Write the Scripture that Max quotes and give its reference.

6) Was it common for people in the mid-eighteenth century to marry at the ages Patrick and Sallie did?

7) Where will Max, Nelson, Clarie, Kate, Nigel, and Liz be on the next part of their missions?

8) Who is with Sallie as she gets ready for the wedding? Who will marry Jane someday? What does Sallie say that her friends' future husbands might do? Who do you think is more nervous, Patrick or Sallie? Why?

9) Which uncle performs the ceremony? Which uncle surprises Patrick by attending? Who does the second uncle bring with him? How far away from the Sheltons will Patrick and Sallie be living? What reason does Mr. Shelton offer for choosing to give them Pine Slash? Why might it have been a good thing for Samuel Davies to have been in London?

10) What does Nelson ask Liz as the ceremony starts? Who does Cupid's arrow strike during the ceremony? With whom is he smitten? Is the wedding ceremony similar to the wedding ceremony still used in most Protestant churches today Look at A WORD FROM THE AUTHOR. Is Elizabeth a historical or fictional character? Do you think the wedding scene in chapter 20 is historical or fictional, or both, and why?

Nigel's Nuggets

Chapter 29: Love and War

You might not know this about me, but I am a true romantic at heart! I find weddings utterly thrilling! Please make a presentation about Patrick and Sallie's wedding. Include typical "wedding planner" details. I am looking for items in your presentation such as an invitation, description of decorations, menu, and post-nuptial entertainments.

Cato's Eagle-Eye View

Chapter 29: Love and War

Gliding: Summarize the chapter in three to five sentences, written or orally.

Soaring: Summarize the chapter in one word, phrase, or sentence and write it on an index card with the chapter number and title written on the other side.

Soaring Flashcard Game: Shuffle all your Soaring flashcards. Player 1 reads the number and/or title of a chapter on one side of a flashcard. Player 2 answers with the Soaring Summarization on the other side of the flashcard. Reshuffle your flashcards, switch players if desired, and play three times.

Eaglet

Chapter 30: Plowshares and Swords

1) Where is Chapter 30 set and when? Samuel Davies has gathered his congregation. What does he tell them Governor Dinwiddie has asked him to support?

2) Samuel Davies calls men to join the battle against the French. What will Patrick's battlefield be?

3) Even if Patrick prepares the land the best he can, upon what is he completely dependent?

4) Samuel Davies mentions that the neglect of the Gospel has spread like a *subtle poison*. How does he describe this poison?

5) Liz feels that Samuel Davies' words should be published on both sides of the Atlantic. What does she propose to send to Governor Dinwiddie? Who will carry it to him?

6) Gillamon is nursing George Washington in the wilderness. From which disease is he suffering? What fort are they trying to reach? How far is it? Who is the commanding general? How far does the general plan to reach the next day?

7) What is George Washington's position for this mission?

8) The British are in high spirits on the morning of July 9, 1755. What do they expect to do?

9) How do the British fight? How do the French and Indians fight?

10) George Washington suggests fighting like the French, but General Braddock refuses his advice. As a result, he is shot and killed. What are his last words to George Washington? Do you think the battle might have gone differently if he had listened to George Washington's advice?

Fledgling

Chapter 30: Plowshares and Swords

1) Where and when is Chapter 30 set? Samuel Davies gathers his congregation. What does he tell them Governor Dinwiddie has asked him to support? Samuel Davies calls men to join the battle against the French. What will Patrick's battlefield be? What will Patrick soon leave?

2) Describe the process of growing tobacco, from January until the tobacco is sent down the river to Yorktown.

3) Samuel Davies calls the people to repent. Recount his reasons why they should. He mentions that the neglect of the Gospel has spread like a *subtle poison*. How does he describe this poison? Liz feels that Samuel Davies' words should be published on both sides of the Atlantic. What does she propose to send to Governor Dinwiddie? Who will carry it to him?

4) Gillamon is nursing George Washington in the wilderness. From which disease is he suffering? What fort are they trying to reach? Who is the commanding general? How far does the general plan to reach the next day? What is George Washington's position?

5) Describe General Braddock as a leader. Who has supplied the army, and with what? Do the British have enough Indian guides? Why or why not?

6) How does General Braddock get his army to Fort Duquesne? What does George Washington propose? What happens as a result? Do the French know the British are coming? Who is the French commander? What is his leadership style?

7) The British are in high spirits on the morning of July 9, 1755. What do they expect to do? What instruction does Gillamon give Max? How do the British fight? How do the French and Indians fight?

8) Contrast General Braddock's assessment of the situation with George Washington's. What would Braddock listen to? Do you think this attitude is wise or foolish in war? Why?

9) Describe the strategy of the French commander and the formation he deploys. What happens after the first French volley?

10) Describe the battle from the time General Braddock races to the front of the column until George Washington reaches him. What are his last words to? Do you think the battle might have gone differently if he had listened to George Washington? Why?

Chapter 30: Plowshares and Swords

1) Where and when is Chapter 30 set? Samuel Davies gathers his congregation. What does he tell them Governor Dinwiddie has asked him to support? Samuel Davies calls men to join the battle against the French. What will Patrick's battlefield be? What will Patrick soon leave?

2) Describe the process of growing tobacco, from January until the tobacco is sent down the river to Yorktown.

3) Samuel calls the people to repent. Recount his reasons why they should. He mentions that the neglect of the Gospel has spread like a *subtle poison*. How does he describe this poison? Liz feels that Samuel Davies' words should be published on both sides of the Atlantic. What does she propose to send Governor Dinwiddie? Who will carry it to him?

4) Gillamon is nursing George Washington in the wilderness. From which disease is he suffering? What fort are they trying to reach? Who is the commanding general? How far does the general plan to reach the next day? What is George Washington's position?

5) Describe General Braddock as a leader. Who has supplied the army, and with what? Do the British have enough Indian guides? Why or why not? What kind of allegiance does General Braddock receive? Why?

6) How does General Braddock get his army to Fort Duquesne? What does George Washington propose? Do the French know the British are coming? Who is the French commander? What is his leadership style? Which commander would you rather follow?

7) The British are in high spirits on the morning of July 9, 1755. What do they expect to do? What instruction does Gillamon give Max? How do the British fight? How do the French and Indians fight? Which style do you think will be more successful? Why?

8) Contrast Braddock's assessment of the situation with George Washington's. What would Braddock listen to? Do you think this attitude is wise or foolish in war? Why?

9) Describe the strategy of the French commander and the formation he deploys. What happens after the first French volley?

10) Describe the battle, from the time General Braddock races to the front of the column until Washington reaches him. What are his last words to George Washington? Do you think the battle might have gone differently if he had listened to George Washington? Why? What is the main genre employed by Jenny L. Cote in Chapter 30? Give examples.

Nigel's Nuggets

Chapter 30: Plowshares and Swords

If you do not possess toy soldiers and accessories, you will want to acquire a set. In order to truly grasp the events of a battle, it is helpful to be able to visualize the battlefield. Right! Now it's time to set up a mock battlefield. Place the British and French in the type of battle positions they generally took, including the terrain. You need not be specific to this battle, but rather represent the two types of strategies as they might have looked pitted against each other.

Cato's Eagle-Eye View

Chapter 30: Plowshares and Swords

Gliding: Summarize the chapter in three to five sentences, written or orally.

Soaring: Summarize the chapter in one word, phrase, or sentence and write it on an index card with the chapter number and title written on the other side.

Soaring Flashcard Game: Shuffle all your Soaring flashcards. Player 1 reads the number and/or title of a chapter on one side of a flashcard. Player 2 answers with the Soaring Summarization on the other side of the flashcard. Reshuffle your flashcards, switch players if desired, and play three times.

Eaglet

Chapter 31: Soldier On

1) How many near misses does George Washington tell his brother, Augustine, he has experienced? What did Governor Dinwiddie call George Washington? What command does George Washington assume? How old is he?

2) Patrick is beside himself with concern for his family and his country. List at least two reasons for his concern.

3) Whom does Samuel Davies see sitting in the lane as he approaches Patrick and Sallie's house? What has Patrick named her for this part of the mission?

4) How old is Sallie? What is the name of their firstborn? What is her nickname?

5) How long had Samuel Davies been in England and Scotland? For which colleges was he raising funds?

6) What does Samuel Davies tell Patrick the drought will teach him?

7) Patrick tells Samuel Davies he wonders if he should be fighting for his country. Where does Samuel Davies tell Patrick he is most needed?

8) Who have the families gathered to honor on August 17, 1755? Where are they gathered?

9) What name has Governor Dinwiddie given to Samuel Davies?

10) What did Patrick say as he watched a line of young men form "ready to answer the call and join Overton's militia?"

Chapter 31: Soldier On

1) How many near misses does George Washington tell his brother, Augustine, he has experienced? What did Governor Dinwiddie call George Washington? What command does George Washington assume? How old is he? Rewrite George Washington's letter to his brother in today's language.

2) Why are the people gathered at Polegreen Church? Patrick is beside himself with concern for his family and his country. List the four reasons for his concern.

3) Whom does Samuel Davies see sitting in the lane as he approaches Patrick and Sallie's house? What has Patrick named her for this part of the mission? How old is Sallie? What is the name of their firstborn? What is her nickname?

4) What weather condition has developed in Virginia? What Bible story does Samuel Davies use to comfort Patrick? Tell the story in two or three sentences.

5) Samuel Davies comforts Patrick with a different Bible story after Patrick shares his concern that he has nine mouths to feed. What is it? Summarize the story.

6) What does Samuel Davies tell Patrick the drought will teach him? Patrick tells Samuel Davies he wonders if he should be fighting for his country. Where does Samuel Davies tell Patrick he is most needed?

7) Who have the families gathered to honor on August 17, 1755? Where are they gathered and why? Is George Overton a real or fictional character?

8) Summarize Samuel Davies' introduction before Liz and Nigel's conversation.

9) What name has Governor Dinwiddie given to Samuel Davies? Why? What does Liz say Patrick wishes to do?

10) Who was Meroz and why was he cursed? How does Patrick respond to the sermon?

Chapter 31: Soldier On

1) How many near misses does George Washington tell his brother, Augustine, he has experienced? What does Governor Dinwiddie call George Washington? What command does George Washington assume? How old is he? Rewrite George Washington's letter to his brother in today's language.

2) Why are the people are gathered at Polegreen Church? Patrick is beside himself with concern for his family and his country. List the four reasons for his concern.

3) Who does Samuel Davies see sitting in the lane as he approaches Patrick and Sallie's house? What has Patrick named her for this part of the mission? How old is Sallie? What is the name of their firstborn? What is her nickname?

4) What weather condition has developed in Virginia? What Bible story does Samuel Davies use to comfort Patrick? Tell the story in one to three paragraphs.

5) Samuel Davies comforts Patrick with a different Bible story after Patrick shares his concern that he has nine mouths to feed. What is it? Summarize the story. How are both stories applicable to Patrick's life?

6) What does Samuel Davies tell Patrick the drought will teach him? Patrick tells Samuel Davies he wonders if he should be fighting for his country. Where does Samuel Davies tell Patrick he is most needed?

7) Whom have the families gathered to honor on August 17, 1755? Where are they gathered and why? Is George Overton a real or fictional character?

8) Summarize Samuel Davies' introduction before Liz and Nigel's conversation. What do the following word/terms mean: unmerited, ardent, good courage, and valiant?

9) What name has Governor Dinwiddie given to Samuel Davies? Why? What does Liz say Patrick wishes to do?

10) Who was Meroz and why was he cursed? How does Patrick respond to the sermon? List examples of all three genres of Jenny L. Cote's writing from the scene of the meeting at Polegreen.

Nigel's Nuggets

Chapter 31: Soldier On

Let's practice those cartography skills you're developing. Make a simple map of Virginia including Jamestown, Williamsburg, Hanover, Polegreen Meetinghouse, Pine Slash Farm, and Mount Brilliant.

Cato's Eagle-Eye View

Chapter 31: Soldier On

Gliding: Summarize the chapter in three to five sentences, written or orally.

Soaring: Summarize the chapter in one word, phrase, or sentence and write it on an index card with the chapter number and title written on the other side.

Soaring Flashcard Game: Shuffle all your Soaring flashcards. Player 1 reads the number and/or title of a chapter on one side of a flashcard. Player 2 answers with the Soaring Summarization on the other side of the flashcard. Reshuffle your flashcards, switch players if desired, and play three times.

Eaglet

Chapter 32: Fire to the Fiddle

1) Where is Chapter 32 set and when? How old is Patsy?

2) Where is Nigel? Where is Liz? What kind of creature runs by her?

3) What do Cato and Nigel spot? What do they do to help?

4) Are all the humans safe? What is left inside the house?

5) Who goes back in to get it?

6) Who saves Sallie and John? Can Patrick save this creature? Why or why not?

7) Does Nelson live? Does he rescue the fiddle? Does he remember how he got out of the burning house?

8) What does Samuel Davies tell Patrick about bitterness?

9) Gillamon tells Liz and Nigel it is time for the Henry family to do something. What is it?

10) At the end of Chapter 32, where does Patrick tell Sallie they are moving?

Chapter 32: Fire to the Fiddle

1) Where is Chapter 32 set and when? How old is Patsy? What bird call is Patrick teaching her? How is Patrick carrying Patsy? Who flies by? How old is Patrick? For whom is his baby son named?

2) Where is Nigel? Where is Liz? What kind of creature runs by her? What kind of accent does it have?

3) What do Cato and Nigel spot? What do they do to help? Is this an accident? If not, who is responsible?

4) Are all the humans safe? What is left inside the house? Who goes to get it and for whom is this creature working? Is it immortal?

5) Does the rat think he has been successful? How did he set the fire? What does the voice from the darkness state it will do to accomplish the mission?

6) Where do the humans spend the night? What does "minion" mean? What happened the last night Liz slept in a stable with a baby and a cow? Does Nelson live? Does he rescue the fiddle? Does he remember how he got out of the burning house?

7) Who comes to visit Patrick and Sallie one week after the fire? What does he bring with him? Where have Patrick and Sallie moved their family? What does Samuel Davies tell Patrick about bitterness?

8) What has happened to Nelson as a result of the fire? What does Liz say about the harvest? Gillamon tells Liz and Nigel it is time for the Henry family to do something. What is it? Where are they going to go? What is Nigel's concern about this location? What two things does Gillamon tell Liz and Nigel about the upcoming move?

9) Describe Patrick's distant memory with his father. Write out the verse from Isaiah 40.

10) Liz leaves two verses for Patrick to discover. Give the reference for each. What insight does the second verse give Patrick?

Chapter 32: Fire to the Fiddle

1) Where is Chapter 32 set and when? How old is Patsey? What bird call is Patrick teaching her? How is Patrick carrying Patsey? Who flies by? How old is Patrick? For whom is his baby son named?

2) Where is Nigel? Where is Liz? What kind of creature runs by her? What kind of accent does it have? Where have we seen this creature before?

3) What do Cato and Nigel spot? What do they do to help? Is this an accident? If not, who is responsible? Who is this creature working for?

4) Are all the humans safe? What is left inside the house? Who goes to get it and for whom is this creature working? Is it immortal? Are the animals in this event historical or fictional?

5) Does the rat think he has been successful? How did he set the fire? What does the voice from the darkness state it will do to accomplish the mission? Do you think this is a good strategy? Why or why not?

6) Where do the humans spend the night? What does "minion" mean? What happened the last night Liz slept in a stable with a baby and a cow? Does Nelson live? Does he rescue the fiddle? Does he remember how he got out of the burning house? How do you think it happened?

7) Who comes to visit Patrick and Sallie one week after the fire? What does he bring with him? Where have Patrick and Sallie moved their family? What does Samuel Davies tell Patrick about bitterness? What does he mean by this?

8) What has happened to Nelson as a result of the fire? What does Liz say about the harvest? Gillamon tells Liz and Nigel it is time for the Henry family to do something. What is it? Where are they going to go? What is Nigel's concern about this location? What four things does Gillamon tell Liz and Nigel about the upcoming move?

9) Describe Patrick's distant memory with his father. Write out the verse from Isaiah 40. What insight does this passage provide to Patrick?

10) Liz leaves two verses for Patrick to discover. Give the reference for each. What insight does each verse give Patrick?

Nigel's Nuggets

Chapter 32: Fire to the Fiddle

My new broadcast venture is going swimmingly. Pop over to the Podcast to find out the latest at www.epicorderoftheseven.com/podcast. You will come back inspired. Do your own broadcast about the dreadful fire at Pine Slash Farm.

Well done! You have now finished Part Two of the VRK and the VRK Study Guide. Have you filled in all the answers to the Fiddle's Riddle that you have discovered so far? How is your eagle feather display coming along? Be sure to send pictures of your eagle feather display, your Fiddle's Riddle Poster, or any other brilliant thing you have created, to:

jenny@epicorderoftheseven.com

Cato's Eagle-Eye View

Chapter 32: Fire to the Fiddle

Gliding: Summarize the chapter in three to five sentences, written or orally.

Soaring: Summarize the chapter in one word, phrase, or sentence and write it on an index card with the chapter number and title written on the other side.

Soaring Flashcard Game: Shuffle all your Soaring flashcards. Player 1 reads the number and/or title of a chapter on one side of a flashcard. Player 2 answers with the Soaring Summarization on the other side of the flashcard. Reshuffle your flashcards, switch players if desired, and play three times.

PART THREE: DESPAIR NOT THE TRAGIC (1759-65)

Eaglet

Chapter 33: The Little Marquis

1) Where are Kate and Al at the start of chapter 33? What is the date?

2) Gillamon tells Kate what she must follow to understand the connection. What is it?

3) What is the name of the fourteenth-century castle Gillamon shows Kate and Al? Where is it located?

4) Kate's next human is a baby boy. What is his birthdate?

5) What does Clarie tell Kate to call her human?

6) Has Kate's human met his father? Why or why not?

7) What did the Virginia militia do in 1758? What did George Washington do after this?

8) Gillamon tells Kate and Al to take note of three other young men at the Battle of Minden. What are their names?

9) What color hair does Gilbert have? What color eyes and what complexion does he have?

10) What does Gilbert run to in the middle of the garden while he and Kate are chasing each other?

Fledgling

Chapter 33: The Little Marquis

1) Where are Kate and Al at the start of chapter 33? What is the date? Gillamon tells Kate and Al why they have been called to the IAMISPHERE. What does he say?

2) Gillamon tells Kate what she must follow to understand the connection. What is it? What is the name of the fourteenth-century castle Gillamon shows Kate and Al? Where is it located?

3) Kate's next human is a baby boy. What is his birthdate? Write out his whole name.

4) What does Clarie tell Kate to call her human? How old is his father? What is his father's military title? Has Kate's human met his father? Why or why not?

5) What year does the chronicle of the Lafayette family history begin? How far back does Clarie say it actually goes?

6) Describe the life of Joan of Arc in one to three paragraphs.

7) What did the Virginia militia do in 1758? What did George Washington do after this? What will happen to Gilbert's father as a result of the war George Washington started? What does Kate ask to do?

8) Gillamon tells Kate and Al to take note of three other young men at the Battle of Minden. What are their names? What are their current ranks? Name the units in which they serve.

9) Briefly describe the Château de Chavaniac and its location. Contrast the different ways the local villagers and the French courtiers view Chavaniac.

10) What does Gilbert run to in the middle of the garden while he and Kate are playing "Chase"? Explain the significance of the statue, including how it got to Chavaniac, who brought it, and the origins of the Lafayette knights.

Chapter 33: The Little Marquis

1) Where are Kate and Al at the start of chapter 33? What is the date? Gillamon tells Kate and Al why they have been called to the IAMISPHERE. What does he say?

2) Gillamon tells Kate what she must follow to understand the connection. What is it? What is the name of the fourteenth-century castle Gillamon shows Kate and Al? Where is it located?

3) Kate's next human is a baby boy. What is his birthdate? Write out his whole name.

4) What does Clarie tell Kate to call her human? How old is his father? What is his father's military title? Has Kate's human met his father? Why or why not?

5) What year does the chronicle of the Lafayette family history begin? How far back does Clarie say it actually goes? Is Clarie's statement historical or fictional?

6) Describe the life of Joan of Arc in three to five paragraphs.

7) What did the Virginia militia do in 1758? What did George Washington do after this? What will happen to Gilbert's father as a result of the war George Washington started? What does Kate ask to do? Are the EO7 allowed to do this? Why or why not?

8) Gillamon tells Kate and Al to take note of three other young men at the Battle of Minden. What are their names? What are their current ranks? Name the units in which they serve. Explain the function of each of these military units in one paragraph per unit.

9) Briefly describe the Château de Chavaniac and its location. Contrast the different ways the local villagers and the French courtiers view Chavaniac. Describe the typical life for many children of European nobility.

10) What does Gilbert run to in the middle of the garden while he and Kate are playing "Chase"? Explain the significance of the statue, including how it got to Chavaniac, who brought it, and the origins of the Lafayette knights.

Nigel's Nuggets

Chapter 33: The Little Marquis

Nigel P. Monaco reporting in. It is now 1759, and this has been an Epic beginning for Part Three of the VRK. Did you enjoy your trip to France? As you know, it is the homeland of my pet, Liz. Please plan a trip to visit Chavaniac and present your itinerary. Do be sure to include photos of the chateâu and the gardens. Especially the gardens!

Cato's Eagle-Eye View

Chapter 33: The Little Marquis

Gliding: Summarize the chapter in three to five sentences, written or orally.

Soaring: Summarize the chapter in one word, phrase, or sentence and write it on an index card with the chapter number and title written on the other side.

Soaring Flashcard Game: Shuffle all your Soaring flashcards. Player 1 reads the number and/or title of a chapter on one side of a flashcard. Player 2 answers with the Soaring Summarization on the other side of the flashcard. Reshuffle your flashcards, switch players if desired, and play three times.

Eaglet

Chapter 34: A Voice in the Tavern

1) Where is chapter 34 set and when?

2) The patrons of the tavern are celebrating British victories over the French. List three of the five places where the British and Americans triumphed.

3) How is Patrick dressed? What is he doing?

4) When is court day held in Hanover County? Where and when are major cases held?

5) Are John Henry and the other "Gentlemen Justices of the Peace" paid for their services? Are they reimbursed for their expenses?

6) Where do Patrick and Sallie live? What are his two jobs?

7) What do Nigel and Liz do to show Patrick that Liz is earning her keep?

8) What new profession does Liz ask Nigel if he supposes Patrick could do?

9) On page 293, Liz tells Nigel that Patrick needs two things. What are they? What will Gillamon provide?

10) What does Liz suggest that Mr. Poindexter do when he tells her Patrick has no foot *and* no horse? Who does Liz mean?

Chapter 34: A Voice in the Tavern

1) Where is chapter 34 set and when? The patrons of the tavern are celebrating British victories over the French. List the five places where the British and Americans triumphed. Write out the words to “God Save the King.” For whom was it first sung? What year was it first sung, and in celebration of which occasion?

2) How is Patrick dressed? What is he doing? When is court day held in Hanover County? Where and when are major cases held? Who hears the court cases? How many of these officeholders are there? List at least four of the other functions the justices perform in addition to local cases.

3) Are John Henry and the other “Gentlemen Justices of the Peace” paid for their services? Are they reimbursed for their expenses? List the reasons people gather for court day. List some of the other activities that occur on court day.

4) Describe the Hanover Tavern building and the activities that go on there. Where do Patrick and Sallie live? What are Patrick’s two jobs?

5) Describe Patrick physically. What is his age? What fascinates Patrick about court days? What does he do on court days?

6) What do Nigel and Liz do to show Patrick that Liz is earning her keep? On page 29, Liz says Patrick needs two things. What are they?

7) Describe the Two Penny Act and the events that surround it. How does Nigel assess the situation? How does Liz? What new profession does Liz ask Nigel if he supposes Patrick could do?

8) How does Nigel say that entrance into this profession is usually attained? What alternative to this method does Liz present? On page 293, Liz tells Nigel that Patrick needs two things. What are they? What will Gillamon provide?

9) Tell the story Jack Poindexter shares with Patrick. What does he say about Patrick and how the story relates to him?

10) Recount Jack and Liz’s conversation. What plan does Liz formulate after their chat?

Chapter 34: A Voice in the Tavern

1) Where is chapter 34 set and when? The patrons of the tavern are celebrating British victories over the French. List the five places where the British and Americans triumphed. Write out the words to "God Save the King." For whom was it first sung? What year was it first sung, and in celebration of which occasion?

2) How is Patrick dressed? What is he doing? When is court day held in Hanover County? Where and when are major cases held? Who hears the court cases? How many of these officeholders are there? List at least four of the other functions the justices perform in addition to local cases.

3) Are John Henry and the other "Gentlemen Justices of the Peace" paid for their services? Are they reimbursed for their expenses? List the reasons people gather for court day. List some of the other activities that occur on court day.

4) Describe the Hanover Tavern building and the activities that go on there. Where do Patrick and Sallie live? What are Patrick's two jobs?

5) Describe Patrick physically. What is his age? What fascinates Patrick about court days? What does he do on court days?

6) What do Nigel and Liz do to show Patrick that Liz is earning her keep? On page 291, Liz says Patrick needs two things. What are they? What does Liz say about Patrick singing in the tavern? What have Liz and Nigel noticed that causes Patrick's face to light up?

7) Describe the Two Penny Act and the events that surround it. How does Nigel assess the situation? How does Liz? How do you assess the situation? What new profession does Liz ask Nigel if he supposes Patrick could do?

8) How does Nigel say that entrance into this profession is usually attained? What alternative to this method does Liz present? On page 293, Liz tells Nigel that Patrick needs two things. What are they? What will Gillamon provide?

9) Tell the story Jack Poindexter shares with Patrick. What does he say about Patrick and how the story relates to him? How does the stop hasten the knight's escape?

10) Recount Jack and Liz's conversation. What plan does Liz formulate after their chat?

Nigel's Nuggets

Chapter 34: A Voice in the Tavern

Ah, the court of law. It utterly takes the biscuit. Logic, reasoning, drama, intrigue, and wisdom! It brings to mind the quips Max insists on making whilst I am trying to display courtly wisdom on the VRK Podcast. You must pop over and listen in. After you do, please make a presentation about Hanover Tavern and court day at Hanover Courthouse.

Cato's Eagle-Eye View

Chapter 34: A Voice in the Tavern

Gliding: Summarize the chapter in three to five sentences, written or orally.

Soaring: Summarize the chapter in one word, phrase, or sentence and write it on an index card with the chapter number and title written on the other side.

Soaring Flashcard Game: Shuffle all your Soaring flashcards. Player 1 reads the number and/or title of a chapter on one side of a flashcard. Player 2 answers with the Soaring Summarization on the other side of the flashcard. Reshuffle your flashcards, switch players if desired, and play three times.

Eaglet

Chapter 35: Happy Christmas, Mr. Henry

1. Where and when is chapter 35 set? Who is the owner of this location? Whom has his niece recently married?

2. How are the elegant ladies and dashing gentlemen dressed?

3. Whom does Patrick spot while he is dancing with Sallie? Whom does this person introduce to Patrick?

4. What advice does Patrick give Thomas Jefferson about wooing women? How does Thomas Jefferson respond?

5. What course of study will Thomas Jefferson pursue?

6. Thomas Jefferson and Patrick both say they cannot live without something. What does each one say that is?

7. To whom has Elizabeth Strong recently become engaged?

8. What three professions does Gillamon say call for the gift of oratory? Which two does Patrick rule out? Which one does that leave?

9. Mr. Gillamon gives Patrick two books to help him study law. Name them.

10. At the end of chapter 35, Patrick tells Sallie what he would like to study to become. What is it? Does Sallie approve?

Chapter 35: Happy Christmas, Mr. Henry

1. Where and when is chapter 35 set? Describe the decorations and the food. Who is the owner of this location? Who is his wife and who was her father? Who has his niece recently married?

2. How are the elegant ladies and dashing gentlemen dressed? Whom does Patrick spot while he is dancing with Sallie? Whom does this person introduce to Patrick? What does this person notice about Patrick? What does he think of Patrick?

3. What does Thomas Jefferson say when Patrick asks him if a fair maiden has captured his heart? What advice does Patrick give him about wooing women? How does he reply? Does Patrick appear to be offended? What course of study will Jefferson pursue?

4. What two things does Mr. Gillamon say the study of law requires? How does this statement cause Jefferson to feel? Jefferson and Patrick each say they cannot live without something? What does each one say that is?

5. How does Jefferson respond to hearing what Patrick cannot live without? Does this statement cause him to reassess his opinion about Patrick?

6. To whom has Elizabeth Strong recently become engaged? How many children do Patrick and Sallie have? How does Jefferson sum up his discussion with Patrick? Define the term "put-down" in a social context.

7. What three professions does Mr. Gillamon say call for the gift of oratory? Which two does Patrick rule out? Which one does that leave? What does Jefferson do when Mr. Gillamon suggests that Patrick study law? What is your assessment of the way Jefferson replies and what he does next?

8. What does Patrick think about Mr. Gillamon's suggestion? What rare combination does Mr. Gillamon say Patrick possesses? What does he say about Patrick struggling for seven years to figure out his calling?

9. Outline Mr. Gillamon's explanation of how Patrick could study law.

10. Mr. Gillamon gives Patrick two books to help him study law. Name them. How does Mr. Gillamon encourage Patrick in his study of law?

Chapter 35: Happy Christmas, Mr. Henry

1) Where and when is chapter 35 set? Describe the decorations and the food. Who is the owner of this location? Who is his wife and who was her father? Whom has his niece recently married?

2) How are the ladies and gentlemen dressed? Whom does Patrick spot while he is dancing? Whom does this person introduce to Patrick? What does this person notice about Patrick? What does he think of him? Contrast Mr. Gillamon's assessment of Patrick with Jefferson's.

3) What does Thomas Jefferson say when Patrick asks him if a fair maiden has captured his heart? What advice does Patrick give Jefferson about wooing women? How does he reply? Does Patrick appear to be offended? What course of study will Jefferson pursue?

4) What does Mr. Gillamon say the study of law requires? How does this statement cause Jefferson to feel physically? Jefferson and Patrick each say they cannot live without something. What does each say that is?

5) How does Jefferson respond to hearing what Patrick cannot live without? Does he reassess his opinion about Patrick? How do you think he feels about Patrick now?

6) To whom has Elizabeth Strong recently become engaged? How many Henry children are there? How does Jefferson sum up his discussion with Patrick? Define the term "put-down" in a social context. Which of Jefferson's responses could be classified as such?

7) What three professions does Mr. Gillamon say call for the gift of oratory? Which two does Patrick rule out? Which one does that leave? What does Jefferson do when Mr. Gillamon suggests that Patrick study law? How does he reply?

8) What does Patrick think about Mr. Gillamon's suggestion? What rare combination does Mr. Gillamon say Patrick possesses? What does he say about Patrick struggling for seven years to figure out his calling?

9) Outline Mr. Gillamon's explanation of how Patrick could study law.

10) Mr. Gillamon gives Patrick two books to help him study law. Name them. How does Mr. Gillamon encourage Patrick in his study of law?

Nigel's Nuggets

Chapter 35: Happy Christmas, Mr. Henry

Splendid! You have now met The Voice of the Revolution, The Sword of the Revolution, and The Pen of the Revolution. Make a presentation that showcases each man in his *revolutionary* role.

Cato's Eagle-Eye View

Chapter 35: Happy Christmas, Mr. Henry

Gliding: Summarize the chapter in three to five sentences, written or orally.

Soaring: Summarize the chapter in one word, phrase, or sentence and write it on an index card with the chapter number and title written on the other side.

Soaring Flashcard Game: Shuffle all your Soaring flashcards. Player 1 reads the number and/or title of a chapter on one side of a flashcard. Player 2 answers with the Soaring Summarization on the other side of the flashcard. Reshuffle your flashcards, switch players if desired, and play three times.

Eaglet

Chapter 36: Sweet on MizP

1) What is Patrick doing at the beginning of Chapter 36?

2) Who is with Patrick?

3) What creature is chewing on Jack Poindexter's fence post? What is its name?

4) What does Liz ask MizP to volunteer to do? Who carries the bucket of molasses?

5) Whom does Liz introduce to MizP?

6) MizP says there is enough blue sky to do something. What is it?

7) What does MizP brush on the fencepost for Bill to lick off?

8) Who approaches Patrick as he is sitting on the porch of Hanover Tavern?

9) What has Patrick's friend, John Lewis, prepared for Patrick?

10) Who is waiting for Patrick at Hanover Tavern? What does Jack Poindexter propose to do with MizP? What does MizP say to Patrick when he asks her if she wants to ride to Williamsburg tomorrow?

Chapter 36: Sweet on MizP

1) What is Patrick doing at the beginning of chapter 36? How is the book *Coke upon Littleton* laid out?

2) Who is studying with Patrick? What does the quotation about history mean?

3) What creature is chewing on Jack Poindexter's fencepost? What is its name? What does Liz ask MizP to volunteer to do? How does Liz propose to accomplish this? How many times does she think it will take?

4) Who carries the bucket of molasses? What is his current mission? How does Nigel describe the molasses?

5) What were the provisions of the Molasses Act of 1733? What were the circumstances surrounding it?

6) Whom does Liz introduce to MizP? Describe Liz's molasses plan. MizP says there is enough blue sky to do something. What is it? What does MizP brush on the fencepost for Bill to lick off?

7) MizP is known for her quips. What is a quip? Quote three from page 312. Which is your favorite and why?

8) Who approaches Patrick as he is sitting on the front porch of Hanover Tavern? Who shows up next and what happens?

9) What has Patrick's friend, John Lewis, prepared for Patrick? Who are the four examiners? What strategy does Lewis advise Patrick to follow when he gets to Williamsburg?

10) Who is waiting for Patrick at Hanover Tavern? What does Jack Poindexter propose to do with MizP? What does Jack say to convince Patrick? What does MizP say to Patrick when he asks her if she wants to ride to Williamsburg tomorrow?

Chapter 36: Sweet on MizP

1) What is Patrick doing at the beginning of chapter 36? How is the book *Coke upon Littleton* laid out? What does Coke's advice to the reader mean?

2) Who is studying with Patrick? What does the quotation about history mean?

3) What creature is chewing on Jack Poindexter's fencepost? What is its name? What does Liz ask MizP to volunteer to do? How does Liz propose to accomplish this? How many times does she think it will take?

4) Who carries the bucket of molasses? What is his current mission? How does Nigel describe the molasses?

5) What were the provisions of the Molasses Act of 1733? What were the circumstances surrounding it? What have the colonies done in response to the law? What has the King of England's response been?

6) Whom does Liz introduce to MizP? Describe Liz's molasses plan. Liz says there is enough blue sky to do something. What is it? What does MizP brush on the fencepost for Bill?

7) MizP is known for her quips. What is a quip? Quote three from page 312. Which is your favorite and why?

8) Who approaches Patrick as he is sitting on the front porch of Hanover Tavern? Who shows up next and what happens? What does Jack think of Patrick's plan to study law?

9) What has Patrick's friend, John Lewis, prepared for Patrick? Who are the four examiners? What strategy does Lewis advise Patrick to follow in Williamsburg?

10) Who is waiting for Patrick at Hanover Tavern? What does Jack Poindexter propose to do with MizP? What does Jack say to convince Patrick? What does MizP say to Patrick when he asks her if she wants to ride to Williamsburg tomorrow? Do you think Patrick has a hard time accepting Jack's offer? Why do you think it might be hard for Patrick to accept such a generous gift?

Nigel's Nuggets

Chapter 36: Sweet on MizP

Nigel here. I am utterly thrilled that you have met our beloved MizP. I say, I am wondering if you have figured out the secret yet. Please do an Internet search by typing this in your search engine: *2019-Spring Newsletter-Patrick Henry's Red Hill.* Read the article. Next read the entry entitled **Patrick's Horse** in A WORD FROM THE AUTHOR. Once you have accomplished both tasks, make a presentation about the real MizP.

Cato's Eagle-Eye View

Chapter 36: Sweet on MizP

Gliding: Summarize the chapter in three to five sentences, written or orally.

Soaring: Summarize the chapter in one word, phrase, or sentence and write it on an index card with the chapter number and title written on the other side.

Soaring Flashcard Game: Shuffle all your Soaring flashcards. Player 1 reads the number and/or title of a chapter on one side of a flashcard. Player 2 answers with the Soaring Summarization on the other side of the flashcard. Reshuffle your flashcards, switch players if desired, and play three times.

Eaglet

Chapter 37: With a Wythe and a Prayer

1) Where is Patrick going at the start of chapter 37 and why? What food does Sallie give him?

2) Whom does Patrick say he and MizP look like?

3) What college does Patrick pass on his way into Williamsburg? How many students are enrolled?

4) What is the name of the most acclaimed of Williamsburg's inns and taverns?

5) What is MizP's concern about Patrick's muddy clothes?

6) Who is the first examiner Patrick sees?

7) How is Mr. Wythe dressed in contrast to Patrick?

8) Does George Wythe sign Patrick's law license?

9) Which examiner does Patrick see next? Does he sign his license?

10) Whom does Patrick determine to see next?

Chapter 37: With a Wythe and a Prayer

1) Where are Patrick and MizP going at the start of chapter 37 and why? What food does Sallie send with him? How long will it take him to get there? Who will go along with Patrick and MizP?

2) Whom does Patrick say he and MizP look like? What college does Patrick pass on his way into Williamsburg? How many students are enrolled? What is the main street that runs through Williamsburg?

3) What is in the Market District? What is a Magazine? What is the name of the print and book shop? What is the name of the most acclaimed of Williamsburg's inns and taverns? For whom is it named?

4) Where does Patrick stay? Who meets MizP in the barn? What is MizP's concern about Patrick's clothes? Do you think MizP's concerns are valid? Why or why not?

5) Who is the first examiner Patrick sees? Where is his home? Describe it from the outside.

6) What does Nigel notice about Patrick's appearance? How is Mr. Wythe dressed in contrast to Patrick?

7) List three questions George Wythe asks Patrick to determine his qualifications.

8) Describe Patrick's cross-examination by George Wythe in one or two paragraphs.

9) What does George Wythe say first regarding Patrick's response to his grilling? What does he see in Patrick? Does he sign Patrick's license?

10) Which examiner does Patrick see next? How does he view Patrick's boldness? Does the second examiner sign Patrick's license? Whom does Patrick determine to see next?

Chapter 37: With a Wythe and a Prayer

1) Where are Patrick and MizP going at the start of chapter 37 and why? How long will it take him to get there? What food does Sallie send with him? Who will go along with Patrick and MizP?

2) Whom does Patrick say he and MizP look like? What college does Patrick pass on his way into Williamsburg? How many students are enrolled? What is the main street that runs through Williamsburg? How long is it? What is at the end of the street?

3) What is in the Market District? What is a Magazine? What is the name of the print and book shop? What is the name of the most acclaimed of Williamsburg's inns and taverns? For whom is it named? Briefly describe him.

4) Where does Patrick stay? Who meets MizP in the barn? What is MizP's concern about Patrick's clothes? Do you think MizP's concerns are valid? Why or why not?

5) Who is the first examiner Patrick sees? Where is his home? Describe it from the outside. What is the name of the room in which they meet? Describe it.

6) What does Nigel notice about Patrick's appearance? How is Mr. Wythe dressed in contrast to Patrick? Why does Patrick mention John Lewis?

7) List three questions George Wythe asks Patrick to determine his qualifications. How does Patrick answer him?

8) Describe Patrick's cross-examination by George Wythe in two or three paragraphs.

9) What does George Wythe say first regarding Patrick's response to his grilling? What does he see in Patrick? Does he sign Patrick's license? Based on this response from George Wythe, what do you think Patrick thinks about his chances for success with the next examiner?

10) Which examiner does Patrick see next? How does he view Patrick's boldness? Why do Patrick's shoulders sink? Does the second examiner sign Patrick's license? Whom does Patrick determine to see next?

Nigel's Nuggets

Chapter 37: With a Wythe and a Prayer

I am frightfully concerned that your cartography skills are getting rusty. Let us hasten to remedy this. Please study existing maps and make a map of Colonial Williamsburg. Your map should reflect the level of Chapter Guide that you did for this current chapter.

Cato's Eagle-Eye View

Chapter 37: With a Wythe and a Prayer

Gliding: Summarize the chapter in three to five sentences, written or orally.

Soaring: Summarize the chapter in one word, phrase, or sentence and write it on an index card with the chapter number and title written on the other side.

Soaring Flashcard Game: Shuffle all your Soaring flashcards. Player 1 reads the number and/or title of a chapter on one side of a flashcard. Player 2 answers with the Soaring Summarization on the other side of the flashcard. Reshuffle your flashcards, switch players if desired, and play three times.

Eaglet

Chapter 38: Barely Passing the Bar

1) Which examiner does Patrick see first the next day?

2) Patrick arrives to find the Randolph household in uproar. Is it a good time to approach Peyton Randolph?

3) Does Peyton Randolph agree to see Patrick?

4) What does Peyton Randolph advise Patrick to do?

5) Who answers the door of John Randolph's home on page 231? What is her disguise?

6) What does the wording of Clarie's introduction of Patrick lead John Randolph to infer?

7) What does John Randolph object to the moment he sees Patrick?

8) Does John Randolph agree to examine Patrick?

9) Does John Randolph end up signing Patrick's law license?

10) What does John Randolph advise Patrick to do after he wins his first few cases?

Chapter 38: Barely Passing the Bar

1) Which examiner does Patrick see first the next day? What position for the Colony of Virginia does he hold? Who is his brother?

2) Patrick arrives to find the house in uproar. Is it a good time for Patrick to approach Peyton Randolph for an interview? What does Patrick do when he finds Peyton Randolph? Does Peyton Randolph agree to see Patrick?

3) What does Peyton Randolph advise Patrick to do? What does Peyton Randolph advise Patrick to tell his brother, John? Can Patrick afford to stay in Williamsburg after today?

4) Who answers the door of John Randolph's home on page 231? What is her disguise? What does she tell John Randolph about Patrick when she introduces him? What does the wording of the introduction lead John Randolph to believe?

5) What does John Randolph object to the moment he sees Patrick? What does he tell him?

6) What argument does Patrick use to persuade John Randolph to examine him? How does Nigel sum up this argument?

7) Briefly describe the interview between John Randolph and Patrick in one paragraph.

8) What does John Randolph pretend to do during the discussion?

9) Describe John Randolph's office library and Patrick's reaction to it.

10) Does John Randolph end up signing Patrick's law license? What does John Randolph realize that he has mistakenly "assumed differently?"

Chapter 38: Barely Passing the Bar

1) What examiner does Patrick see first the next day? What position for the Colony of Virginia does he hold? Who is his brother? What does Patrick hope as he walks toward his first call?

2) Patrick arrives to find the house in uproar. Is it a good time for Patrick to approach Peyton Randolph for an interview? What does Patrick do when he finds Peyton Randolph? Does Peyton Randolph agree to see Patrick? What does Nigel think of Patrick's decision and why?

3) What does Peyton Randolph advise Patrick to do? What does Peyton Randolph advise Patrick to tell his brother, John? Can Patrick afford to stay in Williamsburg after today? What answer does Patrick not *plan* to take?

4) Who answers the door of John Randolph's home on page 231? What is her disguise? What does she tell John Randolph about Patrick when she introduces him? What does the wording of the introduction lead John Randolph to believe?

5) What does John Randolph object to the moment he sees Patrick? What does he tell him?

6) What argument does Patrick use to persuade John Randolph to examine him? How does Nigel sum up this argument? Who were Tom Bell and Bampfylde Moore Carew?

7) Briefly describe the interview between John Randolph and Patrick in one to three paragraphs. What does Patrick say about the heart of man? What does he mean?

8) What does John Randolph pretend to do during the discussion? Why might this tactic be a good one?

9) Describe John Randolph's office library and Patrick's reaction to it. What does John Randolph bellow as he lifts his hand to his extensive collection of law books?

10) Does John Randolph end up signing Patrick's law license? What does John Randolph realize that he has mistakenly "assumed differently?"

Nigel's Nuggets

Chapter 38: Barely Passing the Bar

By Jove, he did it! Read the entry in A WORD FROM THE AUTHOR to get the full scoop. Then recap the next part of the Fiddle's Riddle. Use the entry **Patrick's Law License** in A WORD FROM THE AUTHOR to crack the code with the clues below. Fill in the blanks below.

Use the code below to find the letters to spell the word to insert in the first blank:
First letter of the second word in the entry
Second letter of the second word on the seventh line
Last letter of the sixth word on the twelfth line
Last letter of the seventh word on the fifth line
First letter of the last word on the page upon which the entry begins
Third letter of the third word in the eleventh line

Use the code below to find the letters to spell the word to insert in the second blank:
Fifth letter of the seventh word on the second line
Second letter in the entry
Fourth letter on the eighteenth line
Second to last letter on the tenth line
Sixth letter of the tenth word on the thirteenth line
Second letter of the seventh word on the ninth line
Sixth letter of the second word on the eighth line

Use the code below to find the letters to spell the word to insert in the third blank:
First letter on the seventeenth line
Third letter of the last word in the entry
Sixth letter of the fourth word on the sixth line
Last letter of the fourteenth line
First letter of the fourth word on the sixteenth line
Fourth letter of the twelfth word on the fourth line

Stupendous! You now have the words to fill in to answer the next part of the Fiddle's Riddle.

Patrick Henry found his voice as a ______________ while living in the ______________

__________________.

Cato's Eagle-Eye View

Chapter 38: Barely Passing the Bar

Gliding: Summarize the chapter in three to five sentences, written or orally.

Soaring: Summarize the chapter in one word, phrase, or sentence and write it on an index card with the chapter number and title written on the other side.

Soaring Flashcard Game: Shuffle all your Soaring flashcards. Player 1 reads the number and/or title of a chapter on one side of a flashcard. Player 2 answers with the Soaring Summarization on the other side of the flashcard. Reshuffle your flashcards, switch players if desired, and play three times.

Eaglet

Chapter 39: The Power Behind the Throne

1) Where and when is chapter 39 set? What is the title of the sermon being read? Who preached it?

2) How old was Samuel Davies when he died?

3) Patrick begins to tell Sallie about the first sermon he heard Samuel Davies preach. Finish the sentence Patrick quotes, which begins, "Woe to you, oh land, . . ."

4) How old is King George III?

5) What had King George II done before he died?

6) Over whose heads did the Virginia parsons go?

7) Has Uncle Patrick gotten involved in the case? If so, who does he support? Which side?

8) With the repeal of the Two Penny Act, what has England done for the first time in its history?

9) Al, Gillamon, and Clarie are attending the coronation of King George III. Where does the ceremony take place and on what date?

10) What happens when King George removes his crown to take communion?

Fledgling

Chapter 39: The Power Behind the Throne

1) Where and when is chapter 39 set? What is the title of the sermon being read? Who preached it? Where was the sermon delivered? How old was Samuel Davies when he died? How long after he delivered this sermon did he die?

2) Patrick begins to tell Sallie about the first sermon he heard Samuel Davies preach. Finish the sentence Patrick quotes, which begins, "Woe to you, oh land, . . ." Read the passage up through the words "childish tyranny." What does the passage mean?

3) Write out the second portion of the sermon that Patrick recounts for Sallie. What does it mean?

4) How old is King George III? What is Sallie's concern about his age?

5) What does Patrick say concerns him more? What had King George II done before he died?

6) How much were parsons paid per year in tobacco? How much was the tobacco normally worth? Why was it a financial hardship to pay the usual amount with a poor tobacco crop? What did the parsons do to ensure they got their full amount of tobacco? Whose heads did they have to go over to do so?

7) Why does Patrick say this is wrong? Who does he think is best positioned to govern the people of Virginia and why? Has Uncle Patrick gotten involved? If so, on which side?

8) What does Liz think as she glances at Patrick's fiddle? How long has Patrick been getting prepared for the coming legal battle? With the repeal of the Two Penny Act, what has England done for the first time in its history?

9) Where are Al, Gillamon, and Clarie on September 22, 1761, and why? What is Al doing during the ceremony? Who is Queen Charlotte? How old is she?

10) Write out the prayer the Archbishop of Canterbury prays over King George III. What does it mean? Describe what happens after the prayer. What is Al's reaction?

Chapter 39: The Power Behind the Throne

1) Where and when is chapter 39 set? What is the title of the sermon being read? Who preached it? Where was the sermon delivered? How old was Samuel Davies when he died? How long after he delivered this sermon did he die? Earlier in the VRK Study Guide, you researched the disease which eventually took Samuel Davies' life. Name it.

2) Patrick begins to tell Sallie about the first sermon he heard Samuel Davies preach. Finish the sentence Patrick quotes, which begins, "Woe to you, oh land, . . ." Read the passage up through the words "childish tyranny." What does the passage mean?

3) Write out the second portion of the sermon that Patrick recounts for Sallie. What does it mean?

4) How old is King George III? What is Sallie's concern about his age?

5) What does Patrick say concerns him more? What had King George II done before he died? Why might Patrick and Sallie's concerns be valid?

6) How much were parsons paid per year in tobacco? How much was the tobacco normally worth? Why was it a financial hardship to pay the usual amount with a poor tobacco crop? What did the parsons do to ensure they got their full amount of tobacco? Whose heads did they have to go over to do so? What were the responses of the Bishop of London and the King?

7) Why does Patrick say this is wrong? Who does he think is best positioned to govern the people of Virginia and why? Has Uncle Patrick gotten involved? If so, on which side?

8) What does Liz think as she glances at Patrick's fiddle? How long has Patrick been getting prepared for the coming legal battle? With the repeal of the Two Penny Act, what has England done for the first time in its history?

9) Where are Al, Gillamon, and Clarie on September 22, 1761, and why? What is Al doing during the ceremony? Who is Queen Charlotte? How old is she?

10) Write out the prayer the Archbishop of Canterbury prays over King George III. What does it mean? Describe what happens after the prayer. What is Al's reaction? What does this foreshadow?

Nigel's Nuggets

Chapter 39: The Power Behind the Throne

"Zadok the Priest, and Nathan the Prophet . . .... " Oh, excuse me. Just reliving some of the utterly thrilling coronations I have witnessed. I say, you really must learn about the process. First read the entry about the coronation in A WORD FROM THE AUTHOR. Next, research British Coronation Ceremonies and make a presentation about them. Please make sure to find out who was the most recent British sovereign to be crowned and include information about her coronation. Then, search for the music from this sovereign's ceremony. You should be able to find an album with her coronation music. Why is the background purple? Find and listen to a certain song, from chapter 39, amongst the splendid pieces of music included in the recording.

Cato's Eagle-Eye View

Chapter 39: The Power Behind the Throne

Gliding: Summarize the chapter in three to five sentences, written or orally.

Soaring: Summarize the chapter in one word, phrase, or sentence and write it on an index card with the chapter number and title written on the other side.

Soaring Flashcard Game: Shuffle all your Soaring flashcards. Player 1 reads the number and/or title of a chapter on one side of a flashcard. Player 2 answers with the Soaring Summarization on the other side of the flashcard. Reshuffle your flashcards, switch players if desired, and play three times.

Eaglet

Chapter 40: Two Pennies for Your Thoughts

1) Where is chapter 40 set and when? Who is getting caught up? Where are they?

2) How many cases has Patrick handled over the last three years?

3) What is the name of Patrick and Sallie's new son?

4) Liz is convinced that the next part of the riddle has to do with Patrick using his voice in Hanover Courthouse. What does she think it involves?

5) John Henry makes the first ruling of its kind in Virginia regarding the Two Penny Act. What is his verdict?

6) Who is the lawyer who unsuccessfully argues for the people of Virginia against the parsons? What does he do after the verdict?

7) Nigel is upset because it looks as if the defendants, Johnson and Brown, will have to go it alone. Who does Liz think should take the case?

8) Patrick argues for John Lewis keeping the case. What does he caution John Lewis never to do?

9) To whom does John Lewis propose turning the case over? Does he accept?

10) Patrick asks the Maker if he should call the parsons *"wicked."* What does he decide to call them instead? What does the first of the two words mean?

Chapter 40: Two Pennies for Your Thoughts

1) Where is chapter 40 set and when? Who is getting caught up? Where are they? What is the case being heard? Who is representing the parsons? Who is representing the defendants and what are their names? Who is the presiding judge?

2) How many cases has Patrick handled over the past three years? What is the name of Patrick and Sallie's new son? What kind of lawyer is Patrick in Max's opinion? Liz is convinced that the next part of the riddle has to do with Patrick using his voice in Hanover Courthouse. What does she think it involves?

3) How does Nigel describe the outcome of the case? Why is he upset about the ruling?

4) Who is the lawyer who unsuccessfully argues for the people of Virginia against the parsons? What does he do after the verdict?

5) Who does Max think should have represented Johnson and Brown? Nigel is upset because it looks as if the defendants, Johnson and Brown, will have to go it alone. Who does Liz think should take the case?

6) What does John Lewis say about Patrick's father's ruling on the case? Why does he think he should drop the case?

7) Why does Patrick think Reverend Maury chose Hanover County for the site of his case?

8) Patrick tells Lewis that Maury's strategy has a flaw. Explain Patrick's reasoning. Patrick argues for Lewis keeping the case. What does he caution Lewis never to do? What does Lewis believe the ruling will mean technically?

9) To whom does John Lewis propose turning the case over? What are his reasons for doing what he does? Does he agree to take it?

10) Liz leaves two pennies on a passage in Patrick's Bible. Describe the dream Patrick has next. Sum up the passage. Patrick asks the Maker if he should call the parsons *"wicked."* What does he decide to call them instead? What does the first of the two words mean?

Chapter 40: Two Pennies for Your Thoughts

1) Where is chapter 40 set and when? Who is getting caught up? Where? What is the case being heard? Who is representing the parsons and the defendants? Who is the judge?

2) How many cases has Patrick handled over the past three years? How many cases per year and per month is this? Who is Patrick and Sallie's new son? What kind of lawyer is Patrick in Max's opinion? Liz is convinced that the next part of the riddle has to do with Patrick using his voice in Hanover Courthouse. What does she think it involves?

3) How does Nigel describe the outcome of the case? Why is he upset about the ruling?

4) Who is the lawyer who unsuccessfully argues for the people of Virginia against the parsons? What does he do after the verdict?

5) Whom does Max think should have represented Johnson and Brown? Nigel is upset because it looks as if the defendants, Johnson and Brown, will have to go it alone. Whom does Liz think should take the case? Describe Patrick's reaction as he listens to the case.

6) What does John Lewis say about Patrick's father's ruling on the case? Why does he think he should drop the case? Give one reason that justifies Lewis's position.

7) Why does Patrick think Reverend Maury chose Hanover County for the site of his case? Why might this have been a good strategy?

8) Patrick tells Lewis that Maury's strategy has a flaw. Explain Patrick's reasoning. Patrick argues for Lewis keeping the case. What does he caution Lewis never to do? What does Lewis believe the ruling will mean technically?

9) To whom does John Lewis propose turning the case over? What are his reasons for doing what he does? Does he agree to take it? What does Liz think of this turn of events?

10) Liz leaves two pennies on a passage in Patrick's Bible. Describe the dream Patrick has next. Sum up the passage. How does this apply to Patrick and his situation? Patrick asks the Maker if he should call the parsons *"wicked."* What does he decide to call them instead? What does the first of the two words mean?

Nigel's Nuggets

Chapter 40: Two Pennies for Your Thoughts

My pet, Liz, is quite the determined cat. I am equally determined that you should recreate and present the scene with Patrick, John Lewis, and Liz—putting in "her two cents' worth."

Cato's Eagle-Eye View

Chapter 40: Two Pennies for Your Thoughts

Gliding: Summarize the chapter in three to five sentences, written or orally.

Soaring: Summarize the chapter in one word, phrase, or sentence and write it on an index card with the chapter number and title written on the other side.

Soaring Flashcard Game: Shuffle all your Soaring flashcards. Player 1 reads the number and/or title of a chapter on one side of a flashcard. Player 2 answers with the Soaring Summarization on the other side of the flashcard. Reshuffle your flashcards, switch players if desired, and play three times.

Eaglet

Chapter 41: Cause for the Parsons to Smile

1) When is chapter 41 set? What has Max brought Liz at her request?

2) Who gives Patrick the Scottish Marigolds and what does she do with them?

3) Patsey asks Patrick, "What could be a better way to win than . . .?" Finish her thought.

4) Who is Thomas Jefferson's tutor?

5) Which justice does Patrick meet on his way into court? Who will some of the other justices be?

6) When Uncle Patrick arrives, what does Patrick ask him not to do? What does he ask him to do instead? Does Uncle Patrick agree?

7) Uncle Patrick stops his carriage after two people pass him. What are their names?

8) Who objects to the jurors? Which side does he represent?

9) What does Liz say the case is about for Patrick?

10) Who walks into the courtroom at the end of chapter 42? What is Patrick's physical reaction?

Chapter 41: Cause for the Parsons to Smile

1) When is chapter 41 set? What has Max brought Liz at her request? Who gives Patrick the Scottish Marigolds? What has she done with them? Patsey asks Patrick, "What could be a better way to win than . . .?" Finish her thought.

2) Which group of people stands out in the crowd? How are they dressed?

3) Whom does Patrick speak with before he can get out of his carriage? What does he ask him not to do and why? What does he ask him to do instead? Does that person agree?

4) Where do Liz and Nigel go to watch the trial? Why does Uncle Patrick stop his carriage? What does he do next? How do Max and Cato respond and what do they plan to do?

5) Describe the inside of the courthouse; who sits where? Describe the entrance of the parsons.

6) Nigel is concerned about the jury who will be picked. Why is the jury important?

7) Who objects to the jury? Which side is he representing? Why does he object?

8) What is Patrick's argument for keeping the jury as seated? Is he successful? Name the jurors who are selected.

9) Summarize Peter Lyons's argument to the jury.

10) Summarize Patrick's response to the jury. Who walks into the courtroom at the end of chapter 42? What is Patrick's physical reaction to this?

Chapter 41: Cause for the Parsons to Smile

1) When is chapter 41 set? What has Max brought Liz at her request? Who gives Patrick the Scottish Marigolds? What has she done with them? Patsey asks Patrick, "What could be a better way to win than . . .?" Finish her thought.

2) Which group of people stands out in the crowd? How are they dressed and why?

3) Whom does Patrick speak with before he can get out of his carriage? What does he ask him not to do and why? What does he ask him to do instead? Does the person agree? Do you think Patrick's request is a good idea? Why or why not?

4) Where do Liz and Nigel go to watch the trial? Why does Uncle Patrick stop his carriage? What does he do next? How do Max and Cato respond and what do they plan to do?

5) Describe the inside of the courthouse; who sits where? Describe the entrance of the parsons.

6) Nigel is concerned about the jury who will be picked. Why are the jury important?

7) Who objects to the jury? Which side is he representing? Why does he object? How does Nigel react to this? Why do you think he reacts this way?

8) What is Patrick's argument for keeping the jury as seated? Is he successful? Name the jurors who are selected.

9) Summarize Peter Lyons's argument to the jury. How do Nigel and Liz react to Lyons's arguments?

10) Summarize Patrick's response to the jury. Who walks into the courtroom at the end of chapter 42? What is Patrick's physical reaction to this? What do you think Uncle Patrick intends by walking into the courtroom?

Nigel's Nuggets

Chapter 41: Cause for the Parsons to Smile

Oh, dear, dear, dear. Things are looking bleak. Very bleak indeed. This chapter is most appropriately entitled. I should think Jenny L. Cote has a bang-up time deciding on chapter titles. List five of your favorite VRK titles. Tell why you like each one. After all that fun, there is still more. Please make a flower chain and fashion it into the item of your choice.

Cato's Eagle-Eye View

Chapter 41: Cause for the Parsons to Smile

Gliding: Summarize the chapter in three to five sentences, written or orally.

Soaring: Summarize the chapter in one word, phrase, or sentence and write it on an index card with the chapter number and title written on the other side.

Soaring Flashcard Game: Shuffle all your Soaring flashcards. Player 1 reads the number and/or title of a chapter on one side of a flashcard. Player 2 answers with the Soaring Summarization on the other side of the flashcard. Reshuffle your flashcards, switch players if desired, and play three times.

Eaglet

Chapter 42: A Voice in the Court

1) What look does Uncle Patrick have on his face when he looks at the jury? Liz is concerned for Patrick. What does Nigel say and do?

2) What does Patrick feel in his pocket? What kind of images flash across his mind?

3) What does Liz think when Patrick opens his eyes and lifts his chin?

4) Which is the only group of people of whom Patrick fails to speak highly?

5) Write out Patrick's equation for the jury.

6) What does Patrick say the Burgesses *represent*? What does the Council *represent*? What does the Governor *represent*?

7) What does Mr. Lyons cry out and accuse Patrick of speaking?

8) Nigel realizes Patrick's brilliance. He has turned from a defense attorney into a prosecutor. What is the effect of this?

9) What amount of damages does the jury award Maury?

10) Where does Gillamon send Max at the end of chapter 42? What creature will be in the next part of his mission?

Chapter 42: A Voice in the Court

1) What look does Uncle Patrick have on his face when he looks at the jury? Liz is concerned for Patrick. What does Nigel do? What does Patrick feel inside his pocket? What kind of images flash across his mind? What does Liz think when Patrick opens his eyes and lifts his chin?

2) Of which group of people does Patrick fail to speak highly? What word does Patrick use to describe the original intent of the Two Penny Acts? How does he summarize them?

3) Write out the equation Patrick demonstrates for the jury. How does Patrick relate the equation to government? What does he say happens if the equation is violated?

4) What question does Patrick pose to the jury as he looks up to the ceiling?

5) How does Patrick answer his own question? Who does Patrick say the Burgesses *represent*? What does the Council *represent*? What does the Governor *represent*? Summarize what Patrick says before Mr. Lyons interjects his position.

6) What does Mr. Lyons cry out and accuse Patrick of speaking? Nigel realizes Patrick's brilliance. He has turned from a defense attorney into a prosecutor. What is the effect of this? How do the people react to Patrick's argument? How many justices disapprove? How does Samuel Meredith react? How does John Syme, Jr., react?

7) How does Patrick describe the use of an established church and clergy in society? What does he say happens when the clergy cease to do this? What does he suggest should be happening to Mr. Maury?

8) How do the parsons respond? What does Uncle Patrick say? Does this appear to affect Patrick? Why or why not?

9) How do Liz and Nigel respond to Patrick's arguments to the jury? What amount of damages does the jury award Maury? How does Lyons react? What two things does he request? Which one is he granted?

10) Max explains how Uncle Patrick was delayed. What happened to accomplish this? How old is Patrick? Who else was this age when they discovered their voices?

Chapter 42: A Voice in the Court

1) What look does Uncle Patrick have on his face as he looks at the jury? Liz is concerned for Patrick. What does Nigel do? What is inside Patrick's pocket? What kind of images cross his mind? What does Liz think when Patrick opens his eyes and lifts his chin?

2) Of which group of people does Patrick fail to speak highly? What word does Patrick use to describe the original intent of the Two Penny Acts? How does he summarize them?

3) Write out the equation Patrick demonstrates. Relate the equation to government. What happens if the equation is violated? Has the equation *been* violated? How, by whom?

4) Which question does Patrick pose to the jury as he looks up to the ceiling?

5) How does Patrick answer his own question? What does Patrick say the Burgesses, and the Governor *represent*? Summarize what Patrick says before Mr. Lyons interjects his position.

6) What does Mr. Lyons accuse Patrick of speaking? Nigel realizes Patrick's brilliance in becoming a prosecutor. What is the effect of this? How do the people react to Patrick's argument? How many justices disapprove? How do Samuel Meredith and John Syme, Jr., react? How does Judge John Henry react and why?

7) How does Patrick describe the use of an established church and clergy in society? What happens when the clergy ceases to do this? What does he suggest for Mr. Maury?

8) What do the parsons do? What does Uncle Patrick say? Is Patrick affected? Who do you think Patrick was trying to spare by asking Uncle Patrick not to attend? Do you think Patrick's argument to the jury might impact relationships within the Henry family? How?

9) How do Liz and Nigel respond to Patrick's arguments to the jury? What amount of damages does the jury award Maury? How does Lyons react? What two things does he request? Which one is he granted? What does Patrick do as he leaves the courtroom?

10) Max explains how Uncle Patrick was delayed. What happened to accomplish this? How old is Patrick? Who else was this age when they discovered their voices? What does Nigel put together about how Gillamon had foreshadowed Patrick? Where does Gillamon send Max at the end of chapter 42? What creature will be in the next part of his mission?

Nigel's Nuggets

Chapter 42: A Voice in the Court

Answers to the Fiddle's Riddle are coming quickly. Please update your poster to reflect the answer of Patrick finding his Voice in the Courtroom during the case of the __________________ __________________.

Now to another concern—Patrick's clothing. It is woefully inadequate to the situation. Please make a presentation demonstrating how a proper mid-eighteenth century lawyer should be attired. Absolutely do <u>not</u> use Patrick as your example.

Cato's Eagle-Eye View

Chapter 42: A Voice in the Court

Gliding: Summarize the chapter in three to five sentences, written or orally.

Soaring: Summarize the chapter in one word, phrase, or sentence and write it on an index card with the chapter number and title written on the other side.

Soaring Flashcard Game: Shuffle all your Soaring flashcards. Player 1 reads the number and/or title of a chapter on one side of a flashcard. Player 2 answers with the Soaring Summarization on the other side of the flashcard. Reshuffle your flashcards, switch players if desired, and play three times.

Eaglet

Chapter 43: Soldiers, Smugglers, Sugar, and Stamps

1) Where is chapter 43 set? What is Al's name for this mission? Who is the new Prime Minister of England?

2) Name King George III's quirky "favorite phrase."

3) How much does it cost England to maintain an army of ten thousand *soldiers* per year in the colonies?

4) What is being *smuggled* into the colonies?

5) King George III says the colonists need to be *taught* obedience to the crown. What kind of act does Grenville propose?

6) Al unwittingly gives Grenville the idea for another act. What is it?

7) How many categories will be taxed by the Stamp Act? What is the range of the tax?

8) What popular slogan does James Otis coin?

9) Patrick is building a new house in Louisa County. Liz and Nigel use this information to figure out the location of the next part of the Fiddle's Riddle. What is it?

10) Colonel Isaac Barré coins a term that will name the movement that will come against the Stamp Act. What is it?

Chapter 43: Soldiers, Smugglers, Sugar, and Stamps

1) Where is chapter 43 set? What is Al's name for this mission? Who is the new Prime Minister of England? Name King George III's quirky "favorite phrase." How much does it cost England to maintain an army of ten thousand *soldiers* per year in the colonies? What is being *smuggled* into the colonies?

2) Where does Grenville suggest that smuggling trials be moved to and why? What benefits does he expect from this move?

3) What act does Grenville propose next? What else does he suggest? Al unwittingly gives Grenville an idea. What does he do to inspire Grenville? What does Grenville propose and why?

4) Who is gathered at Mount Brilliant in November, 1764? What are they discussing? How many categories will be covered by this act? What is the range of the tax?

5) What does Clarie say about the Mutiny and Quartering Acts? How does Nigel respond to this information?

6) What popular slogan does James Otis coin? What does Clarie tell Liz and Nigel about Benjamin Franklin? Why is Nigel not joining him at this time?

7) What is Patrick doing about his family's home? Liz and Nigel begin to puzzle out the next part of the Fiddle's Riddle. What do they think?

8) How is Patrick dressed as he and MizP head into Williamsburg? What does MizP say about this? How has Nigel gotten to Williamsburg? Why is Patrick in Williamsburg? Describe the interior of the House of Burgesses. What is the main concern of the burgesses regarding their response to the Stamp Act?

9) Sum up Nigel and Clarie's recap of Patrick's case. What is Nigel's assessment of the outcome for Patrick?

10) Where are Gillamon and Clarie in February, 1765, and why? What does Charles Townshend say about the colonists? Sum up Colonel Isaac Barré's rebuttal. Colonel Barré coins a term that will name the movement that opposes the Stamp Act. Name it.

Chapter 43: Soldiers, Smugglers, Sugar, and Stamps

1) Where is chapter 43 set? What is Al's name? Who is the Prime Minister of England? Name King George III's quirky "favorite phrase." How much does it cost to maintain an army of ten thousand *soldiers* per year? What is being *smuggled* into the colonies?

2) Where does Grenville suggest that smuggling trials be moved and why? What benefits does he expect from this move?

3) What act does Grenville propose? What else does he suggest? Al unwittingly gives Grenville an idea. What is it? What does Grenville propose and why?

4) Who is gathered at Mount Brilliant in November, 1764? What are they discussing? How many categories will be covered by this act? What is the range of the tax?

5) What does Clarie say about the Mutiny and Quartering Acts? How does Nigel respond to this information? Why do you think these moves by England might be unwise?

6) What popular slogan does James Otis coin? What does Clarie tell Liz and Nigel about Benjamin Franklin? Why is Nigel not joining him at this time?

7) What is Patrick doing about his family's home? Liz and Nigel begin to puzzle out the next part of the Fiddle's Riddle. What do they think? Liz is concerned that her proposal for Patrick is not available. What does Clarie tell her?

8) How is Patrick dressed as he and MizP head into Williamsburg? What does MizP say about this? How has Nigel gotten to Williamsburg? Why is Patrick in Williamsburg? Describe the interior of the House of Burgesses. What is the main concern of the burgesses regarding their response to the Stamp Act? What is Patrick's concern? Why?

9) Sum up Nigel and Clarie's recap of Patrick's case. What is Nigel's assessment of the outcome for Patrick? What idea does Cato have?

10) Where are Gillamon and Clarie in February, 1765, and why? What does Charles Townshend say about the colonists? Sum up Colonel Isaac Barré's rebuttal. Colonel Barré coins a term that will name the movement that opposes the Stamp Act. Name it. Whom do you think best understands the colonists and why?

Nigel's Nuggets

Chapter 43: Soldiers, Smugglers, Sugar, and Stamps

Huzzah! The name, *The Sons of Liberty,* has been planted. Make a presentation about this group.

Cato's Eagle-Eye View

Chapter 43: Soldiers, Smugglers, Sugar, and Stamps

Gliding: Summarize the chapter in three to five sentences, written or orally.

Soaring: Summarize the chapter in one word, phrase, or sentence and write it on an index card with the chapter number and title written on the other side.

Soaring Flashcard Game: Shuffle all your Soaring flashcards. Player 1 reads the number and/or title of a chapter on one side of a flashcard. Player 2 answers with the Soaring Summarization on the other side of the flashcard. Reshuffle your flashcards, switch players if desired, and play three times.

Eaglet

Chapter 44: A Voice in the House

1) Where is chapter 44 set and when? Which EO7 members are present? Why is Nigel upset?

2) When will the next session of the House of Burgesses start? Who holds the two seats from Louisa County?

3) How does Nigel respond to MizP's compliment? What does that word mean?

4) Where is Liz on May 20? How has she arrived? What is different about Patrick? What does Liz say when she sees him?

5) Which birthday is Patrick about to celebrate? What position does William Johnson take? How does Nigel describe this profession?

6) What do Patrick's first words in the House of Burgesses do?

7) Patrick asks why the burgesses will not even discuss something. What is it?

8) Why does Patrick think that many of the burgesses have left town already?

9) What does Patrick say the resolves do not represent?

10) Patrick shows his friends something written on a leaf of paper torn from *Coke Upon Littleton*. What is it?

Chapter 44: A Voice in the House

1) Where is chapter 44 set and when? Which EO7 members are present? Why is Nigel upset? What did Benjamin Franklin write about the outcome?

2) When will the next session of the House of Burgesses start? Who holds the two seats from Louisa County?

3) How does Nigel respond to MizP's compliment? What does this word mean? Liz figures out what to do next. What suggestion does MizP make as Liz runs off? Where is Liz on May 20? How has she arrived? What is different about Patrick? What does Liz say when she sees him? Who is the most excited? How is Clarie disguised?

4) Which birthday is Patrick about to celebrate? What position does William Johnson take? How does Nigel describe this profession? Who has helped Patrick get elected? How do Nigel and Liz get inside the house chamber?

5) Where do Liz and Nigel hide during the action? What time does the session begin for the day? What is Patrick's committee? How many burgesses are there? Where have many of them gone? What town had been recently formed?

6) How does Patrick cause a stir with his first speech? What do Patrick's first words in the house do? What had this person proposed?

7) Who supports Patrick, and which enemies does he make? How does Patrick spend the following days?

8) Describe Patrick's conversation with his new friends at Lewis's Tavern up to the point where Munford leaves.

9) What does Patrick conclude after Munford leaves? Why does Patrick think that many of the burgesses have left town already? What is Patrick's concern if they "remain silent?" What background for this concern has he just expressed? What does Patrick say and do next? What have the resolves not done in Patrick's opinion?

10) What will happen if time runs out? Patrick shows his friends something written on a leaf of paper torn from *Coke Upon Littleton*. What is it?

Chapter 44: A Voice in the House

1) Where is chapter 44 set and when? Which EO7 members are present? Why is Nigel upset? What did Benjamin Franklin write about the outcome?

2) When do the burgesses meet next? Who holds the seats from Louisa County?

3) How does Nigel respond to MizP's compliment? What does this word mean? Liz figures out what to do next. What suggestion does MizP make as Liz runs off? Where is Liz on May 20? How has she arrived? What is different about Patrick? What does Liz say when she sees him? Who is the most excited? How is Clarie disguised?

4) Which birthday is Patrick about to celebrate? What position does William Johnson take? How does Nigel describe this profession? Who helps Patrick get elected? How do Nigel and Liz get in the House? What are the qualifications to vote in Colonial Virginia?

5) Where do Liz and Nigel hide in the house? What time does the session begin for the day? What is Patrick's committee? How many burgesses are there? Where have many of them gone? What town has just been formed? What petition particularly interests Nigel? Why?

6) How does Patrick cause a stir with his first speech? What do Patrick's first words in the house do? What had this person proposed?

7) Who supports Patrick, and which enemies does he make? How does Patrick spend the following days?

8) Describe Patrick's conversation with his new friends at Lewis's Tavern up to the point where Munford leaves.

9) What does Patrick conclude after Munford leaves? Why does Patrick think that many of the burgesses have left town already? What is Patrick's concern if they "remain silent?" What background for this concern has he just expressed? What does Patrick say and do next? What have the resolves not done in Patrick's opinion?

10) What will happen if time runs out? Patrick shows his friends something written on a leaf of paper torn from *Coke Upon Littleton*. What is it? Is this a true historical event?

Nigel's Nuggets

Chapter 44: A Voice in the House

It looks as if our Patrick has stamped his presence upon the Virginia House of Burgesses. Make a poster describing the government of the Colony of Virginia. It should include the structure of all branches of government and a brief description of the typical officeholder.

Cato's Eagle-Eye View

Chapter 44: A Voice in the House

Gliding: Summarize the chapter in three to five sentences, written or orally.

Soaring: Summarize the chapter in one word, phrase, or sentence and write it on an index card with the chapter number and title written on the other side.

Soaring Flashcard Game: Shuffle all your Soaring flashcards. Player 1 reads the number and/or title of a chapter on one side of a flashcard. Player 2 answers with the Soaring Summarization on the other side of the flashcard. Reshuffle your flashcards, switch players if desired, and play three times.

Eaglet

Chapter 45: If This Be Treason

1) Liz has figured out a portion of the next part of the Fiddle's Riddle. What is it? What portion does she not understand?

2) Liz says that the burgesses will do everything in their power to dampen something. What is it?

3) The burgesses are meeting on Patrick's birthday. How old is Patrick turning? Who will give the gift, and what will it be?

4) Who objects to the reading of any further statements? Who says that Patrick may proceed?

5) What does Patrick say is the true mark of British freedom?

6) What happens in the chamber immediately after Patrick finishes reading the seventh resolve?

7) What does Patrick say in response to accusations of treason?

8) Why is the fifth resolve so controversial?

9) Why are the burgesses eventually able to strike the fifth resolve?

10) Liz proposes sending copies of the resolutions to newspapers in the other colonies. What exactly will be sent?

Chapter 45: If This Be Treason

1) What part of the Fiddle's Riddle has Liz solved? How is Fleming's copy of the resolves laid out? What do Patrick's friends suggest to him about the resolves?

2) What does Nigel say about the fifth resolve? Liz says that the burgesses will do everything in their power to dampen something. What is it? As the session begins on May 29, Patrick thinks to himself, "It was one thing . . ." Finish the thought.

3) Who will give the gift on Patrick's birthday, and what will it be? Who proposes a Stamp Act discussion? Why is Speaker Robinson upset? Will the burgesses discuss it?

4) Who objects to the reading of any further statements? Who says Patrick may proceed? Summarize the first and second resolves in one sentence each.

5) Summarize the third and fourth resolves in one to two sentences each. What does Patrick say is the true mark of British freedom? Summarize the fifth resolve in one to two sentences.

6) Summarize the sixth and seventh resolves in one to two sentences each. What happens in the chamber after Patrick reads the seventh resolve? What is Thomas Jefferson's reaction? What is Nigel's? What is Liz's?

7) Write out Patrick's words beginning with "Caesar had . . ." until he is interrupted. Of what is he accused? How does he finish his point? What is his response to the accusation?

8) Why is the fifth resolution so controversial? What does Patrick plan to do next? Liz instructs Nigel to hurry and do something. What is it?

9) What does the old guard persuade the governor to do? What is Peter Randolph sent to do, and why is he chosen? What happens to the first four resolves? How are the burgesses able to strike the fifth resolve?

10) What happens to the journal entry for the day? Why are the resolves not enough as passed? What does Liz propose to do? How does Nigel respond? What does Liz say with a sly grin?

Chapter 45: If This Be Treason

1) What part of the Fiddle's Riddle has Liz solved? How is Fleming's copy of the resolves laid out? What do Patrick's friends suggest to him about the resolves?

2) What does Nigel say about the fifth resolve? Liz says that the burgesses will do everything in their power to dampen something. What is it? As the session begins on May 29, Patrick thinks to himself, "It was one thing . . ." Finish the thought. What is a signet ring? How would using it make things difficult for Patrick?

3) Who will give the gift on Patrick's birthday, and what will it be? Who proposes a Stamp Act discussion? Why is Speaker Robinson upset? Will the burgesses discuss it?

4) Who objects to the reading of any further statements? Who says Patrick may proceed? Summarize the first and second resolves in one sentence each.

5) Summarize the third and fourth resolves in one to two sentences each. What does Patrick say is the true mark of British freedom? Summarize the fifth resolve in one or two sentences. How is the fifth resolve taking things "one step further?"

6) Summarize the sixth and seventh resolves in one to two sentences each. What happens in the chamber after Patrick reads the seventh resolve? What is Thomas Jefferson's reaction? What is Nigel's? What is Liz's? What does a "verbal bloodbath" mean?

7) Write out Patrick's words beginning with "Caesar had . . ." until he is interrupted. Of what is he accused? How does he finish his point? What is his response to the accusation? What does Peyton Randolph say about a single vote?

8) Why is the fifth resolution so controversial? What does Patrick plan to do next? Liz instructs Nigel to hurry and do something. What is it?

9) What does the old guard persuade the governor to do? What is Peter Randolph sent to do? What happens to the first four resolves? How do the burgesses strike the fifth resolve?

10) What happens to the journal entry for the day? Why are the resolves not enough as passed? What does Liz propose to do? How does Nigel respond? What does Liz say with a sly grin? Give one example of each of Jenny L. Cote's three genres from chapter 45.

Nigel's Nuggets

Chapter 45: If This Be Treason

Extra, Extra, read all about it! So much to do betwixt updating your Fiddle's Riddle poster and writing a newspaper article to be published by Nigel's News Nuggets. Your article should convey the import of the moment. When you have completed your assignment, prepare yourself. Scary things await you in France. *Au revoir* and *Bon voyage!*

Cato's Eagle-Eye View

Chapter 45: If This Be Treason

Gliding: Summarize the chapter in three to five sentences, written or orally.

Soaring: Summarize the chapter in one word, phrase, or sentence and write it on an index card with the chapter number and title written on the other side.

Soaring Flashcard Game: Shuffle all your Soaring flashcards. Player 1 reads the number and/or title of a chapter on one side of a flashcard. Player 2 answers with the Soaring Summarization on the other side of the flashcard. Reshuffle your flashcards, switch players if desired, and play three times.

Eaglet

Chapter 46: The Beast of the Gévaudan

1) Where is Chapter 46 set and when? What does Jeanne Boulet do?

2) To whom is Gilbert reading? How old is she? How are they related?

3) What does Marie want Gilbert to do? Why?

4) Marie has overheard the adults talking this morning. What is the latest news? How far away did this happen?

5) What is Kate's name for this mission?

6) How many young women and children have been attacked?

7) Who spurs a group of children to surround a wolf until it lets its victim go? How old is this person?

8) What does Kate sniff and look up to see? What does she notice?

9) Who has the right to bear arms in France?

10) What does the man do when Gilbert turns to leave? Does Gilbert see this happen? For whom do you think he is working?

Chapter 46: The Beast of the Gévaudan

1) Where is chapter 46 set and when? What does Jeanne Boulet do? Write out the translation of *Clair de la lune*.

2) To whom is Gilbert reading? How old is she? How are they related? Who lives with Gilbert? Where is his mother? What does Gilbert love to read? Give two examples. What does Marie like? Define *genre*. What is this new *genre* called?

3) What does Marie want Gilbert to do? Why? Translate the following titles into French: The Tales of Mother Goose, Cinderella, Puss in Boots, and The Sleeping Beauty. From which story does Gilbert read aloud? Marie has overheard the adults talking this morning. What is the latest news? How far away did this happen?

4) What is Kate's name for this mission? How many young women and children have been attacked? What does a French writer note about the "marvelous?"

5) Tell the story of Jacques Portefaix. Who hears Gilbert and Marie's conversation? Who else hears?

6) What do the village children call Gilbert? Why is he going to the village? What does Kate sniff, and look up and see? What does she notice?

7) What does the man say after he tells Gilbert that the whole village is terrified? What happened when the King sent out hunters? Who has the right to bear arms in France?

8) What does the King want to reward? How did he reward Portefaix?

9) What does the Governor, Comte d'Eu, say about the heroes? Who is Madame Varlet? What has she done?

10) Finish the man's statement: "We may be peasants . . ." How does this challenge Gilbert? What does the man do when Gilbert turns to leave? Does Gilbert see this happen? For whom do you think the man is working?

Chapter 46: The Beast of the Gévaudan

1) Where is chapter 46 set and when? What does Jeanne Boulet do? Write out the translation of *Clair de la lune*.

2) To whom is Gilbert reading? How old is she? How are they related? Who lives with Gilbert? Where is his mother? What does Gilbert love to read? Give two examples. What does Marie like? Define *genre*. What is this *genre* called? Sum up the "exciting" part.

3) What does Marie want Gilbert to do? Why? Translate the following titles into French: The Tales of Mother Goose, Cinderella, Puss in Boots, and The Sleeping Beauty. From which story does Gilbert read aloud? Marie has overheard the adults talking this morning. What is the latest news? How far away did this happen?

4) What is Kate's name for this mission? How many young women and children have been attacked? What does a French writer note about the "marvelous?" How could these stories affect people?

5) Tell the story of Jacques Portefaix. Who hears Gilbert and Marie's conversation? Who else hears? What do you think this is?

6) What do the village children call Gilbert? Why is he going to the village? What does Kate sniff and look up to see? What does she notice?

7) What does the man say after he tells Gilbert that the whole village is terrified? What happened when the King sent out hunters? Who has the right to bear arms in France?

8) What does the King want to reward? How did he reward Portefaix?

9) What does the Governor, Comte d'Eu, say about the heroes? Who is Madame Varlet? What has she done?

10) Finish the man's statement: "We may be peasants . . ." How does this challenge Gilbert? What does the man do when Gilbert turns to leave? Does Gilbert see this happen? For whom do you think the man is working? What is Kate thinking as the chapter ends?

Nigel's Nuggets

Chapter 46: The Beast of the Gévaudan

Draw a picture of a scene from one of the fairy tales mentioned in Chapter 46.

Cato's Eagle-Eye View

Chapter 46: The Beast of the Gévaudan

Gliding: Summarize the chapter in three to five sentences, written or orally.

Soaring: Summarize the chapter in one word, phrase, or sentence and write it on an index card with the chapter number and title written on the other side.

Soaring Flashcard Game: Shuffle all your Soaring flashcards. Player 1 reads the number and/or title of a chapter on one side of a flashcard. Player 2 answers with the Soaring Summarization on the other side of the flashcard. Reshuffle your flashcards, switch players if desired, and play three times.

Eaglet

Chapter 47: Marquis and the Beast

1) Write the definition of "glory" as Gilbert read it.

2) Who was King Arthur's best friend? What was his nationality?

3) What is the Lafayette family motto? What does it mean?

4) Does Kate approve of Gilbert's decision when she sees him pick up his father's musket?

5) What does Gilbert eat and drink for breakfast?

6) Does Gilbert tell his grand-mère all his plans?

7) Who goes with Gilbert and Kate? Does Gilbert know he is there?

8) What tips off Max and Kate to the presence of the beastie? What is the beastie? How long and tall is it? How much does it weigh?

9) How does Max defeat the beastie?

10) From which other beast does Kate wish to protect the marquis?

Chapter 47: Marquis and the Beast

1) What does Gilbert ask Abbé Fayon? Write the definition of "glory" as Gilbert read it. List a few synonyms for "glory."

2) What does Abbé say about King Arthur? Who was King Arthur's best friend? What was his nationality? What is the Lafayette family motto? What does it mean? What does Lafayette say he wants to be? What does Abbé say? What is the last piece of advice Abbé gives Gilbert before he sends him to bed?

3) Describe what Gilbert sees on the wall on his way to bed. Why does he feel responsible? What does he think when he looks at his father's musket? Kate frowns at this. Why?

4) What does Gilbert eat and drink for breakfast? Does Gilbert tell his grand-mère all his plans?

5) What is unusual about the morning as Kate follows Gilbert down the well-worn path? Who is going with Gilbert and Kate? Does Gilbert know he is there?

6) What have Max and Kate been doing for months now? What do they know about the wolf attacks? What does Kate tell Max about the stranger in the village?

7) How does the stranger make Kate feel? What tips off Max and Kate to the presence of the beastie? What is the beastie? How long and tall is it? How much does it weigh?

8) Describe Max and Kate's encounter with the big wolf. Why does Kate leave Max? Describe her next encounter.

9) What happens when Kate reaches Gilbert? Where does she go as soon as she is able?

10) What does Max tell Kate about the encounter he had with the wolf after she left? From which other beast does Kate wish to protect the marquis?

Chapter 47: Marquis and the Beast

1) What does Gilbert ask Abbé Fayon? Write the definition of "glory" as Gilbert read it. What are some synonyms for glory?

2) What does Abbé say about King Arthur? Who was King Arthur's best friend? What was his nationality? What is the Lafayette family motto? What does it mean? What does Lafayette say he wants to be? What does Abbé say? What is the last piece of advice Abbé gives Gilbert before he sends him to bed? Summarize the tales of King Arthur and Lancelot in three to five paragraphs.

3) What does Gilbert see on the wall on his way to bed? Why does he feel responsible? What does he think when he looks at his father's musket? Kate frowns at this. Why? Find a picture of the Lafayette family crest. Make a poster with a picture of the crest and an explanation of each portion.

4) What does Gilbert eat and drink for breakfast? Does Gilbert tell his grand-mère all his plans? Make and enjoy French hot *chocolat*.

5) What is unusual about the morning as Kate follows Gilbert down the well-worn path? Who is going with Gilbert and Kate? Does Gilbert know he is there?

6) What have Max and Kate been doing for months now? What do they know about the wolf attacks? What does Kate tell Max about the stranger in the village? What does this foreshadow?

7) How does the stranger make Kate feel? What tips off Max and Kate to the presence of the beastie? What is the beastie? How long and tall is it? How much does it weigh?

8) Describe Max and Kate's encounter with the big wolf. Why does Kate leave Max? Describe her next encounter.

9) What happens when Kate reaches Gilbert? Where does she go as soon as she is able?

10) What does Max tell Kate about the encounter he had with the wolf after she left? From which other beast does Kate wish to protect the marquis? Who do you think is with the wolf after his encounter with Max? What happens to the wolf?

Nigel's Nuggets

Chapter 47: Marquis and the Beast

Eeek! Is it safe to look? This episode with the beast is positively terrifying. Please read the entry about the Marquis and the Beast in A WORD FROM THE AUTHOR. Present a project about the wolves who caused trouble in France.

Right. Now it is time to celebrate! You have finished Part Three of the VRK Study Guide. I will see you in Part Four. The greatest challenges yet await Patrick and the EO7 as Patrick fully finds his voice.

Cato's Eagle-Eye View

Chapter 47: Marquis and the Beast

Gliding: Summarize the chapter in three to five sentences, written or orally.

Soaring: Summarize the chapter in one word, phrase, or sentence and write it on an index card with the chapter number and title written on the other side.

Soaring Flashcard Game: Shuffle all your Soaring flashcards. Player 1 reads the number and/or title of a chapter on one side of a flashcard. Player 2 answers with the Soaring Summarization on the other side of the flashcard. Reshuffle your flashcards, switch players if desired, and play three times.

PART FOUR:
LIBERTY OR DEATH (1765-75)

Eaglet

Chapter 48: Sons of Liberty

1) Who is being toasted at the beginning of Chapter 48?

2) Are the young burgesses able to get all of Patrick's resolves passed? Where are they passed *unanimously?*

3) From which colony and in which paper were the resolves published first?

4) Gillamon says the Stamp Act is the first thing to unite the Colonies on anything besides another event. Name it.

5) What name have Boston's "Loyal Nine" taken?

6) Which is the only colony that still has a stamp distributor?

7) What did King George do with Grenville? What did he do after that?

8) Gillamon says Patrick's fiery words have done something. What is it?

9) Gillamon says the Stamp Act is the Colonies' dress rehearsal for something. What is it?

10) What are Gilbert and the other boys celebrating in Chavaniac?

Chapter 48: Sons of Liberty

1) Who is being toasted at the beginning of Chapter 48? Why is he being toasted? Where has the voice in the House been heard?

2) Where has the fire ignited by Patrick in the House of Burgesses spread? Are the young burgesses able to get all of Patrick's resolves passed? Where are they passed *unanimously?*

3) What assumption has helped spread the fire of Patrick's resolves? What did the Governor of Massachusetts write to London?

4) What does Gillamon say about perception? What does this saying mean? Gillamon says the Stamp Act is the first thing to unite the Colonies on anything besides another event. Name it. What is happening in New York regarding the Stamp Act?

5) What name has Boston's "Loyal Nine" taken? Describe the actions of this group in response to the Stamp Act.

6) What has happened in the other colonies as a result of the actions in Massachusetts? Which is the only colony that still has a stamp distributor?

7) What did the *London Chronicle* do? What did King George do with Grenville? What did he do after that? What are the colonists doing that the merchants of London do not like?

8) What does Gillamon say the *voice* started? Gillamon says Patrick's fiery words have done something. What is it?

9) Gillamon says the Stamp Act is the colonists' dress rehearsal for something. What is it? What does he mean by this?

10) What are Gilbert and the other boys celebrating in Chavaniac? Define the words "vigilant" and "vigilante," explaining the origins. Who must remain vigilant and why? How are the two words different despite looking similar?

Chapter 48: Sons of Liberty

1) Who is being toasted at the beginning of Chapter 48? Why is he being toasted? Where has the voice in the House been heard?

2) Where has the fire ignited by Patrick in the House of Burgesses spread? Are the young burgesses able to get all of Patrick's resolves passed? Where are they passed *unanimously?*

3) What assumption helped spread the fire of Patrick's resolves? What did the Governor of Massachusetts write to London? Define "disaffected."

4) What does Gillamon say about perception? What does this saying mean? Gillamon says the Stamp Act is the first thing to unite the Colonies on anything besides another event. Name it. What is happening in New York regarding the Stamp Act?

5) What name has Boston's "Loyal Nine" taken? Describe the actions of this group in response to the Stamp Act.

6) What has happened in the other colonies as a result of the actions in Massachusetts? Which is the only colony that still has a stamp distributor?

7) What did the *London Chronicle* do? What did King George do with Grenville? What did he do after that? What are the colonists doing that the merchants of London do not like? How would this affect London merchants?

8) What does Gillamon say the *voice* started? Gillamon says Patrick's fiery words have done something. What is it?

9) Gillamon says the Stamp Act is the colonists' dress rehearsal for something. What is it? What does he mean by this?

10) What are Gilbert and the other boys celebrating in Chavaniac? Define the words vigilant and vigilante, explaining the origins. How are the two words different despite looking similar? Who must remain vigilant and why?

Nigel's Nuggets

Chapter 48: Sons of Liberty

Patrick has moved his family to Roundabout. Make a presentation about Roundabout. In addition, add Roundabout to the map of Virginia you created in Chapter 31.

Cato's Eagle-Eye View

Chapter 48: Sons of Liberty

Gliding: Summarize the chapter in three to five sentences, written or orally.

Soaring: Summarize the chapter in one word, phrase, or sentence and write it on an index card with the chapter number and title written on the other side.

Soaring Flashcard Game: Shuffle all your Soaring flashcards. Player 1 reads the number and/or title of a chapter on one side of a flashcard. Player 2 answers with the Soaring Summarization on the other side of the flashcard. Reshuffle your flashcards, switch players if desired, and play three times.

Eaglet

Chapter 49: Hard Acts to Follow

1) Where is Chapter 49 set and when? From which paper is Nigel reading?

2) How much has the colonial boycott of British goods cost in trade? When was the Stamp Act repealed? When did the Colonies get word?

3) Do the colonists think the King supports the repeal of the Stamp Act?

4) What do the Declaratory Acts stipulate?

5) Who is King George III's fourth Prime Minister?

6) Does King George support the Stamp Act? What kind of acts will follow?

7) What does Patrick Henry's name mean?

8) Which house?

9) Where will Max be going? Whom will he join? What will Nigel do eventually?

10) What creature comes to Nigel's memory when he hears the word *shuccshesshful?*

Chapter 49: Hard Acts to Follow

1) Write out Anti-Sejanus's quotation. What does it mean?

2) What things do the newspapers that Liz and Nigel are reading contain? What has the reaction in London been? How much has the colonial boycott of British goods cost in trade? When was the Stamp Act repealed? When did the Colonies get word?

3) Who is visiting Patrick and Sally? Where is this couple's home? How many acres does Roundabout consist of? What crops does Patrick grow?

4) What have the Sons of Liberty vowed to do every year? What do they also plan to do? What do the Declaratory Acts stipulate?

5) What has Britain realized? What would be the effect of the Colonies in *rebellion?*

6) What part of the riddle is puzzling Liz and Nigel as they think about it? How does Gillamon answer their question? What are the *Acts* in *harder Acts*? Does King George support the repeal of the Stamp Act?

7) How has Governor Fauquier reacted to Patrick's effect on the House? How long has this action been in effect? Using a dictionary for the meaning of names, explain what each part of Patrick Henry's name means.

8) To which house is the riddle referring? What full meaning does Nigel realize?

9) Write out Gillamon's response to Nigel's question.

10) Where will Max be going? Whom will he join? What will Nigel do eventually? What creature comes to Nigel's memory when he hears the word *shuccshesshful?*

Chapter 49: Hard Acts to Follow

1) Write out Anti-Sejanus's quotation. What does it mean?

2) What things do the newspapers that Liz and Nigel are reading contain? What has the reaction in London been? How much has the colonial boycott of British goods cost in trade? When was the Stamp Act repealed? When did the Colonies get word?

3) Who is visiting Patrick and Sally? Where is this couple's home? How many acres does Roundabout consist of? What crops does Patrick grow?

4) What have the Sons of Liberty vowed to do every year? What do they also plan to do? What do the Declaratory Acts stipulate?

5) What has Britain realized? What would be the effect of the Colonies in *rebellion?* Write one to three paragraphs about the life of William Pitt, also known as Pitt the Elder.

6) What part of the riddle is puzzling Liz and Nigel as they think about it? How does Gillamon answer their question? What are the *Acts* in *harder Acts*? Does King George support the repeal of the Stamp Act?

7) How has Governor Fauquier reacted to Patrick's effect on the House? How long has this action been in effect? Using a dictionary for the meaning of names, explain what each part of Patrick Henry's name means.

8) To which house is the riddle referring? What full meaning does Nigel realize?

9) Write out Gillamon's response to Nigel's question. What does Gillamon mean?

10) Where will Max be going? Whom will he join? What will Nigel do eventually? What creature comes to Nigel's memory when he hears the word *shuccshesshful?*

Nigel's Nuggets

Chapter 49: Hard Acts to Follow

Noble ruler of the house—an apt way to describe Patrick Henry, and one of my favorites. Alas, not all names are as happily constructed. Locate a dictionary that defines names. Define the meaning of the following VRK characters' first and last names: George Washington, Thomas Jefferson (please include the definition of Jeffrey), Benjamin Franklin, Samuel Crowley, John Syme, Peyton Randolph, and Gilbert Lafayette.

Cato's Eagle-Eye View

Chapter 49: Hard Acts to Follow

Gliding: Summarize the chapter in three to five sentences, written or orally.

Soaring: Summarize the chapter in one word, phrase, or sentence and write it on an index card with the chapter number and title written on the other side.

Soaring Flashcard Game: Shuffle all your Soaring flashcards. Player 1 reads the number and/or title of a chapter on one side of a flashcard. Player 2 answers with the Soaring Summarization on the other side of the flashcard. Reshuffle your flashcards, switch players if desired, and play three times.

Eaglet

Chapter 50: Threatening Skies and Seizing Liberty

1) Where is Chapter 50 set and when?

2) What has Governor Fauquier finally done after eighteen months?

3) How many delegates are new to the House of Burgesses?

4) List three of the things Benjamin Franklin is currently doing.

5) Richard Henry Lee asks Patrick what gave him confidence to assert his resolves. Write out the last sentence of Patrick's reply.

6) What has been installed in the chamber of the House of Burgesses?

7) What is Al doing in his dream right before thunder awakens him?

8) Where is Max on June 10, 1768? Whom does he join? What does he see a mob doing?

9) What is Clarie catching? Whom is she trying to protect?

10) What has Massachusetts Governor Bernard requested to be sent from London? Does Max think this move could spell trouble?

Chapter 50: Threatening Skies and Seizing Liberty

1) Write out the words to the advertisement from the *Virginia Gazette* found at the beginning of Chapter 50.

2) What has Governor Fauquier finally done after eighteen months? What has forced him to do this? What has happened to many of the burgesses who opposed the Stamp Act resolves? How many delegates are new to the House of Burgesses? Who is the new Speaker of the House?

3) What has Benjamin Franklin's discovery done? List three of the things Benjamin Franklin is currently doing.

4) Richard Henry Lee asks Patrick what gave him confidence to assert his resolves. Write out Patrick's reply. What has been installed in the chamber of the House of Burgesses? Write out the rest of Richard's statement beginning, "But just as Dr. Franklin . . ."

5) Describe Al's BOOMING dream.

6) What has happened to Prime Minister William Pitt? What has Charles Townshend done/? Where does King George boast that the Colonies will be? Is Al happy with what he hears? What does he do next?

7) What does King George say about Townshend as he raises his glass? What is Edmund Burke's response to the new acts? Why does Al decline to eat the food that drops on the floor?

8) Where is Max on June 10, 1768? Whom does he join? What does he see a mob doing? Describe what Max observes after this and up to the point he sees Clarie.

9) How is Clarie disguised? What is Clarie trying to protect in general and which individual specifically? How does Clarie recap recent events in Boston up to the point when Max asks whose idea this was?

10) What has happened to John Hancock's boat? For which crime is he being threatened? Who will defend him in court? What has Samuel Adams done?

Chapter 50: Threatening Skies and Seizing Liberty

1) Write out the words to the advertisement from the *Virginia Gazette* found at the beginning of Chapter 50. What do they mean?

2) What has Governor Fauquier finally done after eighteen months? What has forced him to do this? What has happened to many of the burgesses who opposed the Stamp Act resolves? How many delegates are new to the House of Burgesses? Who is the new Speaker of the House?

3) What has Benjamin Franklin's discovery done? List three of the things Benjamin Franklin is currently doing.

4) Richard Henry Lee asks Patrick what gave him confidence to assert his resolves. Write out Patrick's reply. What has been installed in the chamber of the House of Burgesses? Write out the rest of Richard's statement beginning, "But just as Dr. Franklin . . ."

5) Describe Al's BOOMING dream.

6) What has happened to Prime Minister William Pitt? What has Charles Townshend done? Where does King George boast that the Colonies will be? Is Al happy with what he hears? What does he do next?

7) What does King George say about Townshend as he raises his glass? What is Edmund Burke's response to the new acts? Why does Al decline to eat the food that drops on the floor?

8) Where is Max on June 10, 1768? Whom does he join? What does he see a mob doing? Describe what Max observes after this and up to the point when he sees Clarie.

9) How is Clarie disguised? What is Clarie trying to protect in general and which individual specifically? How does Clarie recap recent events in Boston up to the point when Max asks whose idea this was?

10) What has happened to John Hancock's boat? For which crime is he being threatened? Who will defend him in court? What has Samuel Adams done?

Nigel's Nuggets

Chapter 50: Threatening Skies and Seizing Liberty

AAAAACK! What a fright! It makes me want to jump into a corner and hide, just thinking about it. Poor chap. Dastardly thing that BOOMING dream. Please make a picture of the whole hair-raising experience.

Cato's Eagle-Eye View

Chapter 50: Threatening Skies and Seizing Liberty

Gliding: Summarize the chapter in three to five sentences, written or orally.

Soaring: Summarize the chapter in one word, phrase, or sentence and write it on an index card with the chapter number and title written on the other side.

Soaring Flashcard Game: Shuffle all your Soaring flashcards. Player 1 reads the number and/or title of a chapter on one side of a flashcard. Player 2 answers with the Soaring Summarization on the other side of the flashcard. Reshuffle your flashcards, switch players if desired, and play three times.

Eaglet

Chapter 51: Coach and Six or Ten-Shilling Jackets

1) Where is Chapter 51 set and when? What color is the coach? How many horses are pulling it? What color are they?

2) What do Cato, Nigel, and Lord Botetourt have in common? What has Cato been thinking regarding this status? Does Nigel feel the same way?

3) Patrick spots a tall, red-headed, twenty-six-year-old young man who is a new burgess. Who is he?

4) How does Richard Henry Lee describe the Townshend Acts?

5) How does Nigel describe Nero?

6) Patrick proposes drafting resolves against the Townshend Acts. How many are adopted, and with which kind of vote?

7) How does the governor respond? What does Patrick say to do when the messenger knocks on the door?

8) What action does the governor take when he meets with the burgesses? What do they do next?

9) What does George Washington propose as the ex-burgesses meet at the Raleigh Tavern the next day?

10) What is Nigel concerned will happen if Patrick's prophecy comes true?

Chapter 51: Coach and Six or Ten-Shilling Jackets

1) Describe the new governor's coach. What is his name?

2) What do Cato, Nigel, and Lord Botetourt have in common? What has Cato been thinking regarding this status? Does Nigel feel the same way? Patrick says the king's approach to Virginia is different from his approach to Massachusetts. How?

3) Finish Patrick's statement beginning with "We shall also see . . ...." What does it mean?

4) What does Lord Botetourt do after the opening of the assembly? How does Richard Henry Lee describe the Townshend Acts?

5) What are the "telling words" about the Townshend Acts? How does Nigel describe Nero? Finish Richard Henry Lee's statement, ". . .... Virginia led the other colonies . . ." Who speaks next? Summarize his statement.

6) What does Patrick propose? Summarize his reason for doing so. What is the outcome and how do the burgesses vote?

7) How does the governor respond? What does Patrick say to do when the messenger knocks on the door and why? What does Thomas Jefferson think of this? What does Speaker Randolph decide to do?

8) Define the following terms from the fourth resolution: *nemine contradicente*, "inviolable," and "interposition." What action does the governor take when he meets with the burgesses? What do the burgesses do next?

9) What does George Washington propose as the ex-burgesses meet at the Raleigh Tavern the next day? Summarize his proposal including the provisions it contains.

10) What does George Washington tell Patrick and Richard he has written to his London merchants? What has happened in Boston? What is Patrick's prophecy? What is Nigel concerned will happen if Patrick's prophecy comes true?

Chapter 51: Coach and Six or Ten-Shilling Jacket

1) Describe the new governor's coach. What is his name? How is he dressed?

2) What do Cato, Nigel, and Lord Botetourt have in common? What has Cato been thinking regarding this status? Does Nigel feel the same way? Patrick says the king's approach to Virginia is different from his approach to Massachusetts. How?

3) Finish Patrick's statement beginning with "We shall also see . . ." What does it mean?

4) What does Lord Botetourt do after the opening of the assembly? How does Richard Henry Lee describe the Townshend Acts?

5) What are the "telling words" about the Townshend Acts? How does Nigel describe Nero? Finish Richard Henry Lee's statement, ". . . Virginia led the other colonies . . ." Who speaks next? Summarize his statement.

6) What does Patrick propose? Summarize his reason for doing so. What is the outcome and how do the burgesses vote?

7) How does the governor respond? What does Patrick say to do when the messenger knocks on the door and why? What does Thomas Jefferson think of this? What does Speaker Randolph decide to do? Do you agree with Jefferson? Why or why not?

8) Define the following terms from the fourth resolution: *nemine contradicente*, "inviolable," and "interposition." What action does the governor take when he meets with the burgesses? What do the burgesses do next?

9) What does George Washington propose as the ex-burgesses meet at the Raleigh Tavern the next day? Summarize his proposal including the provisions it contains.

10) What does George Washington tell Patrick and Richard he has written to his London merchants? What has happened in Boston? What is Patrick's prophecy? What is Nigel concerned will happen if Patrick's prophecy comes true? Nigel scurries away to do something. What is it and why?

Nigel's Nuggets

Chapter 51: Coach and Six or Ten-Shilling Jackets

Huzzah! All three *revolutionary* patriots are in the same room. I say, it is utterly thrilling at moments like this to be the Mouse in the House. You simply must do a broadcast about the stupendous events in Chapter 51. Send it to me at the Nigel's News Nuggets studio. You have learned about the studio on the VRK Podcast, have you not? If not, scamper over and prepare to be amazed.

Cato's Eagle-Eye View

Chapter 51: Coach and Six or Ten-Shilling Jackets

Gliding: Summarize the chapter in three to five sentences, written or orally.

Soaring: Summarize the chapter in one word, phrase, or sentence and write it on an index card with the chapter number and title written on the other side.

Soaring Flashcard Game: Shuffle all your Soaring flashcards. Player 1 reads the number and/or title of a chapter on one side of a flashcard. Player 2 answers with the Soaring Summarization on the other side of the flashcard. Reshuffle your flashcards, switch players if desired, and play three times.

Eaglet

Chapter 52: Comfort and Joy

1) Where is Chapter 52 set and when? What is Nigel drinking from his thimble?

2) Which colonies have adopted the Townshend Resolves in full? Which colonies have copied the essence of them? Please answer with the current two-letter state abbreviations.

3) What had Lord Botetourt done in November?

4) Lord Botetourt has given a ball. What did the guests wear?

5) What is Patrick's time commitment for his appointment to the General Court?

6) How often, when, and for how long does the House of Burgesses meet?

7) Who are Patrick's current law students?

8) Liz frowns as she studies Sallie's face. What does she notice about her?

9) Liz scans the advertisements in the *Virginia Gazette* and is inspired with a question for Nigel. What is it?

10) What is the name of the home Liz finds for the Henrys? Whom does she think would be a perfect fit for this home, and a comfort to Sallie?

Fledgling

Chapter 52: Comfort and Joy

1) Where is Chapter 52 set and when? What is Nigel drinking from his thimble? Which colonies have adopted the Townshend Resolves in full? Which colonies have copied the essence of them? Please answer with the current two-letter state abbreviations.

2) How is the association among the Colonies working? How has it affected imports into America? How has Great Britain been affected? Define "pompous."

3) How are things in Boston? What is happening to cause a tempest in London? What had Lord Botetourt done in November?

4) What does Liz say the governor wishes to accomplish? Lord Botetourt has given a ball. What did the guests wear?

5) What is Patrick's time commitment for his appointment to the General Court? How often, when, and for how long does the House of Burgesses meet?

6) Who are Patrick's current law students? Liz says Patrick is living up to his name. How so? Liz frowns as she studies Sallie's face. What does she notice about her?

7) What possible cause does Nigel suggest? How does Liz respond?

8) Liz scans the advertisements in the *Virginia Gazette* and is inspired with a question for Nigel. What is it? Describe the object of her interest.

9) To whose estate does Scotchtown belong? What does Liz think about the price? What does she think it would give Sallie?

10) Whom does Liz think will be perfect at Scotchtown and why?

Chapter 52: Comfort and Joy

1) Where is Chapter 52 set and when? What is Nigel drinking from his thimble? Which colonies have adopted the Townshend Resolves in full? Which colonies have copied the essence of them? Please answer with the current two-letter state abbreviations.

2) How is the association among the Colonies working? How has it affected imports into America? How has Great Britain been affected? Define "pompous."

3) How are things in Boston? What is happening to cause a tempest in London? What had Lord Botetourt done in November?

4) What does Liz say the governor wished to accomplish? Lord Botetourt has given a ball. What did the guests wear? What are the names and ages of Patrick and Sallie's children?

5) What is Patrick's time commitment for his appointment to the General Court? How often, when, and for how long does the House of Burgesses meet?

6) Who are Patrick's current law students? Liz says Patrick is living up to his name. How so? Liz frowns as she studies Sallie's face. What does she notice about her?

7) What possible cause does Nigel suggest? How does Liz respond? With whom do you agree and why?

8) Liz scans the advertisements in the *Virginia Gazette* and is inspired with a question for Nigel. What is it? Describe the object of her interest.

9) To whose estate does Scotchtown belong? What does Liz think about the price? What does she think it would give Sallie?

10) Who does Liz think will be perfect at Scotchtown and why? What is Liz's concern at the end of Chapter 52? Do you think she has reason to be concerned?

Nigel's Nuggets

Chapter 52: Comfort and Joy

Patrick has been appointed to the General Court of Colonial Virginia. Please make a presentation about the Court. Do be sure to include the proper attire for a mid-eighteenth-century lawyer. Do I have a wig? Do I have a wig? I shall endeavor not to be personally insulted. Naturally, an erudite Mouse of the World such as myself has a proper wig! As you are perfectly aware, MizP cannot tolerate shabbily dressed barristers in her presence. Her fashion tips are essential in one's quest to be properly attired. Please assure that your lawyer's attire will please MizP.

Cato's Eagle-Eye View

Chapter 52: Comfort and Joy

Gliding: Summarize the chapter in three to five sentences, written or orally.

Soaring: Summarize the chapter in one word, phrase, or sentence and write it on an index card with the chapter number and title written on the other side.

Soaring Flashcard Game: Shuffle all your Soaring flashcards. Player 1 reads the number and/or title of a chapter on one side of a flashcard. Player 2 answers with the Soaring Summarization on the other side of the flashcard. Reshuffle your flashcards, switch players if desired, and play three times.

Eaglet

Chapter 53: Innocent Blood

1) Where is Chapter 53 set and when?

2) Who has recruited young boys as apprentices to stir up trouble with merchants?

3) What could happen to loyalist merchants if the mob gets out of control?

4) What is the name of the gruff-looking man Max and Clarie encounter? What is his job?

5) Does Robinson make things better or worse with the boys?

6) The boys hurl things and something hits Richardson's wife in the face. What is it and where specifically is she hit?

7) What group of people joins the mob? What does Richardson's daughter do?

8) Richardson grabs his musket. What does he do? Is anyone harmed? Why or why not?

9) What happens to Richardson's wife just before Richardson sends his family to the back of the house?

10) What happens to Christopher Seider next?

Chapter 53: Innocent Blood

1) Where is Chapter 53 set and when? What do Max and Clarie view as they walk up?

2) Why are the boys not in school? Whom have they been recruited by, and for what purpose?

3) What could happen to loyalist merchants if the mob gets out of control? What does this process involve?

4) What is the name of the gruff-looking man Max and Clarie encounter? What does he try to get the mob to do? What is his job? What does this job involve?

5) Does Richardson make things better or worse with the boys? Why is Clarie worried? What do the boys shout at Richardson's door?

6) What does Richardson's wife attempt to do? Is she successful? What does *King's highway* mean? The boys hurl things and something hits Richardson's wife. What is it and where is she hit?

7) What group of people join the mob? What does Richardson's daughter do? What does the sailor do in return? What happens when Max sniffs the air?

8) Richardson grabs his musket. What does he do? Is anyone harmed? Why or why not? Why does Clari7e's smile fade? What does this person do?

9) Describe what happens to Christopher Seider. What does Clarie do with him?

10) What does Max do after Clarie runs away from the crowd? What does he see?

Chapter 53: Innocent Blood

1) Where is Chapter 53 set and when? What do Max and Clarie view as they walk up?

2) Why are the boys not in school? Whom have they been recruited by and for what purpose?

3) What could happen to loyalist merchants if the mob gets out of control? What does this process involve?

4) What is the name of the gruff-looking man Max and Clarie encounter? What does he try to get the mob to do? What is his job? What does this job involve?

5) Does Richardson make things better or worse with the boys? Why is Clarie worried? What do the boys shout at Richardson's door? Are Christopher Seider and Ebenezer Richardson historical or fictional characters?

6) What does Richardson's wife attempt to do? Is she successful? What does *King's highway* mean? The boys hurl things and something hits Richardson's wife. What is it and where is she hit?

7) What group of people join the mob? What does Richardson's daughter do? What does the sailor do in return? What happens when Max sniffs the air?

8) Richardson grabs his musket. What does he do? Is anyone harmed? Why or why not? Why does Clarie's smile fade? What does this person do?

9) Describe what happens to Christopher Seider. What does Clarie do with him?

10) What does Max do after Clarie runs away from the crowd? What does he see? Is this man a historical, fictional, or fantasy character? Give reasons to support your answer.

Nigel's Nuggets

Chapter 53: Innocent Blood

Sadly, the events of Chapter 53 actually happened with a few fictional fill-ins. Make a presentation about Christopher Seider, Ebenezer Richardson, and the tragic events of February 22, 1770.

Cato's Eagle-Eye View

Chapter 53: Innocent Blood

Gliding: Summarize the chapter in three to five sentences, written or orally.

Soaring: Summarize the chapter in one word, phrase, or sentence and write it on an index card with the chapter number and title written on the other side.

Soaring Flashcard Game: Shuffle all your Soaring flashcards. Player 1 reads the number and/or title of a chapter on one side of a flashcard. Player 2 answers with the Soaring Summarization on the other side of the flashcard. Reshuffle your flashcards, switch players if desired, and play three times.

Chapter 54: Bloody Boston

Please note that all three Chapter Guide levels are the same for Chapter 54.

1) Who is the nineteen-year-old working at Wharton and Bowe Booksellers?

2) Who is the first customer who walks in? With which unit is he serving? How old is he?

3) Henry Knox's old sergeant comes in. What is his name and who is with him?

4) Captain Preston sees the article in the *Boston Gazette* about Christopher Seider's funeral. How many people attended?

5) How did Sam Adams prey on people's emotions?

6) Jock Frost says Bostonians are passionate about something. What is it?

7) Jock Frost tells Knox to be on his guard. Finish his warning: "Remember, it only takes a single spark . . ."

8) Who published an etching entitled, *"The Bloody Massacre?"*

9) How does Clarie define "propaganda?"

10) Who will handle the defense for Captain Preston and the soldiers?

Nigel's Nuggets

Chapter 54: Bloody Boston

Fill in the blanks using pages 473–77 of the VRK. Each blank may contain multiple words. Please leave the title blank for now. An Answer Key is provided in the Answer Key section.

____

Title

*Captain John Goldfinch heads to ________________ to break up a brawl.

*________________ falsely accuses ________________ of not paying his ________________.

* ________________ confronts ________________.

*Edward Garrick and ________________ enter the ________________ to eat dinner.

*Edward Garrick taunts ________________.

*________________ hits Garrick on the side of his head with ________________.

*Garrick and Broaders ________________ about what has happened, drawing ________________.

*Private White ________________ as a crowd gathers around him. ________________ advises him not to fire.

*The crowd surrounding ____ begins to ___________________________.

* ___________________________, a town ________________, stands ________________ ______________________ telling them to stop throwing snowballs.

*A group of __________________ led by ______________________ has just finished working at __________________ when they hear about the brawl at Murray's Barracks and that there is trouble at the ________________________, and heads in that direction. They are armed with ______________________

*The _______________________ begin ringing, and people rush outside thinking there is a _________________. There is no _________________.

*The crowd swells to ___________. They quickly learn about the events of the evening.

*Private White sends for ____________________. Captain __________________________ sends ______________________ and follows shortly.

*The soldiers form a _________________ around Private White. The crowd throws ____ at the soldiers.

* _____________________ walks ____ and orders the crowd to disperse.

*Local innkeeper ________________________, armed with _______________________, confronts Captain Preston demanding reassurance that the soldiers will not ___________.

*Captain Preston responds that ____

and reminds Palmes that he is standing ___________________________________.

*The crowd continues to taunt the soldiers and ___________________ at them.

* ________________________ grabs ________________________________,

jerking it back and forth and yelling, ____

__________________________.

*_________________________ is struck _____________________________ by

_____________________ thrown from ____________________________________

__________ and is knocked____.

*People in the crowd yell at the soldiers in the crowd to _____________ and also tell them

_________________________ do so, and issue shouts to __________________.

*Montgomery gets to his feet, ____________________________________, yells

____________________, and ______________________________________.

*___________________________________ swings his _________________

_____, striking Montgomery ___________________________________. He swings

again, aiming for ________________________, but slips and strikes him on ______

_____, knocking him to the ground.

*The other soldiers ______________________________ and ___________________ people are shot.

*____ gets to his feet and holds his sword ____ to keep them _____________________________ and orders them _____________________ ____.

*The town ____________________, _____________________ orders the crowd to disperse.

*_________________________________, _________________________________, and ____________________________ are dead; _____________________________________ and _________________________ lay mortally wounded.

Cato's Eagle-Eye View

Chapter 54: Bloody Boston

Gliding: Summarize the chapter in three to five sentences, written or orally.

Soaring: Summarize the chapter in one word, phrase, or sentence and write it on an index card with the chapter number and title written on the other side.

Soaring Flashcard Game: Shuffle all your Soaring flashcards. Player 1 reads the number and/or title of a chapter on one side of a flashcard. Player 2 answers with the Soaring Summarization on the other side of the flashcard. Reshuffle your flashcards, switch players if desired, and play three times.

Eaglet

Chapter 55: A Darkness Begins

1) Where is Chapter 55 set? Who is present?

2) What have the colonists done in response to the Townshend Acts? Who has become King George's sixth Prime Minister?

3) How does Lord North sum up the king's wishes regarding taxes in the Colonies?

4) What happened the same day as the Boston Massacre?

5) Patrick and the Colony of Virginia have opposed the king with words. How have the Sons of Liberty opposed the King?

6) What does John Adams say about *facts?* Is Captain Preston cleared of charges? How many men are convicted? On what charge(s)?

7) What has happened to Governor Botetourt? Where has Patrick's family moved to? What hangs over Sallie after the birth of Neddy? Who will join Liz and Sallie?

8) Who has Gilbert lost? What training will he begin?

9) Who will become Virginia's next royal governor?

10) How will Dunmore help the cause of American Independence?

Fledgling

Chapter 55: A Darkness Begins

1) Where is Chapter 55 set? Who is present? What have the colonists done in response to the Townshend Acts? Who has become King George's sixth Prime Minister? What does Gillamon say the British lion seeks to do?

2) Write out the king's instructions to Lord North. How does he sum them up?

3) What happened the same day as the Boston Massacre? Patrick and the Colony of Virginia have opposed the king with words. How have the Sons of Liberty opposed the king? What does Gillamon say the young colonies must learn to do without? What will there need to be for this to happen?

4) How was John Adams used as a counterbalance? Write out his words in defense of Captain Preston and his men. How many men are convicted and on what charges?

5) What do John Adams' words mean? Use his words to fill in the Title for chapter 54 Nigel's Nuggets. List some facts that helped clear Preston. List some facts Paul Revere omitted in his etching. What is due process? How did it apply in this case?

6) What does Patrick say his eyes have been opened to see? What has helped the value of land in Pennsylvania? What will Britain not allow the Colonies to end? To what do freedom and liberty lead?

7) What has happened to Governor Botetourt? Where has Patrick's family moved? What hangs over Sallie after the birth of Neddy? What does this expression mean? Who will join Liz and Sallie? What will she be able to do?

8) What has the Marquis de Lafayette become? How? What training will he begin?

9) Who will become Virginia's next royal governor? Describe his "temper tantrum."

10) Clarie is alarmed about Virginia's new governor. What does Gillamon say to reassure her? How will Dunmore help the cause of American Independence?

Chapter 55: A Darkness Begins

1) Where is Chapter 55 set? Who is present? What have the colonists done in response to the Townshend Acts? Who has become King George's sixth Prime Minister? What does Gillamon say the British lion seeks to do?

2) Write out the king's instructions to Lord North. How does he sum them up?

3) What happened the same day as the Boston Massacre? Patrick and the Colony of Virginia have opposed the king with words. How have the Sons of Liberty opposed the king? What does Gillamon say the young colonies must learn to do without? What will there ever need to be for this to happen? Define "mob rule" and "anarchy." How do they apply here?

4) How was John Adams used as a counterbalance? Write out his words in defense of Captain Preston and his men. How many men are convicted and on what charges?

5) What do John Adams' words mean? Use his words to fill in the title for Chapter 54 Nigel's Nuggets. List some facts that helped clear Preston. List some facts Paul Revere omitted in his etching. What is due process? How did John Adams ensure it? Research and use your findings to list John Adams' reasons for taking this case.

6) What does Patrick say his eyes have been opened to see? What has helped the value of land in Pennsylvania? What will Britain not allow the Colonies to end? To what do freedom and liberty lead?

7) What has happened to Governor Botetourt? Where has Patrick's family moved? What hangs over Sallie after the birth of Neddy? What does this expression mean? Who will join Liz and Sallie? What will she be able to do?

8) What has the Marquis de Lafayette become? How? What training will he begin? What does this position entail?

9) Who will become Virginia's next royal governor? Describe his "temper tantrum."

10) Clarie is alarmed about Virginia's new governor. What does Gillamon say to reassure her? How will Dunmore help the cause of American Independence?

Nigel's Nuggets

Chapter 55: A Darkness Begins

The Henry Family has moved to Scotchtown. Plan a one-day visit and present your itinerary. Also, place Scotchtown on your map of Virginia.

Cato's Eagle-Eye View

Chapter 55: A Darkness Begins

Gliding: Summarize the chapter in three to five sentences, written or orally.

Soaring: Summarize the chapter in one word, phrase, or sentence and write it on an index card with the chapter number and title written on the other side.

Soaring Flashcard Game: Shuffle all your Soaring flashcards. Player 1 reads the number and/or title of a chapter on one side of a flashcard. Player 2 answers with the Soaring Summarization on the other side of the flashcard. Reshuffle your flashcards, switch players if desired, and play three times.

Eaglet

Chapter 56: Gasping for Liberty

1) Where is Chapter 56 set and when? What is Patrick's concern about Sallie?

2) How has Sallie acted toward the children? Her condition is a source of two things. What are they? How is her condition regarded?

3) What have the people of Rhode Island done to the H.M.S. Gaspée after luring it into shallow waters, scuffling with the crew, and bringing them to shore? Had Lieutenant Dudington done anything to incur wrath?

4) What appeal from the House of Burgesses had the king ignored?

5) Whose funeral is Patrick attending on February 2, 1773? Who conducts the ceremony?

6) What had John asked Patrick to "Hold on ta?" Whom does Patrick meet at the end of the funeral?

7) Whom does Patrick bring to Scotchtown? Where has Nigel gone? Whom will he be helping?

8) Among which group has the Dissenter movement been birthed in Hanover?

9) Finish Liz's statement: ". . . our Patrick has a large heart for . . ."

10) Sallie's condition is worsening. What institution will Patrick tour? Does Liz think it is the answer?

Fledgling

Chapter 56: Gasping for Liberty

1) Where is Chapter 56 set and when? What is Patrick's concern about Sallie? How has Sallie acted toward the children? Her condition is a source of two things. What are they? How is her condition regarded?

2) Describe the events on the H.M.S. Gaspée. Was anyone charged with a crime? Why or why not?

3) Patrick knows it is only a matter of time before another incident occurs. What does he think the colonists must do and for what must they prepare?

4) What appeal from the House of Burgesses has the king ignored? Read Patrick's letter to Mr. Pleasants. Summarize each of paragraphs 2 through 5 in one to sentences each. Use today's language.

5) Read the words Uncle Patrick reads from the *Book of Common Prayer*. What does each sentence mean?

6) Summarize Patrick's last conversation with his father.

7) Whom does Patrick meet at the funeral? Which humans does Patrick bring to Scotchtown? Which EO7 members? Where has Nigel gone? Whom will he be helping and with what? What will the Lassies be doing?

8) Summarize Liz and MizP's answer to Kate's question: "How does he capture the humans he speaks ta?"

9) Recount Liz's retelling of Patrick's "finest moment."

10) Sallie's condition is worsening. What type of institution will Patrick visit? Describe one of these facilities as they existed in the mid-eighteenth century. Does Liz think this is the answer?

Chapter 56: Gasping for Liberty

1) Where is Chapter 56 set and when? What is Patrick's concern about Sallie? How has Sallie acted toward the children? Her condition is a source of two things. What are they? How is her condition regarded? Why is this so?

2) Describe the events on the H.M.S. Gaspée. Was anyone charged with a crime? Why or why not?

3) Patrick knows it is only a matter of time before another incident occurs. What does he think the colonists must do and for what must they prepare? What does trading one form of tyranny for another mean and how does it apply in this instance?

4) What appeal from the House of Burgesses has the king ignored? Read Patrick's letter to Mr. Pleasants. Summarize each of paragraphs 2 through 5 in one to sentences each. Use today's language.

5) Read the words Uncle Patrick reads from the *Book of Common Prayer*. What does each sentence mean?

6) Summarize Patrick's last conversation with his father.

7) Whom does Patrick meet at the funeral? Which humans does Patrick bring to Scotchtown? Which EO7 members? Where has Nigel gone? Whom will he be helping and with what? What will the Lassies be doing?

8) Summarize Liz and MizP's answer to Kate's question: "How does he capture the humans he speaks ta?"

9) Recount Liz's retelling of Patrick's "finest moment."

10) Sallie's condition is worsening. What will Patrick visit? Describe one of these facilities as they existed in the mid-eighteenth century. Does Liz think this is the answer?

Nigel's Nuggets

Chapter 56: Gasping for Liberty

Bravo! You have now completed your map of Virginia. It is time to plan an expedition. Plan a trip to visit all of the American sites for which you have itineraries, then present it. Please include costs such as hotel, car rental, and flights. I shall be packing my bags!

Cato's Eagle-Eye View

Chapter 56: Gasping for Liberty

Gliding: Summarize the chapter in three to five sentences, written or orally.

Soaring: Summarize the chapter in one word, phrase, or sentence and write it on an index card with the chapter number and title written on the other side.

Soaring Flashcard Game: Shuffle all your Soaring flashcards. Player 1 reads the number and/or title of a chapter on one side of a flashcard. Player 2 answers with the Soaring Summarization on the other side of the flashcard. Reshuffle your flashcards, switch players if desired, and play three times.

Eaglet

Chapter 57: Troubling Letters

1) Al is decorating his cat bed for Christmas. What is he putting on the holly points? Who is watching Al? What does he pull from other decorations to give to Al?

2) What is the hazard of decorating with food?

3) Nigel explains the next part of the mission to Al. What is it? Who is currently in possession of these items?

4) To which street does Al take Nigel? What does Al tell him about this street?

5) What is Al's concern with Nigel's plan?

6) Franklin realizes who ordered troops to Boston. Who is it?

7) What has Samuel Adams proposed throughout Massachusetts? Where else does Patrick say they are needed? What does Liz say Patrick has just suggested?

8) Where does Patrick go to visit on South Francis Street in Williamsburg?

9) Will Patrick put Sallie in this place?

10) Who has opened the packet of letters Benjamin Franklin sent to Thomas Cushing?

Chapter 57: Troubling Letters

1) Where is Chapter 57 set and when? Is the opening scene before or after the events of Chapter 56? Al is decorating his cat bed for Christmas. What is he putting on the holly points? Who is watching Al? What does he pull from other decorations to give to Al?

2) What is the hazard of decorating with food? Nigel explains the next part of the mission to Al. What is it? Who is currently in possession of these items?

3) Who wrote the letters? What was his position at the time? Where does Al say they should begin to look and why? To which street does Al take Nigel? What does Al tell him about the street?

4) What is Al's concern? How does Nigel respond to Al?

5) What does Benjamin Franklin pick up? What is curious about this item? Nigel is concerned as he reads Franklin's letter. What is his concern?

6) Why are Patrick and his fellow burgesses in Williamsburg? What have the governor and the old guard done to earn Patrick's harsh criticism?

7) What has Samuel Adams proposed throughout Massachusetts? What have citizens of Massachusetts done as a result of this? Where else does Patrick say this is needed? What does Liz say Patrick has just suggested? What does Liz ponder?

8) What does Patrick learn about the future living conditions and treatments for patients at the asylum?

9) How does Patrick react to seeing the first room? Does he finish his tour? What does he vow to Sallie?

10) Who has opened the packet of letters Franklin sent to Cushing? Do you think he will honor Franklin's request? Why or why not?

Chapter 57: Troubling Letters

1) Where is Chapter 57 set and when? Is the opening scene before or after the events of Chapter 56? Al is decorating his cat bed for Christmas. What is he putting on the holly points? Who is watching Al? What does he pull from other decorations to give to Al?

2) What is the hazard of decorating with food? Nigel explains the next part of the mission to Al. What is it? Who is currently in possession of these items?

3) Who wrote the letters? What was his position at the time? Where does Al say they should begin to look and why? To which street does Al take Nigel? What does Al tell him about the street?

4) What is Al's concern? How does Nigel respond to Al? How do you think Nigel feels about Al's suggestion and why?

5) What does Benjamin Franklin pick up? What is curious about this item? Nigel is concerned as he reads Franklin's letter. What is his concern? Do you think Al has reason to be concerned? Why or why not?

6) Why are Patrick and his fellow burgesses in Williamsburg? What have the governor and the old guard done to earn Patrick's harsh criticism? What practice is Patrick concerned might become a precedent as a result of the governor's actions?

7) What has Samuel Adams proposed throughout Massachusetts? What have citizens of Massachusetts done as a result of this? Where else does Patrick say this is needed? What does Liz say Patrick has just suggested? What does Liz ponder?

8) What does Patrick learn about the future living conditions and treatments for patients at the asylum?

9) How does Patrick react to seeing the first room? Does he finish his tour? What does he vow to Sallie?

10) Who has opened the packet of letters Franklin sent to Cushing? Do you think he will honor Franklin's request? Why or why not?

Nigel's Nuggets

Chapter 57: Troubling Letters

Nigel here, straight from recording the latest utterly thrilling episode of VRK the Podcast. Max was at his best, even if it was at my expense. Reviewing Chapter 57, I am reminded of Al accusing me of making us bank robbers. We absolutely were *not* bank robbers. I cannot even take a chance with that scene. Therefore, please create a picture of me and Al as my favorite kitty decorates for Christmas.

Cato's Eagle-Eye View

Chapter 57: Troubling Letters

Gliding: Summarize the chapter in three to five sentences, written or orally.

Soaring: Summarize the chapter in one word, phrase, or sentence and write it on an index card with the chapter number and title written on the other side.

Soaring Flashcard Game: Shuffle all your Soaring flashcards. Player 1 reads the number and/or title of a chapter on one side of a flashcard. Player 2 answers with the Soaring Summarization on the other side of the flashcard. Reshuffle your flashcards, switch players if desired, and play three times.

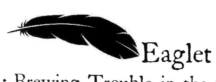

Eaglet

Chapter 58: Brewing Trouble in the Cat's-Paw

1) How is Clarie disguised at the start of Chapter 58? Who is next to her? Who delivered Benjamin Franklin's letters to Samuel Adams? Did Samuel Adams publish them or Honor Franklin's request?

2) The colonists are acting less like Englishmen and more like Americans. Is Benjamin Franklin doing the same?

3) What is the figure of speech that means "that someone is used unknowingly by another to accomplish the other's own purposes?"

4) What will the East India Tea Company become?

5) Clarie says tea is a perfect drink for something. What is it?

6) Who is standing at the front of the Old South Meeting House conducting a meeting? Will governor Hutchinson let the ships leave Boston Harbor without unloading their cargo?

7) What do the Bostonians do to protest the Tea Act? Who will stand trial for their actions?

8) Does Franklin approve of the Bostonians?

9) Nigel puts quotations into Franklin's pocket from two sources. Name the sources.

10) Finish the statement: "When Benjamin Franklin set foot in the Cockpit . . ."

Chapter 58: Brewing Trouble in the Cat's-Paw

1) Where is Chapter 58 set and when? How is Clarie disguised at the start of Chapter 58? Who is next to her? Who delivered Benjamin Franklin's letters to Samuel Adams? What has happened since Samuel Adams got the letters?

2) What good will come of this episode? What will the storm of Hutchinson's letters accomplish? What does Al read in the *Boston Gazette*?

3) What is a *cat's-paw?* What will the East India Tea Company become? What will the Colonies admit by paying the tea tax? What will happen as a result of this?

4) Why is the king upset? For what is the Massachusetts assembly calling? What is all of London wondering? Finish Nigel's statement: "The Colonies are shifting . . ."

5) Max asks Clarie if she is heading to a costume party. How does she respond? What will be served at this event? Clarie says it is perfect for something. What is it?

6) Who is standing at the front of the Old South Meeting House conducting a meeting? Will governor Hutchinson let the ships leave Boston Harbor without unloading their cargo? What does Samuel Adams say upon hearing this news? What does Max watch in stunned disbelief? How is this action different from other actions by the Bostonians? How would the Bostonians have made a case for the property destruction during their Tea Party being justified?

7) What do the Bostonians do before they leave the scene of the Tea Party? Who will stand trial for their actions? What does Franklin admit to doing?

8) Parliament has called Benjamin Franklin to do something. What is it? Finish King George's statement: "We'll let *Franklin* be . . ." Does Franklin approve of the actions of the Bostonians?

9) Nigel puts quotations into Franklin's pocket from two sources. Write out both quotations. Explain the first.

10) Describe Wedderburn's grilling of Franklin. What disgusts Nigel? What is the eventual outcome in the Privy Council? How have King George, Lord North, Alexander Wedderburn, and the Privy Council been unwittingly used? Finish the statement: "When Benjamin Franklin set foot in the Cockpit . . ."

Chapter 58: Brewing Trouble in the Cat's-Paw

1) Where is Chapter 58 set and when? How is Clarie disguised? Who is next to her? Who delivered Benjamin Franklin's letters to Samuel Adams? What has happened since then?

2) What good will come of this episode? What will the storm of Hutchinson's letters accomplish? What does Al read in the *Boston Gazette*?

3) What is a *cat's-paw*? What will the East India Tea Company become? What will the Colonies admit by paying the tea tax? What will happen as a result of this?

4) Why is King George upset? For what is the Massachusetts assembly calling? What is all of London wondering? Finish Nigel's statement: "The Colonies are shifting . . ." Explain the meaning of Nigel's statement.

5) Max asks Clarie if she is heading to a costume party. How does she respond? What will be served at this event? Clarie says it is perfect for something. What is it?

6) Who is standing at the front of the Old South Meeting House conducting a meeting? Will governor Hutchinson let the ships leave Boston Harbor without unloading their cargo? What does Samuel Adams say upon hearing this news? What does Max watch in stunned disbelief? How is this action different from other actions by the Bostonians? How would the Bostonians have made a case for the property destruction during their Tea Party being justified?

7) What do the Bostonians do before they leave the scene of the Tea Party? Who will stand trial for their actions? What does Franklin admit to doing?

8) What has Parliament called Benjamin Franklin to do? Finish King George's statement: "We'll let *Franklin* be . . ." Does Franklin approve of the Bostonians' actions?

9) Nigel puts quotations into Franklin's pocket from two sources. Write out both quotations. Explain both of the quotations.

10) Describe Wedderburn's grilling of Franklin. What disgusts Nigel? What is the eventual outcome in the Privy Council? How have King George, Lord North, Alexander Wedderburn, and the Privy Council been unwittingly used? Finish the statement: "When Benjamin Franklin set foot in the Cockpit . . ." What does this mean?

Nigel's Nuggets

Chapter 58: Brewing Trouble in the Cat's-Paw

Right. There is obviously only one thing remaining to do for Chapter 58. Please file your news report from the field. Turn it in to me at Nigel's News Nuggets, or you can reach me via Jenny L. Cote at her website: jenny@epicorderoftheseven.com

Cato's Eagle-Eye View

Chapter 58: Brewing Trouble in the Cat's-Paw

Gliding: Summarize the chapter in three to five sentences, written or orally.

Soaring: Summarize the chapter in one word, phrase, or sentence and write it on an index card with the chapter number and title written on the other side.

Soaring Flashcard Game: Shuffle all your Soaring flashcards. Player 1 reads the number and/or title of a chapter on one side of a flashcard. Player two answers with the Soaring Summarization on the other side of the flashcard. Reshuffle your flashcards, switch players if desired, and play three times.

Eaglet

Chapter 59: A Voice That Is Hungry

1) Where is Chapter 59 set and when? What is Kate reading to Liz?

2) Finish Kate's sentence: "Aye, but puttin' a hedge around someone . . ."

3) Gillamon tells Kate that Sallie will respond to her. What does she ask if she should do? Does Liz tell her yes or no?

4) What is England going to do to the port of Boston?

5) Who has been ordered returned to England in iron fetters?

6) What does Richard Henry Lee suggest calling? Does Patrick think the burgesses are ready for such an action?

7) Patrick, Richard Henry Lee, and Thomas Jefferson draft a resolution calling for something. What is it?

8) Governor Dunmore's face turns red when he reads the burgesses' resolution. On which date will this take place, and to coincide with which event?

9) After Dunmore dissolves the burgesses they meet in the Raleigh Tavern and sign another agreement to halt something. What is it?

10) George Mason calls Patrick the first man upon this continent. What does Nigel say the first man will get?

Chapter 59: A Voice That Is Hungry

1) Write out the two quotations Kate reads at the beginning of Chapter 59. Of what does "Liberty's Goddess" speak?

2) Finish Kate's sentence: "Aye, but puttin' a hedge around someone . . ." What does she mean? What does Kate worry about Sallie? What does this help Liz realize? What is overdue?

3) Summarize Gillamon's message for Liz and Kate in three to five sentences. Gillamon tells Kate that Sallie will respond to her. What does she ask if she should do? Does Liz tell her yes or no?

4) What is England going to do to the port of Boston? What does Richard Henry Lee tell the men he has heard from his brother in London? Who has been ordered returned to England in iron fetters?

5) What is the *last* thing Patrick says Dunmore should be given? What does Richard Henry Lee suggest about Dunmore? Summarize Patrick's answer and what he is thinking.

6) What does Lee suggest? How does Patrick answer him and what does he propose? What does Lee say in response?

7) Patrick, Lee, and Thomas Jefferson draft a resolution calling for something. What is it? What do Nigel and Al overhear King George declare? What are each of the four Intolerable Acts, and what does each act stipulate?

8) What does Liz say will happen when General Gage takes over? What must happen first?

9) Governor Dunmore's face turns red when he reads the burgesses' resolution. On which date will this take place, and to coincide with which event? What does Dunmore do?

10) After Dunmore dissolves the burgesses they meet in the Raleigh Tavern and sign another agreement to halt something. What is it? Write out George Mason's words about Patrick.

Chapter 59: A Voice That Is Hungry

1) Write out the two quotations Kate reads at the beginning of Chapter 59. Of what does "Liberty's Goddess" speak?

2) Finish Kate's sentence: "Aye, but puttin' a hedge around someone . . ." What does she mean? What does Kate worry about Sallie? What does this help Liz realize? What is overdue?

3) Summarize Gillamon's message for Liz and Kate in one to three paragraphs. Gillamon tells Kate that Sallie will respond to her. What does she ask if she should do? Does Liz tell her yes or no?

4) What is England going to do to the port of Boston? What does Richard Henry Lee tell the men he has heard from his brother in London? Who has been ordered returned to England in iron fetters?

5) What is the *last* thing Patrick says Dunmore should be given? What does Richard Henry Lee suggest about Dunmore? Summarize Patrick's answer and what he is thinking.

6) What does Lee suggest? How does Patrick answer him and what does he propose? What does Lee say in response?

7) Patrick, Lee, and Thomas Jefferson draft a resolution calling for something. What is it? What do Nigel and Al overhear King George declare? What does this mean? What are each of the four Intolerable Acts, and what does each act stipulate?

8) What does Liz say will happen when General Gage takes over? What must happen first?

9) Governor Dunmore's face turns red when he reads the burgesses' resolution. On which date will this take place, and to coincide with which event? What does Dunmore do?

10) After Dunmore dissolves the burgesses they meet in the Raleigh Tavern and sign another agreement to halt something. What is it? Write out George Mason's words about Patrick. What does Nigel say Patrick will get?

Nigel's Nuggets

Chapter 59: A Voice That Is Hungry

Well, I am all for this day of fasting, humiliation, and prayer. However, fasting reminds me of that from which we are abstaining. In that activity, I have been appallingly remiss. Although, you may have included epicurean experiences in your VRK Study Guide itineraries.

Oh, dear. Wherever were we? Ah, yes, the Raleigh Tavern! You simply must plan a trip to patronize this worthy establishment to enjoy a delicious feast for the culinary senses. Make sure your plans include the selections for your repast. I should expect that you will partake of an appetizer, entrée, dessert, and a drink. I will need to know the costs you incur with any local and state taxes, and a tip of at least 15 percent.

After you finish your delectable challenge, please do not overlook the import of the moment. You have solved another portion of The Fiddle's Riddle! Neglect not the filling in of your poster.

Cato's Eagle-Eye View

Chapter 59: A Voice That Is Hungry

Gliding: Summarize the chapter in three to five sentences, written or orally.

Soaring: Summarize the chapter in one word, phrase, or sentence and write it on an index card with the chapter number and title written on the other side.

Soaring Flashcard Game: Shuffle all your Soaring flashcards. Player 1 reads the number and/or title of a chapter on one side of a flashcard. Player 2 answers with the Soaring Summarization on the other side of the flashcard. Reshuffle your flashcards, switch players if desired, and play three times.

Eaglet

Chapter 60: To Philadelphia

1) Where is Chapter 60 set and when? What have the Virginia churches collected for the Bostonians?

2) What begins August 1, 1774, in Williamsburg? Is Lord Dunmore in town?

3) Where does the convention meet?

4) Finish the statement: "UNITED . . ."

5) What did the delegates agree to cancel, to deny, and to ban?

6) Complete the middle of Patrick's statement: "I will keep . . . when riding with Mr. Pendleton."

7) Who does Sallie say talks to her?

8) What does Patrick tell Liz and Kate to do while he is in Philadelphia?

9) What is Clarie's disguise on September 1, 1774?

10) Where does Max go at the end of Chapter 60? Where does Clarie go?

Chapter 60: To Philadelphia

1) Where is Chapter 60 set and when? What have Virginia churches collected for the Bostonians? What begins August 1, 1774, in Williamsburg? Is Lord Dunmore in town?

2) Where does the convention meet? What had the freeholders done at Hanover Courthouse July 20, 1774?

3) Summarize the list of instructions from the freeholders of Hanover County.

4) What did the delegates agree to cancel, to deny, and to ban? How many delegates does the convention send to the Continental Congress in Philadelphia? Name them. Describe their political philosophies and give one reason they were chosen.

5) What were the delegates instructed to do in Philadelphia?

6) What does George Washington invite Patrick to do? Who else will be present? Complete the middle of Patrick's statement: "I will keep . . . when riding with Mr. Pendleton."

7) What does Sallie mutter as she stares at the animals? Whom does she mean? What does Patrick tell Liz and Kate to do while he is in Philadelphia?

8) Who is in Boston on September 1, 1774? What has just happened? What had the British thought? What do the Minute Men show them instead?

9) What does Clarie say will happen when the Americans will not back down? What does she mean by this?

10) Where does Max go at the end of Chapter 60? Whom will he join and what will they prevent? Where does Clarie go?

Chapter 60: To Philadelphia

1) Where is Chapter 60 set and when? What have Virginia churches collected for the Bostonians? What begins August 1, 1774, in Williamsburg? Is Lord Dunmore in town?

2) Where does the convention meet? What had the freeholders done at Hanover Courthouse on July 20, 1774?

3) Summarize the list of instructions from the freeholders of Hanover County.

4) What did the delegates agree to cancel, to deny, and to ban? How many delegates does the convention send to the Continental Congress in Philadelphia? Name them. Describe their political philosophies and give one reason they were chosen.

5) What were the delegates instructed to do in Philadelphia?

6) What does George Washington invite Patrick to do? Who else will be present? Complete the middle of Patrick's statement: "I will keep . . . when riding with Mr. Pendleton." Why would Patrick need to do this? What were Pendleton's political views at the time?

7) What does Sallie mutter as she stares at the animals? Whom does she mean? What does Patrick tell Liz and Kate to do while he is in Philadelphia? Do you think Patrick believes Sallie? Why or why not?

8) Who is in Boston on September 1, 1774? What has just happened? What had the British thought? What do the Minute Men show them instead?

9) What does Clarie say will happen when the Americans will not back down? What does she mean by this?

10) Where does Max go at the end of Chapter 60? Whom will he join and what will they prevent? Where does Clarie go? In which colony was this place located in 1774? Where is it today?

Nigel's Nuggets

Chapter 60: To Philadelphia

Let me just say this about that. Max can be most unjust in his portrayal of yours truly in the VRK Podcast. It is positively outrageous! Although, I must give the old chap credit where credit is due—he is positively hilarious. Now where were we? Ah, yes, Point Pleasant. Please make a presentation about the battle that occurred on this fair land.

Cato's Eagle-Eye View

Chapter 60: To Philadelphia

Gliding: Summarize the chapter in three to five sentences, written or orally.

Soaring: Summarize the chapter in one word, phrase, or sentence and write it on an index card with the chapter number and title written on the other side.

Soaring Flashcard Game: Shuffle all your Soaring flashcards. Player 1 reads the number and/or title of a chapter on one side of a flashcard. Player 2 answers with the Soaring Summarization on the other side of the flashcard. Reshuffle your flashcards, switch players if desired, and play three times.

Eaglet

Chapter 61: A Voice Unified

1) Where is Chapter 61 set and when? What does Cato tell Nigel he is thinking about doing?

2) How does Nigel tell Cato he can return to Virginia?

3) Which EO7 members are in the crowd waiting to greet the delegates?

4) Finish Patrick's statement: "Not that I desire war either, Colonel . . ."

5) After Patrick reads Colonel Stephens' letter, he realizes that it is not just about Virginia, but *America*. Finish the thought: "Not just . . ."

6) On what date do the delegates have a quorum?

7) Where does the First Continental Congress meet? What other building do they choose not to use?

8) What is the first question to spark a debate in Congress?

9) John Adams marvels at Patrick's statements to Congress. Whom will he write about this insightful man?

10) How do the delegates finally agree to vote?

Chapter 61: A Voice Unified

You have two options for Chapter 61. For Option 1, answer the questions below. For Option 2, find Plutarch's* Cato the Younger, *and read the entire book, which is approximately forty-two pages. Summarize the book in one to three pages. In addition, please complete all Eaglet level questions, Nigel's Nuggets, and Cato's Eagle-Eye View.

1) Read a summary of Plutarch's *Cato the Younger* and give a one to three paragraph recap of what you have read.

2) Write out Cato's quotation at the beginning of Chapter 61. What does he say the quotation means? Who else is thinking about love in addition to Juba?

3) What does Cato want to do? How long would he need to stay in Philadelphia? How does Nigel react? How does Nigel tell Cato he can return to Virginia? Which EO7 members are in the crowd waiting for the delegates to arrive?

4) Explain Patrick's meaning regarding his and George Washington's "exclusive club." Finish Patrick's statement: "Not that I desire war, Colonel . . ."

5) Richard Henry Lee gives Patrick a letter that Gillamon has brought to Philadelphia for him. Who wrote the letter? Summarize its contents.

6) Where does the First Continental Congress meet? Describe this location including its designer, its members, and some of its uses.

7) Why did the First Continental Congress choose not to meet at the Pennsylvania State House?

8) What is the first question to spark a debate in Congress? Finish Patrick's statement, then tell what he is suggesting should happen: "It would be a great injustice if . . ." Who is John Sullivan and how does he counter Patrick's argument?

9) John Adams marvels at Patrick's statements to Congress. Explain the meaning of Adams' thoughts. Which colony does he represent?

10) How do the delegates finally agree to vote? What news breaks at the end of Chapter 61? How do the delegates and townspeople react?

Chapter 61: A Voice Unified

You have two options for Chapter 61. For Option 1, answer the questions below. For Option 2, find Plutarch's* Cato the Younger, *and read the entire book, which is approximately forty-two pages. Summarize the book in three to five pages. In addition, please complete all Eaglet level questions, Nigel's Nuggets, and Cato's Eagle-Eye View.

1) Read a summary of Plutarch's *Cato the Younger* and give a three to five paragraph recap of what you have read.

2) Write out Cato's quotation at the beginning of Chapter 61. What does he say the quotation means? Who else is thinking about love in addition to Juba?

3) What does Cato want to do? How long would he need to stay in Philadelphia? How does Nigel react? How does Nigel tell Cato he can return to Virginia? Which EO7 members are in the crowd waiting for the delegates to arrive?

4) Explain Patrick's meaning regarding his and George Washington's "exclusive club." Finish Patrick's statement: "Not that I desire war, Colonel . . ."

5) Richard Henry Lee gives Patrick a letter that Gillamon has brought to Philadelphia for him. Who wrote the letter? Summarize its contents. What is the original reference for "the gates of hell?" What does it mean?

6) Where does the First Continental Congress meet? Describe this location including its designer, its members, and some of its uses.

7) Why did the First Continental Congress choose not to meet at the Pennsylvania State House?

8) What question sparks the first debate in Congress? Finish Patrick's statement, then tell what he is suggesting: "It would be a great . . ." How does John Sullivan counter Patrick?

9) John Adams marvels at Patrick's statements to Congress. Explain the meaning of Adams' thoughts. Which colony does he represent?

10) How do the delegates agree to vote? What news breaks at the end of Ch 61? How do the delegates and townspeople react? What do the last two sentences of Ch 61 foreshadow?

Nigel's Nuggets

Chapter 61: A Voice Unified

Nigel here, still astounded by the wonder that is Carpenter's Hall. Including the chairs. Especially the chairs. Chairs are ever so important. Patrick has a most magnificent specimen. But I digress. In general, we do not sit on the artifacts, such as Patrick's chair. However, a replica of any artifact is a jolly good thing! Make a presentation about the chairs at Carpenter's Hall. Include information regarding the chair in which one is allowed to sit. Include a picture or pictures, especially if you have a photograph of yourself reposing in said chair. Naturally, Jenny L. Cote will want to see them. She is a connoisseur of all chairs historic, be they replicas or the genuine items.

Absolutely do not forget to update your Fiddle's Riddle Poster to reflect your recent discoveries.

Cato's Eagle-Eye View

Chapter 61: A Voice Unified

Gliding: Summarize the chapter in three to five sentences, written or orally.

Soaring: Summarize the chapter in one word, phrase, or sentence and write it on an index card with the chapter number and title written on the other side.

Soaring Flashcard Game: Shuffle all your Soaring flashcards. Player 1 reads the number and/or title of a chapter on one side of a flashcard. Player 2 answers with the Soaring Summarization on the other side of the flashcard. Reshuffle your flashcards, switch players if desired, and play three times.

Eaglet

Chapter 62: God Bless America

1) Where is Chapter 62 set and when? Panic has set in over a report of an attack upon Boston. Is the report true?

2) What does Max tell Gillamon he will do?

3) Congress decided to keep their meetings secret. What will they not allow? What else will they do?

4) What does Thomas Cushing propose? Whom does Samuel Adams suggest? What is his posting?

5) Which Psalm does Reverend Duché read?

6) How do the Quakers and Dissenters receive the reading of the Psalm?

7) From which position does Patrick join Duché in prayer? Is the prayer pre-written?

8) What does the false rumor about Boston do?

9) Whom does Gillamon invite to dinner?

10) What does Paul Revere deliver on September 18, 1774? Are they supported?

Chapter 62: God Bless America

1) Where is Chapter 62 set and when? Panic has set in over a report of an attack upon Boston. Is the report true? What does Max tell Gillamon he will do?

2) What does Gillamon tell Max and Nigel about war? What does he excuse himself to do next?

3) What does Congress decide to do? What will they not allow? How will they accomplish this?

4) What does Thomas Cushing suggest and why? How does John Jay respond and why? Whom does Samuel Adams recommend? Who has given him this idea?

5) Which book does Reverend Duché open to begin the session of Congress? Which Psalm does he read?

6) How do the Quakers and Dissenters receive the reading of the Psalm? From which position does Patrick join Duché in prayer? Is the prayer pre-written?

7) Pick three separate sentences from the prayer and explain the meaning of each.

8) What does the false rumor about Boston do? Whom does Gillamon invite to dinner?

9) What does Paul Revere deliver on September 18, 1774? Are they supported? What do these resolves state that Americans should not do? What should they do instead?

10) What does John Adams write in his diary after the Suffolk Resolves win support? Summarize his letter to Abigail.

Chapter 62: God Bless America

1) Where is Chapter 62 set and when? Panic has set in over a report of an attack upon Boston. Is the report true? What does Max tell Gillamon he will do?

2) What does Gillamon tell Max and Nigel about war? What does he excuse himself to do next?

3) What does Congress decide to do? What will they not allow? How will they accomplish this?

4) What does Thomas Cushing suggest and why? How does John Jay respond and why? Whom does Samuel Adams recommend? Who has given him this idea?

5) Which book does Reverend Duché open to begin the session of Congress? Which Psalm does he read? What do the verses on page 547 mean to you?

6) How do the Quakers and Dissenters receive the reading of the Psalm? From which position does Patrick join Duché in prayer? Is the prayer pre-written?

7) Pick five separate sentences from the prayer and explain the meaning of each.

8) What does the false rumor about Boston do? Whom does Gillamon invite to dinner?

9) What does Paul Revere deliver on September 18, 1774? Are they supported? What do these resolves state that Americans should not do? What should they do instead?

10) What does John Adams write in his diary after the Suffolk Resolves win support? Summarize his letter to Abigail. What happens in the last paragraph of Chapter 62? What is this creature planning and for whom?

Nigel's Nuggets

Chapter 62: God Bless America

Make a presentation about the Suffolk Resolves. Include biographical information about Dr. Joseph Warren from his birth through 1774, but not beyond.

Cato's Eagle-Eye View

Chapter 62: God Bless America

Gliding: Summarize the chapter in three to five sentences, written or orally.

Soaring: Summarize the chapter in one word, phrase, or sentence and write it on an index card with the chapter number and title written on the other side.

Soaring Flashcard Game: Shuffle all your Soaring flashcards. Player 1 reads the number and/or title of a chapter on one side of a flashcard. Player 2 answers with the Soaring Summarization on the other side of the flashcard. Reshuffle your flashcards, switch players if desired, and play three times.

Eaglet

Chapter 63: Unjust Desserts and Passing the Mantle

1) Where is Chapter 63 set and when? Whom does Patrick see upon arrival?

2) George Washington says he would like a dog such as Max on his farm because they are well bred to round up something. What is it?

3) How many people reside in Philadelphia? How many in London?

4) Which play will the men join Mr. Gillamon to see? Who has Mr. Gillamon commissioned to make a new cloak?

5) What has happened to Mr. Gillamon's cook this afternoon? What does Max growl and decide to do?

6) What is the new cook's name? What has possibly made the regular cook sick? What does the new cook pull out of her pocket? What does she do with it?

7) What is Charlotte intending to do to the men? Is she able to accomplish it?

8) When is the next Continental Congress scheduled to convene? What does Cato name his eaglets?

9) Where will Max go next and who will go with him?

10) What does Mr. Gillamon leave for Patrick and what does he leave inside?

Fledgling

Chapter 63: Unjust Desserts and Passing the Mantle

1) Where is Chapter 63 set and when? Patrick asks Mr. Gillamon how he has been there for so many key moments of Patrick's life's journey. How does Mr. Gillamon answer him?

2) Who does Patrick see upon his arrival? George Washington says he would like a dog such as Max on his farm because they are well bred to round up something. What is it? How many people reside in Philadelphia? How many in London?

3) Which play will the men join Mr. Gillamon to see? Whom has Mr. Gillamon commissioned to make a new cloak? What do the men discuss during the first course of dinner? What should be going on by now? Who is there?

4) What has happened to Mr. Gillamon's cook this afternoon? What has possibly made this happen? What does Max growl and decide to do? What is the new cook's name?

5) What does Charlotte pull out of her pocket? What does she do with it? What does Max say to Charlotte? What does he do? What does she call Max?

6) How does Charlotte respond to Gillamon's rebuke? What is she intending to do to the men? Is Charlotte able to do what she intends?

7) What has the First Continental Congress accomplished by October 20, 1774? When is the next Continental Congress scheduled to convene? What does Cato name his eaglets?

8) Recount Cato and Nigel's viewing of the play, *Cato.* What does the play inspire the eagle to do? Where will Max go next and who will go with him?

9) Summarize Major Joseph Hawley's letter in today's language.

10) Summarize Mr. Gillamon's note to Patrick.

Chapter 63: Unjust Desserts and Passing the Mantle

1) Where is Chapter 63 set and when? Patrick asks Mr. Gillamon how he has been there for so many key moments of Patrick's life's journey. How does Mr. Gillamon answer him?

2) Whom does Patrick see upon his arrival? George Washington says he would like a dog such as Max on his farm because they are well bred to round up something. What is it? How many people reside in Philadelphia? How many in London?

3) Which play will the men join Mr. Gillamon to see? Whom has Mr. Gillamon commissioned to make a new cloak? What do the men discuss during the first course of dinner? What should be going on by now? Who is there?

4) What has happened to Mr. Gillamon's cook this afternoon? What has possibly made this happen? What does Max growl and decide to do? What is the new cook's name?

5) What does Charlotte pull out of her pocket? What does she do with it? What does Max say to Charlotte? What does he do? What does she call Max? Why do you think she uses this term?

6) How does Charlotte respond to Gillamon's rebuke? What is she intending to do to the men? Is Charlotte able to do what she intends? Do you think Gillamon has known about Charlotte all along?

7) What has the First Continental Congress accomplished by October 20, 1774? When is the next Continental Congress scheduled to convene? What does Cato name his eaglets?

8) Recount Cato and Nigel's viewing of the play, *Cato*. What does the play inspire the eagle to do? Where will Max go next and who will go with him?

9) Summarize Major Joseph Hawley's letter in today's language.

10) Summarize Mr. Gillamon's note to Patrick. What is the significance of the enclosed item?

Nigel's Nuggets

Chapter 63: Unjust Desserts and Passing the Mantle

And this is why I love the chap! Max and I certainly engage in quite the fair amount of verbal sparring. However, he is the fiercest of protectors. This chapter was a close call. I very well could say that our Patrick and the other men were saved by a whisker. Max's whisker. Please submit to Nigel's News Nuggets a newscast about the hair-raising events.

Cato's Eagle-Eye View

Chapter 63: Unjust Desserts and Passing the Mantle

Gliding: Summarize the chapter in three to five sentences, written or orally.

Soaring: Summarize the chapter in one word, phrase, or sentence and write it on an index card with the chapter number and title written on the other side.

Soaring Flashcard Game: Shuffle all your Soaring flashcards. Player 1 reads the number and/or title of a chapter on one side of a flashcard. Player 2 answers with the Soaring Summarization on the other side of the flashcard. Reshuffle your flashcards, switch players if desired, and play three times.

Eaglet

Chapter 64: Winds Of War

1) Where is Chapter 64 set and when? Whom do the scouts set out to warn when they see Indian warriors move onto the warpath?

2) One of the scouts is wounded. Where is his wound? Who comes to his aid? In which form? What is the first name of the scout? Will he survive?

3) Patrick is having dinner with Colonel Samuel Overton. What does Overton ask Patrick? Does Patrick answer essentially a yes or a no?

4) Who is visiting Patrick at Scotchtown on November 15, 1774? Who is his wife?

5) William describes the Battle of Point Pleasant to Patrick. With what type of muskets and rifles were the Indians armed?

6) Patrick finds out the identity of the scout who is killed in the Battle of Point Pleasant. Who is it? Patrick says he "counts" this man as something. What is that something?

7) Clarie tells Liz and Kate that one of Samuel and Elizabeth's children will play a role in the future. What is that role? What is the name of the child?

8) Finish Kate's statement: "The winds of , , ,"

9) Where has Max gone? Who has gone with him?

10) Complete the verse from Ecclesiastes Liz quotes at the end of Chapter 64: "There is a time and a season . . ."

Chapter 64: Winds Of War

1) Where is Chapter 64 set and when? Whom do the scouts set out to warn when they see Indian warriors move onto the warpath? One of the scouts is wounded. Where is his wound? Who comes to his aid? In which form? What is the first name of the scout? Will he survive?

2) Patrick is having dinner with Colonel Samuel Overton. What does Overton ask Patrick? How does Patrick answer? Is this answer essentially a "yes" or a "no"?

3) What does another man ask worriedly? How does Patrick respond? What alarming possibility does this suggest?

4) Who is visiting Patrick at Scotchtown on November 15, 1774? Who is his wife? Where had she and Patrick's mother been when the hostilities began? Where did they go?

5) As William explains the unfolding of the Battle of Point Pleasant, he relates several suspicious coincidences. List them (page 564).

6) What defense of Dunmore's innocence does William consider aloud to Patrick?

7) Patrick finds out the identity of the scout who was killed in the Battle of Point Pleasant. Who is it? Patrick says he 'counts' this man as something. What is that something? Present a one-paragraph summation that gives reasons for the Battle of Point Pleasant being considered the first Revolutionary War battle.

8) Clarie tells Liz and Kate that one of Samuel and Elizabeth's children will play a role in the future. What is that role? What is the name of the child? Whom does this foreshadow?

9) What is Liz's lament to Clarie? How does Clarie answer? What is Kate's comment? Does Clarie agree? What does she say?

10) Where has Max gone? Who has gone with him? Complete the verse from Ecclesiastes that Liz quotes at the end of Chapter 64: "There is a time and a season . . ."

Chapter 64: Winds Of War

1) Where is Chapter 64 set and when? Whom do the scouts set out to warn when they see Indian warriors move onto the warpath? One of the scouts is wounded. Where is his wound? Who comes to his aid? In which form? What is the first name of the scout? Will he survive?

2) Patrick is having dinner with Colonel Samuel Overton. What does Overton ask Patrick? How does Patrick answer? Is this answer essentially a "yes" or a "no"? How do you know this?

3) What does another man ask worriedly? How does Patrick respond? What alarming possibility does this suggest?

4) Who is visiting Patrick at Scotchtown on November 15, 1774? Who is his wife? Where had she and Patrick's mother been when the hostilities began? Where did they go?

5) As William explains the unfolding of the Battle of Point Pleasant, he relates several suspicious coincidences. List them (page 564).

6) What defense of Dunmore's innocence does William consider aloud to Patrick?

7) Patrick finds out the identity of the scout who was killed in the Battle of Point Pleasant. Who is it? Patrick says he 'counts' this man as something. What is that something? Present a one- to three-paragraph summation which gives reasons for the Battle of Point Pleasant being considered the first Revolutionary War battle.

8) Clarie tells Liz and Kate that one of Samuel and Elizabeth's children will play a role in the future. What is it? What is the name of the child? Whom does this foreshadow?

9) What is Liz's lament to Clarie? How does Clarie answer? What is Kate's comment? Does Clarie agree? What does she say?

10) Where has Max gone? Who has gone with him? Complete the verse from Ecclesiastes that Liz quotes at the end of Chapter 64: "There is a time and a season . . ." What does this foreshadow?

Nigel's Nuggets

Chapter 64: Winds Of War

Lassie Power! Once again the Lassies have taken center stage. Please file a newscast taken from Chapter 64. Present your newscast in voice character as one, two, or all three of the Lassies. I look forward to receiving your report. Cheerio!

Cato's Eagle-Eye View

Chapter 64: Winds Of War

Gliding: Summarize the chapter in three to five sentences, written or orally.

Soaring: Summarize the chapter in one word, phrase, or sentence and write it on an index card with the chapter number and title written on the other side.

Soaring Flashcard Game: Shuffle all your Soaring flashcards. Player 1 reads the number and/or title of a chapter on one side of a flashcard. Player 2 answers with the Soaring Summarization on the other side of the flashcard. Reshuffle your flashcards, switch players if desired, and play three times.

Eaglet

Chapter 65: Farewell, My Love

1) Where is Chapter 65 set and when? Dinah is making a straight-dress for Sallie. What is different about the sleeves of a straight-dress?

2) Patrick asks Dinah if she thinks Sallie remembers her children. Does Dinah think so?

3) Patrick tells Patsey he looks like an old man. Patsey disagrees. What does Patrick say Sallie will always be?

4) What does Lord Dunmore hear as he sits at his desk on December 24, 1774?

5) Dunmore and all the royal governors will soon receive a letter instructing them to do something. What is it?

6) What does Al hope Benjamin Franklin will do and why?

7) What does William Pitt try to convince Parliament to avoid? Is he successful? Where does Franklin realize he must go now? In what endeavor will he join his fellow Americans?

8) Sallie appears to be having a lucid moment on February 25, 1775. What does she tell Patrick? What does she ask of him before her face goes blank?

9) Sallie begins to slip away. What does she tell Liz and Kate?

10) What are Sallie's last words to Patrick? Liz says it took something to give Sallie liberty. What was it?

Chapter 65: Farewell, My Love

1) Where is Chapter 65 set and when? Dinah is making a straight-dress for Sallie. What is different about the sleeves of a straight-dress? How does Dinah care for Sallie? Why does Sallie need the straight-dress?

2) Patrick makes a comment about fetters. What does he say and what does he mean? What question does Patrick ask Patsey? How does she answer him?

3) Patrick tells Patsey he looks like an old man. What does she say to counter this? What does Patrick say Sallie will always be?

4) What does Lord Dunmore hear as he sits at his desk on December 24, 1774? What is Dunmore doing? Summarize his letter in one paragraph.

5) What will Dunmore and the other royal governors soon receive? What will it instruct them to do? How will Dunmore handle this assignment?

6) How does King George instruct Lord North to respond to Virginia's resolves? What does Al hope Benjamin Franklin will do and why?

7) What does William Pitt try to convince Parliament to avoid? Is he successful? Read the passage Franklin writes. Define "calamities" and "imprudences." What does Franklin mean? Where does he realize he must go now? In which endeavor will he join his fellow Americans?

8) What does Patrick notice about Sallie as he begins to help her eat on February 25, 1775? What does Sallie tell Patrick? Does she mean her straight-dress?

9) What does Sallie say when Patrick leaves the room? What do you think she is seeing? What does she say to Liz and Kate?

10) What does Patrick say when he returns and fears he is losing Sallie? What are her last words to Patrick? What does Kate observe? What is Liz's response?

Chapter 65: Farewell, My Love

1) Where is Chapter 65 set and when? Dinah is making a straight-dress for Sallie. What is different about the sleeves of a straight-dress? How does Dinah care for Sallie? Why does Sallie need the straight-dress?

2) Patrick makes a comment about fetters. What does he say and what does he mean? What question does Patrick ask Patsey? How does she answer him?

3) Patrick tells Patsey he looks like an old man. What does she say to counter this? What does Patrick say Sallie will always be?

4) What does Lord Dunmore hear as he sits at his desk on December 24, 1774? What is Dunmore doing? Summarize his letter in one to three paragraphs.

5) What will Dunmore and the other royal governors soon receive? What will it instruct them to do? How will Dunmore handle this assignment?

6) How does King George instruct Lord North to respond to Virginia's resolves? What does Al hope Benjamin Franklin will do and why? Do you agree with Al's assessment? Why or why not?

7) What does William Pitt try to convince Parliament to avoid? Is he successful? Read the passage Franklin writes. Define "calamities" and "imprudences." What does Franklin mean? Where does he realize he must go now? In which endeavor will he join his fellow Americans?

8) What does Patrick notice about Sallie as he begins to help her eat on February 25, 1775? What does Sallie tell Patrick? Does she mean her straight-dress? What does she mean?

9) What does Sallie say when Patrick leaves the room? What do you think she is seeing? What do you think is happening to her? What does she say to Liz and Kate?

10) What does Patrick say when he returns and fears he is losing Sallie? What are her last words to Patrick? What does Kate observe? What is Liz's response?

Nigel's Nuggets

Chapter 65: Farewell, My Love

There is nothing like writing a scene "on location." Please peruse pages xxii and 611. You shall find contained therein, no fewer than three mentions of Jenny L. Cote writing a scene in the exact spot where it originally happened. Utterly thrilling! Review the VRK in your mind, and think about one of your favorite scenes that you would like to write on location. Make a presentation about the scene, the location, and your plans for composing an *epic* retelling of the event.

Cato's Eagle-Eye View

Chapter 65: Farewell, My Love

Gliding: Summarize the chapter in three to five sentences, written or orally.

Soaring: Summarize the chapter in one word, phrase, or sentence and write it on an index card with the chapter number and title written on the other side.

Soaring Flashcard Game: Shuffle all your Soaring flashcards. Player 1 reads the number and/or title of a chapter on one side of a flashcard. Player 2 answers with the Soaring Summarization on the other side of the flashcard. Reshuffle your flashcards, switch players if desired, and play three times.

Eaglet

Chapter 66: Cloak and Dagger

1) Where is Chapter 66 set? How long ago was Sallie's death? Where is Patrick going?

2) Patrick thinks the Second Virginia Convention should act as the government of Virginia. Whom will this bypass? How might King George view this action? What could it launch?

3) Gillamon tells the team their next tasks. Who will be in Richmond and in Scotchtown?

4) Liz asks Gillamon if Patrick will die. Finish writing the first sentence of his answer: "Death happens in far more ways . . ."

5) Once they arrive in Richmond, Liz and Nigel figure out that the fragment from Plutarch's "Winged Victory" has become something now in Patrick's possession. What is it?

6) Liz and Nigel realize several things about Kakia, the cat Liz rescued from the Tower of London.

Fill in the blanks to list the revelations in chapter 66:

The footprints on Plutarch's terrace were _________. She is not a ______________ being. Kakia in the Greek means, ______________, trouble, and __________________ ______ ____________ ______. Someone ______________________ young George Washington on Barbados with smallpox, and there was an attempt on _____________________________ and ______________ _____________ in Philadelphia. The ___________________ that failed to kill Patrick was ______ _____________. Kakia could be like ___________________ for the EO7. She might be able to change __________________ like ___________________ and ___________________.

7) Liz and Nigel realize they must search for Kakia. How can Cato search?

8) Cato finds Kakia and they have a fierce fight. Cato breaks free and flies to pick up the letter opener. What has been done to it? What will happen to Cato if he picks it up?

9) Kakia gives Cato a choice regarding picking up the letter opener. What does he choose?

10) Finish the following two sentences about the Second Virginia Convention from page 588: "And it was in a church in Jamestown that . . ." "The cause of liberty could find no better sanctuary than a church, for . . ."

Chapter 66: Cloak and Dagger

1) Where is Chapter 66 set? How long ago was Sallie's death? Where is Patrick going? Write out Patrick's resolutions, which Liz reads as he sleeps.

2) Patrick thinks the Second Virginia Convention should act as the government of Virginia. Whom will this bypass? How might King George view this action? What could it launch? Patrick scribbles something in Latin. Write it in both Latin and English.

3) Summarize Gillamon's response to Kate about it being time for the Revolution to begin. Gillamon tells the team their next tasks. Who will be in Richmond and who in Scotchtown?

4) Liz asks Gillamon if Patrick will die. How does he respond? What does a voice say as the notes cease floating in the air?

5) Once they arrive in Richmond, Liz and Nigel figure out that the fragment from Plutarch's "Winged Victory" has become something that is now in Patrick's possession. What is it? Liz and Nigel realize several things about Kakia, the cat Liz rescued from the Tower of London.

Fill in the blanks to list the revelations in chapter 66:

The footprints on Plutarch's terrace were ________. She is not a _____________ being. Kakia in the Greek means ______________, trouble, and ___________________ _____ ___________ ______. Someone ______________________ young George Washington on Barbados with smallpox, and there was an attempt on ______________________________ and ______________ ____________ in Philadelphia. The ____________________ that failed to kill Patrick was ______ ____________. Kakia could be like ____________________ for the EO7. She might be able to change __________________ like ____________________ and ____________________.

6) After these discoveries, Liz's mind races. What is she thinking? Summarize the next portion of Liz and Nigel's conversation until Nigel gives a determined answer. Liz and Nigel realize they must search for Kakia. How can Cato search?

7) Cato finds Kakia and they have a fierce fight. Cato breaks free and flies to pick up the letter opener. What has been done to it? What will happen to Cato if he picks it up? What has Kakia done to Cato that has put him in danger?

8) Kakia tells Cato that he has a choice to make, but there are plenty of options from which to choose. List the choices she presents.

9) Cato's heart races as he ponders his decision. What are his thoughts? What does Cato decide to do with the letter opener? How does Kakia respond?

10) Where is the Second Virginia Convention meeting? Who built the town? What is the eponym of this town? Define the term eponym. Finish the following two sentences about the Second Virginia Convention from page 588: "And it was in a church in Jamestown that . . ." "The cause of liberty could find no better sanctuary than a church, for . . ."

Chapter 66: Cloak and Dagger

1) Where is Chapter 66 set? How long ago was Sallie's death? Where is Patrick going? Write out Patrick's resolutions, which Liz reads as he sleeps.

2) Patrick thinks the Second Virginia Convention should act as the government of Virginia. Whom will this bypass? How might King George view this action? What could it launch? Patrick scribbles something in Latin. Write it in both Latin and English.

3) Summarize Gillamon's response to Kate about it being time for the Revolution to begin. Gillamon tells the team their next tasks. Who will be in Richmond and who in Scotchtown?

4) Liz asks Gillamon if Patrick will die. How does he respond? What does a voice say as the notes cease floating in the air? Who says this and what does it foreshadow?

5) Once in Richmond, Liz and Nigel figure out that the fragment from Plutarch's "Winged Victory" has become something that is now in Patrick's possession. What is it? Liz and Nigel realize several things about Kakia, the cat Liz rescued from the Tower of London.

Fill in the blanks to list the revelations in chapter 66:

The footprints on Plutarch's terrace were ________. She is not a ____________ being. Kakia in the Greek means ______________, trouble, and __________________ _____ ___________ ______. Someone _____________________ young George Washington on Barbados with smallpox, and there was an attempt on ____________________________ and ______________ ____________ in Philadelphia. The __________________ that failed to kill Patrick was ______ ____________. Kakia could be like __________________ for the EO7. She might be able to change _________________ as do __________________ and ___________________.

6) After these discoveries, Liz's mind races. What is she thinking? Summarize the next portion of Liz and Nigel's conversation until Nigel gives a determined answer. Liz and Nigel realize they must search for Kakia. How can Cato search?

7) Cato finds Kakia and they have a fierce fight. Cato breaks free and flies to pick up the letter opener. What has been done to it? What will happen to Cato if he picks it up? What has Kakia done to Cato that has put him in danger?

8) Kakia tells Cato that he has a choice to make, but there are plenty of options from which to choose. List the choices she presents. Briefly describe the effects the poison will have on Cato.

9) Cato's heart races as he ponders his decision. What are his thoughts? What does Cato decide to do with the letter opener? How does Kakia respond?

10) Where is the Second Virginia Convention meeting? Who built the town? What is the eponym of this town? Define the term eponym. Finish the following two sentences about the Second Virginia Convention from page 588: "And it was in a church in Jamestown that . . ." "The cause of liberty could find no better sanctuary than a church, for . . ." Why do you think American liberty might have needed an altar of grace?

Nigel's Nuggets

Chapter 66: Cloak and Dagger

There is a veritable smorgasbord of artistic inspiration to be found in Chapter 66. Please pick your favorite scene from "Cloak and Dagger" and *immortalize* it in art.

Cato's Eagle-Eye View

Chapter 66: Cloak and Dagger

Gliding: Summarize the chapter in three to five sentences, written or orally.

Soaring: Summarize the chapter in one word, phrase, or sentence and write it on an index card with the chapter number and title written on the other side.

Soaring Flashcard Game: Shuffle all your Soaring flashcards. Player 1 reads the number and/or title of a chapter on one side of a flashcard. Player 2 answers with the Soaring Summarization on the other side of the flashcard. Reshuffle your flashcards, switch players if desired, and play three times.

Eaglet

Chapter 67: Liberty or Death

1) Whom does Liz see at the beginning of Chapter 66? What is being carried?

2) Who gave the letter opener to Max? What had been done to it before it was given to Max?

3) Who will get to the opposite side of the church? What has been placed under a window for him?

4) Clarie gives Liz instructions on page 590. What are they?

5) Max tells Liz to remember what Gillamon always says. What is it?

6) Patrick is recognized by Peyton Randolph and he calls for the Colony of Virginia to immediately be put into a state of something. What is it?

7) Who offers a rebuttal to Patrick's resolutions?

8) Patrick's most famous speech is presented on pages 592 to 598. Find a partner and read the entire speech aloud. Write out the final *seven* words of Patrick's speech.

9) Peyton Randolph calls for a vote after Patrick's speech. Finish his admonition to those voting "aye:" ". . . you will be potentially accused of . . ."

10) Liz, Nigel, and Max do not stay to hear the results of the vote because Clarie tells them to get to someone. Who is it and where do they go?

Chapter 67: Liberty or Death

1) Whom does Liz see at the beginning of Chapter 66? What is being carried? Who gave the letter opener to Max? What had been done to it before it was given to Max?

2) Who will get to the opposite side of the church? What has been placed under a window for him? Clarie gives Liz instructions on page 590. What are they?

3) Max tells Liz to remember what Gillamon always says. What is it? Patrick is recognized by Peyton Randolph and calls for the Colony of Virginia to immediately be put into a state of something. What is it? Who offers a rebuttal to Patrick's resolution?

4) ***The following question counts for questions 4-7.***
5)
6)
7) Patrick's most famous speech is presented on pages 592-598. Find a partner and read the entire speech aloud. After reading Patrick's masterpiece, select five to seven of Patrick's arguments. Summarize each point and tell what it means.

8) How does Edward Carrington react to Patrick's speech? Is Carrington a historical or fictional character? Was his request eventually honored? Who speaks up in support of Patrick's resolutions? What does the last of the three pledge?

9) What does Peyton Randolph call for after the resolutions have been seconded? What admonition does he give?

10) Liz, Nigel, and Max do not stay to hear the results of the vote because Clarie tells them to get to someone. Who is it and where do they go?

Chapter 67: Liberty or Death

1) Whom does Liz see at the beginning of Chapter 66? What is being carried? Who gave the letter opener to Max? What had been done to it before it was given to Max?

2) Who will get to the opposite side of the church? What has been placed under a window for him? Clarie gives Liz instructions on page 590. What are they?

3) Max tells Liz to remember what Gillamon always says. What is it? Patrick is recognized by Peyton Randolph and he calls for the Colony of Virginia to immediately be put into a state of something. What is it? Who offers a rebuttal to Patrick's resolution?

4) ***The following question counts for questions 4-7.***
5)
6)
7) Patrick's most famous speech is presented on pages 592-598. Find a partner and read the entire speech aloud. After reading Patrick's masterpiece, select five to seven of Patrick's arguments. Summarize each point and tell what it means.

8) How does Edward Carrington react to Patrick's speech? Is Carrington a historical or fictional character? Was his request eventually honored? Who speaks up in support of Patrick's resolutions? What does the last of the three pledge?

9) What does Peyton Randolph call for after the resolutions have been seconded? What admonition does he give?

10) Liz, Nigel, and Max do not stay to hear the results of the vote because Clarie tells them to get to someone. Who is it and where do they go? What do you think Liz fears at the end of Chapter 67?

Nigel's Nuggets

Chapter 67: Liberty or Death

"TO ARMS! TO ARMS!" That was such a stirring speech. Patrick undoubtedly takes the biscuit as far as orators are concerned! I was honored to be the mouse in the house to witness such a pivotal moment in history. Praise be the Maker! I was almost a mouse in the pocket, which simply would not have done. But I digress. We have important business at hand. You have not demonstrated your *voice* yet. We must remedy this glaring omission posthaste. Please recite a portion of Patrick's "Liberty or Death" speech. Dress in period costume to the best of your ability. A hat is an ideal starting point. Record yourself giving your rendition of "Liberty or Death." Do make sure to send it to Jenny L. Cote: jenny@epicorderoftheseven.com Neglect *not* the letter opener!

Cato's Eagle-Eye View

Chapter 67: Liberty or Death

Gliding: Summarize the chapter in three to five sentences, written or orally.

Soaring: Summarize the chapter in one word, phrase, or sentence and write it on an index card with the chapter number and title written on the other side.

Soaring Flashcard Game: Shuffle all your Soaring flashcards. Player 1 reads the number and/or title of a chapter on one side of a flashcard. Player 2 answers with the Soaring Summarization on the other side of the flashcard. Reshuffle your flashcards, switch players if desired, and play three times.

Eaglet

Chapter 68: On Eagle's Wings

1) Liz, Max, and Nigel are rushing to find Cato. How is Nigel traveling?

2) Max suggests looking for Cato in the sky. Where does Nigel say they should look to find him instead?

3) Cato tries to ask Liz something when she reaches his side. How does she answer him?

4) Max says, "We've got ta save him!" What is Nigel's reply?

5) Liz thanks Cato for his sacrifice. He answers Liz with four words. What are they?

6) Finish Cato's statement: "What a pity . . ."

7) What does Cato do with all his remaining strength? For whom?

8) Finish Nigel's statement: "The price of being immortal is . . ."

9) ***Fill in the blanks from page 604:***

"Extraordinary. While _________________ was dying on the _____________________ of the church, _______________________ was 'dying' on the ___________________ of the church." "__________ ___________" has also been dying on the _____________ from the weight of a ______________ ___________________. . ." "Yet the ____________ of the Revolution threw off his own chains of _______________ to exclaim Cato's words and rally a _ _________________ to ___________________,"

10) ***Fill in the blanks from page 605:***

"Aye. Amazin' wha' this _____________________ finally led ta." "Jest _____________ little words." "Give me _______________ or give me _______________," "I do believe the ________ ____________ of those ________________ little _____________ will forever _____________ ______ through the air of ____________________." "*Oui,*"__________ _________________ _________________."

Fledgling

Chapter 68: On Eagle's Wings

1) How is Nigel traveling as they rush to Cato? What does Nigel shout into Max's ear?

2) Max suggests looking for Cato in the sky. Where does Nigel say they should look to find him instead? Liz spots Cato. Describe his location and how he is positioned. Cato tries to ask Liz something. How does she answer him?

3) Max says, "We've got ta save him!" What is Nigel's reply? What does Cato ask next?

4) Liz thanks Cato for his sacrifice. Write his answer. Finish this statement: "What a pity . . ."

5) What is Cato's last action? What are his last words?

6) What does Clarie ask when she walks up? What is Max's concern about Liz? Nigel sums up the price of being immortal. What does he say?

7) What does Liz say as she hears Clarie, Max, and Nigel approach?

8) Have Patrick's resolutions passed? What is the vote? Write out Isaiah 40:31.

9) ***Fill in the blanks from page 604:***

"Extraordinary. While ___________ was dying on the _______________ of the church, ______ ______ was 'dying' on the ________ of the church." "_____ ____________" has also been dying on the ______ from the weight of a _______ ____________. . ." "Yet the _______ of the Revolution threw off his own chains of ________________ to exclaim Cato's words and rally a _ ____________ to _______________________."

10) ***Fill in the blanks from page 605:***

"Aye. Amazin' wha' this ________________ finally led ta." "Jest _____________ little words." "Give me __________ or give me _________." "I do believe the ____________________ of those ______________ little ______________ will forever ________ through the air of _________ ____________." "*Oui,*"___________ __________________ _________________."

Chapter 68: On Eagle's Wings

1) How is Nigel traveling as they rush to Cato? What does Nigel shout into Max's ear?

2) Max suggests looking for Cato in the sky. Where does Nigel say they should look to find him instead? Liz spots Cato. Describe his location and how he is positioned. Cato tries to ask Liz something. How does she answer him?

3) Max says, "We've got ta save him!" What is Nigel's reply? What does Cato ask next?

4) Liz thanks Cato for his sacrifice. Write his answer. Finish the statement: "What a pity ..."

5) What are Cato's last action and his last words?

6) What does Clarie ask when she walks up? What is Max's concern about Liz? Nigel sums up the price of being immortal. What does he say? How would you feel about this part of being "immortal?"

7) What does Liz say as she hears Clarie, Max, and Nigel approach?

8) Have Patrick's resolutions passed? What is the vote? Write out Isaiah 40:31.

9) ***Fill in the blanks from page 604:***

"Extraordinary. While ___________ was dying on the _______________ of the church, ______ ______ was 'dying' on the ________ of the church." "____ ___________" has also been dying on the ______ from the weight of a _______ _____________ . . ." "Yet the ____________ of the Revolution threw off his own chains of ________________ to exclaim Cato's words and rally a _ ____________ to _____________________."

10) ***Fill in the blanks from page 605:***

"Aye. Amazin' wha' this ________________ finally led ta." "Jest ______________ little words." "Give me __________ or give me ________." "I do believe the _____________________ of those ______________ little ______________ will forever _______ through the air of _________ ____________." "*Oui,*" "__________ ___________________ ___________________."

Nigel's Nuggets

Chapter 68: On Eagle's Wings

Despair not the tragic. Cato soars with the angels. It has been my honor to complete this mission with you. I trust you have fully filled in your Fiddle's Riddle Poster. Jolly good job on that!

In honor of Cato, your Nigel's Nuggets Challenge for this last chapter of the VRK Study Guide involves all your "Soaring" Cato Index cards upon which you have summarized each chapter in one word, phrase, or sentence. You have put in the work, now for the fun. As you know, brevity is the soul of wit. Keeping this *maxim* in mind, compose a synopsis of Jenny L. Cote's *The Voice, The Revolution and The Key*. Next you shall perform your compilation. It must clock in at three minutes or less! Do not forget the wit. You must be absolutely hilarious whilst maintaining decorum and respect at all times. Do send a copy of your *magnum opus* to Jenny L. Cote: jenny@epicorderoftheseven.com

Continue to be on the lookout for a thrilling announcement on the website in March. This is Nigel P. Monaco, for the entire Epic Order of the Seven, and friends, signing off.

Keep soaring with the Eagles!

Cato's Eagle-Eye View

Chapter 68: On Eagle's Wings

Gliding: Summarize the chapter in three to five sentences, written or orally.

Soaring: Summarize the chapter in one word, phrase, or sentence and write it on an index card with the chapter number and title written on the other side.

Soaring Flashcard Game: Shuffle all your Soaring flashcards. Player 1 reads the number and/or title of a chapter on one side of a flashcard. Player 2 answers with the Soaring Summarization on the other side of the flashcard. Reshuffle your flashcards, switch players if desired, and play three times.

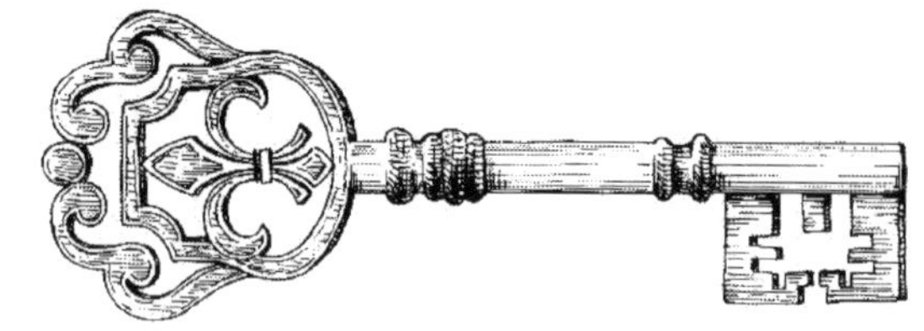

ANSWER KEY

ANSWER KEY

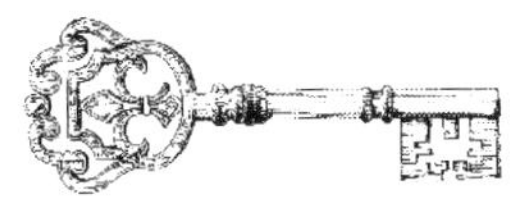

Getting Started

QUESTION	PAGE NUMBER	ANSWER
1	Internet Search	EAGLET: From the time an eagle hatches until it leaves the nest, at about 10 to 12 weeks FLEDGLING: From the time an eagle has gotten enough feathers to fly, and it is large enough to begin hunting for prey, until the time it is able to be totally independent, at about 120 days EAGLE: From the time an eagle reaches full maturity and is able is able to reproduce, about 4 or 5 years of age
2	Table of Contents Internet Search	140, 70 Chapter Guides, and 70 Nigel's Nuggets Approximately 7,000
3	Internet Search	No. It is illegal to possess an Eagle Feather in the United States.

PAGE NUMBER	CHARACTER NAME	ANSWER
xxv–xxvi	Gillamon	D
xxv–xxvi	Max	F
xxv–xxvi	Al	A
xxv–xxvi	Liz	G
xxv–xxvi	Kate	B
xxv–xxvi	Nigel	C
xxv–xxvi	Clarie	E

ANSWER KEY

Prologue: Jewels in Her Crown

EAGLET:

QUESTION	PAGE NUMBER	ANSWER
1	p. xxvii	New York City
2	p. xxvii	1944
3	Internet Search	World War II
4	p. xxix	Patrick Henry
5	Internet Search	Revolutionary War
6	p. xxix	Voice: Patrick Henry Sword: George Washington Pen: Thomas Jefferson
7	p. xxxi	"Give me liberty or give me death."
8	pp. xxvii, xxix	The Statue of Liberty
9	p. xxviii	St. Patrick's Day
10	p. xxviii	Hot dogs, pretzels, and cotton candy

FLEDGLING:

QUESTION	PAGE NUMBER
1	p. xxvii
2	p. xxix
3	p. xxxi
4	Internet Search
5	Personal Opinion
6	p. xix
7	p. xxviii
8	pp. xxvii, xxix
9	p. xxviii
10	pp. xxvii, xxviii

EAGLE:

QUESTION	PAGE NUMBER
1	p. xxvii; xxviii
2	VRK book cover; p. xxix
3	p. xxvii; xxviii; xxv
4	Personal Opinion
5	p. xxxi; xxix
6	p. xxvii; xxx; xxi
7	p. xxxi
8	p. xxxi; xxxii
9	p. xxxi
10	p. 607

ANSWER KEY

Chapter 1: Down to the Letter

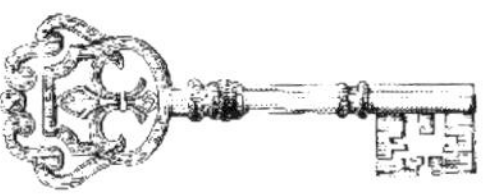

EAGLET:

QUESTION	PAGE NUMBER	ANSWER
1	p. 3	London, England; March 23, 1743
2	p. 3	Handel's *Messiah*
3	p. 3	Sharp White Cheddar
4	p. 3	He stood
5	p. 5	The unseen realm of how the Maker observed time—past, present, and future—all happening at once
6	pp. 8–9	Patrick Henry, Liz
7	p. 8	Al, King George III
8	p. 9	Benjamin Franklin
9	pp. 11–12	George Washington
10	pp. 6, 12	David Henry

FLEDGLING:

QUESTION	PAGE NUMBER
1	p. 3
2	p. 5
3	pp. 8, 12
4	pp. 6, 12
5	pp. 12–13 John, Chapter 1 (The Bible)
6	p. 11
7	p. 12
8	Research
9	p. 12
10	p. 13

EAGLE:

QUESTION	PAGE NUMBER
1	p. 3
2	pp. 4, 6
3	p. 5
4	pp. 8, 12; Prologue
5	pp. 6, 12
6	pp. 12, 13
7	pp. 12, 13
8	pp. 11, 12; Research
9	p. 13
10	p. 13

ANSWER KEY

Chapter 2: Conquering Scots and Rising Tides

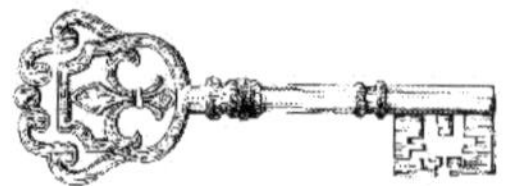

EAGLET:

QUESTION	PAGE NUMBER	ANSWER
1	p. 14	Off the Virginia coast; 1743
2	pp. 14, 16	Max, Liz, Nigel, Clarie; 8 weeks
3	p. 15	Aberdeen, Scotland; French, Scottish, and English
4	p. 15	"A good name is more to be desired than great wealth, Favor is better than silver or gold."
5	p. 16	A courier
6	p. 16	Hanover; "Studley"
7	p. 16, 17	Three
8	pp. 17	John; Colonel of the Hanover Militia; Vestryman for St. Paul's Parish
9	p. 17	Middle
10	p. 18	David Henry's letter

FLEDGLING:

QUESTION	ANSWER
1	p. 14
2	p. 15
3	p. 17
4	p. 15; Proverbs 22 (The Bible)
5	pp. 16, 18
6	p. 16
7	pp. 16, 17
8	pp. 17, 18
9	pp. 18 –19
10	pp. 18, 19

EAGLE:

QUESTION	ANSWER
1	p. 14; Prologue
2	p. 15
3	p. 15
4	p. 15
5	pp. 16, 17
6	pp. 17–18
7	pp. 17–18
8	pp. 18–19
9	pp. 19–20
10	p. 18, 19

ANSWER KEY

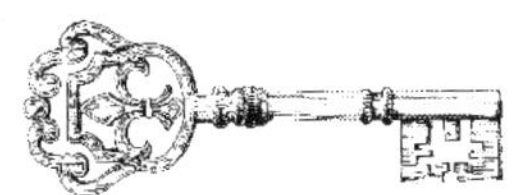

Chapter 3: Forest-Born Demosthenes

EAGLET:

QUESTION	PAGE NUMBER	ANSWER
1	p. 21	Hanover County, Virginia; May 29, 1743
2	Map of Virginia	Richmond
3	p. 21	To go fishing
4	p. 22	Birds
5	p. 22	Max, Liz, and Nigel
6	p. 23	Liz
7	p. 23	A Chickadee; reader's choice starting p. 23
8	p. 25	Max
9	pp. 25–26	A catfish
10	p. 26	Take them home

FLEDGLING:

QUESTION	PAGE NUMBER
1	pp. 21, 26
2	p. 21
3	Map of Virginia
4	p. 22
5	p. 21, 22, 23, 25
6	pp. 25, 26
7	pp. 22, 24
8	p 22; VRK book cover
9	pp. 23, 25
10	p. 26

EAGLE:

QUESTION	PAGE NUMBER
1	pp. 21, 26; Map of Virginia
2	p. 21
3	p. 22
4	pp. 21, 25
5	pp. 22, 23, 25–26
6	p. 23 and Research
7	p. 22
8	p. 22; VRK book cover
9	p. 26
10	p. 26

ANSWER KEY

Chapter 4: Settled at Studley

EAGLET:

QUESTION	PAGE NUMBER	ANSWER
1	p. 27	Black Locust Tree
2	pp. 27, 29	Jane, Anne, Sarah, Susannah
3	p. 27	Uncle Patrick Henry
4	p. 29	The barn
5	p. 29	Dried beef and fish
6	p. 29	John Syme, Jr. and William
7	p. 30	Pat
8	p. 30	A small panther
9	p. 30	Clarie as a courier
10	p. 31	Maximillian and Elizabeth; Max and Liz

FLEDGLING:

QUESTION	PAGE NUMBER
1	p. 27
2	p. 27-28
3	pp. 27, 29
4	pp. 27
5	pp. 29
6	p. 30
7	p. 31
8	pp. 30, 31
9	p. 32
10	p. 28

EAGLE:

QUESTION	PAGE NUMBER
1	p. 27
2	p. 27; Research
3	Research
4	pp. 27, 28, 29
5	p. 27
6	p. 29
7	p. 30
8	p. 31
9	pp. 30, 31
10	pp. 28, 32

ANSWER KEY

Chapter 5: Great Awakenings

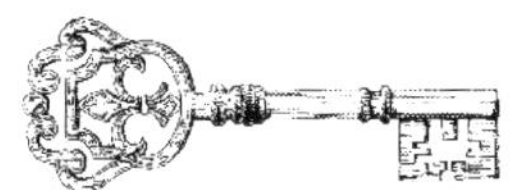

EAGLET:

QUESTION	PAGE NUMBER	ANSWER
1	p. 33	His uncle; Patrick Henry; Pastor of St. Paul's Parish
2	p. 34	Virginia, 1607
3	p. 34	Pilgrims
4	p. 35	Dissenters; Methodist, Baptist, Lutheran, Presbyterian, and Quaker
5	p. 36	Samuel Davies
6	p. 37	Anglican and Presbyterian
7	p. 39	Rise up and change history
8	p. 40	A musket
9	p. 608	Rome
10	p. 42	May 29th

FLEDGLING:

QUESTION	ANSWER
1	pp. 33, 42
2	pp. 34, 35
3	p. 34
4	p. 35
5	pp. 33, 35, 36
6	p. 37
7	p. 37
8	p. 35
9	p. 39
10	pp. 40, 608

EAGLE:

QUESTION	PAGE NUMBER
1	pp. 33, 40, 42, 608
2	pp. 34, 35
3	Research
4	p. 35
5	p. 36
6	pp. 35, 37
7	p. 38 and Research
8	pp. 38, 39
9	p. 40
10	p. 41

ANSWER KEY

Chapter 6: Back in St. Andrew's Day

EAGLET:

QUESTION	PAGE NUMBER	ANSWER
1	p. 43	Gillamon and Clarie
2	p. 43	A mountain goat and a lamb
3	p. 43	John the Baptist and two of his followers
4	pp. 43, 44	Jesus; "Behold the Lamb of God!"
5	pp. 44, 44–46	Andrew and John; Jesus; Simon and James
6	p. 47	Loaves and fishes; yes; fish
7	p. 48	An X-shaped Cross
8	p. 48	Robert the Bruce; Max; a St. Andrew's Cross
9	p. 49	They fish and follow Jesus; nothing escapes their attention
10	p. 49	Walking down the streets of Hanover, Virginia

FLEDGLING:

QUESTION	PAGE NUMBER
1	p. 43
2	pp. 43, 44
3	p. 44
4	p. 45
5	pp. 45–46
6	p. 46
7	p. 47
8	p. 48
9	p. 49
10	p. 49

EAGLE:

QUESTION	PAGE NUMBER
1	p. 43
2	pp. 43, 44
3	Research
4	Bible Research
5	pp. 45-46
6	pp. 46-48
7	Bible Research
8	Bible Research; pp. 48, 49
9	p. 49
10	p. 49

ANSWER KEY

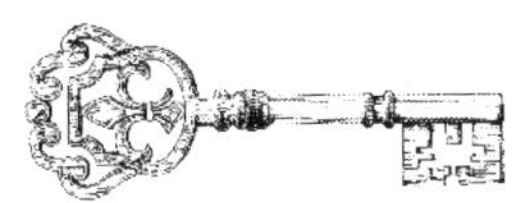

Chapter 7: Magical Meetings

Part 1

EAGLET:

QUESTION	PAGE NUMBER	ANSWER
1	p. 50	Any three of the following: savory chicken, sides of beef, ham biscuits, cheese wafers, corn pudding, three-bean relish, melon balls, spoon bread, curried shrimp, oyster fritters, plum pudding, roasted artichokes, brandied peaches, ploughman's pastry pies, sweet potato muffins, Sally Lunn bread, almond macaroons, cranberry-orange bread, lemon tartlets, gingerbread, apple pies, pumpkin pies, and cherry pies
2	p. 50	Any three of the following: cider, ale, rum punch, and wassail
3	p. 50	Reader's opinion
4	p. 51	A maple walking stick with a carved mountain goat as a handle
5	p. 52	Young ladies can meet husbands at the St. Andrew's Day festival
6	p. 52	Any two of the following: races for gingerbread cakes, a horse race for a hunting saddle, boxing for a fine hat, wrestling for silver-buckled shoes, dancing for a handsome pair of shoes, a pair of silk stockings for the prettiest maiden, fiddling for a fiddle
7	p. 53	Nigel's violin
8	p. 53	Into his hat
9	p. 54	Patrick, William, John Syme, Jr.
10	p. 55	Samuel Meredith

ANSWER KEY

Chapter 7: Magical Meetings

Part 2

FLEDGLING:

QUESTION	ANSWER
1	p. 50
2	p. 50; Bible Research
3	p. 51
4	p. 52
5	p. 52
6	p. 53
7	p. 53
8	p. 54
9	p. 54
10	p. 55

EAGLE:

QUESTION	ANSWER
1	p. 50; Bible Research
2	p. 51
3	p. 52
4	p. 52
5	p. 53
6	p. 53
7	p. 54
8	p. 55
9	p. 55
10	p. 55

ANSWER KEY

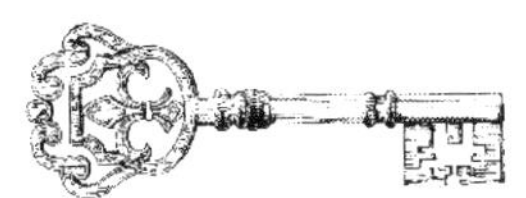

Chapter 8: Life Lessons and Fiery Fiddling

EAGLET:

QUESTION	PAGE NUMBER	ANSWER
1	p. 56	With Jane and the others
2	p. 56	His hat
3	p. 57	Sarah Shelton; Sallie
4	p. 57	Jimmy; he is poor
5	p. 58	He gets shoved to the ground
6	p. 58	He could share the food with his family
7	p. 58	Enoch; he cheated
8	p. 59	A daisy chain necklace
9	p. 59	Uncle Langloo; gives it to Patrick
10	p. 62	A fiddle to woo a lass; a gun to provide for her and protect her with

FLEDGLING:

QUESTION	PAGE NUMBER
1	pp. 56–57
2	p. 57
3	p. 58
4	pp. 58–59
5	p. 59
6	pp. 59–60
7	p. 60
8	p. 61
9	pp. 61, 62
10	p. 62

EAGLE:

QUESTION	PAGE NUMBER
1	pp. 56-57
2	p. 57
3	p. 58
4	p. 58, 59
5	p. 59
6	p. 59, 60
7	p. 60
8	pp. 61-62
9	p. 62
10	p. 63

ANSWER KEY

Chapter 9: Fiddle a Riddle

EAGLET:

QUESTION	PAGE NUMBER	ANSWER
1	p. 64	Sitting on a stool by the hearth
2	p. 64	The type of music played
3	p. 65	A pineapple
4	p. 65	He flies
5	p. 66	The notes Liz played
6	p. 66	The bow
7	pp. 67–69	Various answers from the list beginning on p. 67
8	pp. 69–70	Various answers from the list on pp. 69–70
9	p. 71	With all thy soul love God above, And as thyself thy neighbor love
10	p. 73	Training time with Uncle Langloo

FLEDGLING:

QUESTION	PAGE NUMBER
1	p. 64
2	p. 65
3	p. 66
4	pp. 67–68
5	p. 68
6	p. 69
7	pp. 69, 70
8	p. 72
9	pp. 67, 73
10	pp. 72, 73

EAGLE:

QUESTION	PAGE NUMBER
1	p. 64
2	pp. 65, 66
3	p. 67–68
4	p. 68, 69
5	p. 69, 70
6	p. 71
7	pp. 69–70 for a pattern, Bible verses and original work
8	p. 72
9	p. 72
10	pp. 67, 72, 73

ANSWER KEY

Chapter 10: A Voice in the Wilderness

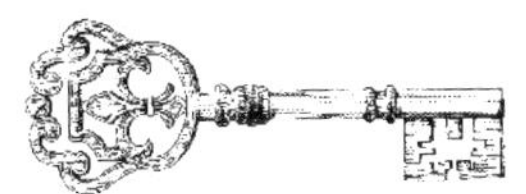

EAGLET:

QUESTION	PAGE NUMBER	ANSWER
1	p. 74	Always keep your powder dry and your gun loaded and at the ready at night.
2	p. 75	A predator was nearby.
3	p. 75	Sharp and pointed
4	p. 76	Claw marks
5	p. 76	A cat
6	p. 77	He is working for the Maker.
7	p. 78	A snake
8	p. 79	A red cloak
9	p. 82	One
10	p. 82	Sometimes it's not just what you say but how you say it.

FLEDGLING:

QUESTION	PAGE NUMBER
1	p. 75
2	pp. 75–76
3	p. 76
4	pp. 76–77
5	pp. 77–78
6	p. 79
7	pp. 80–81
8	p. 81
9	pp. 81–82
10	p. 82

EAGLE:

QUESTION	PAGE NUMBER
1	pp. 74–75
2	pp. 75–76
3	p. 76, Research
4	pp. 76–77; Research
5	p. 77
6	p. 77
7	p. 77; Research and opinion
8	p. 80–81
9	p. 81–82
10	p. 83

ANSWER KEY

Chapter 11: Plutarch's Nine Lives

EAGLET:

QUESTION	PAGE NUMBER	ANSWER
1	p. 85	Cato the Younger
2	p. 86	Liberty or death
3	p. 86	"Nike" or "Winged Victory"
4	p. 87	Biographies
5	p. 87	"A man's true character was revealed in his private life rather than his public deeds."
6	pp. 87–88	Her wing
7	p. 88	Cato
8	p. 88	Justice and honesty
9	p. 89	A pair of eyes peering in the window to study her and Plutarch
10	p. 90	Volume 1 is there; Volume 2 is missing

FLEDGLING:

QUESTION	PAGE NUMBER
1	p. 85
2	p. 85
3	p. 86
4	p. 86
5	p. 87
6	p. 87
7	p. 87
8	p. 88
9	p. 89
10	p. 90

EAGLE:

QUESTION	PAGE NUMBER
1	p. 85
2	p. 85
3	p. 86
4	p. 86
5	p. 87
6	p. 87
7	p. 87; Research
8	p. 88
9	p. 89; Opinion
10	p. 90

ANSWER KEY

Chapter 12: A Tragedy in London

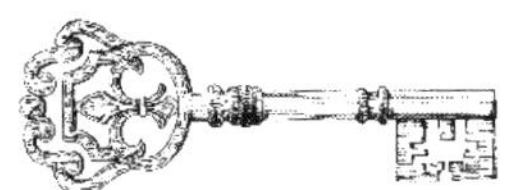

EAGLET:

QUESTION	PAGE NUMBER	ANSWER
1	p. 91	London; May 30, 1745; along the banks of the Thames
2	p. 91	Londinium; the center of power for the entire world
3	p. 92	Prince Frederick, Princess Augusta, and their many children including their oldest son, George
4	p. 92	He is being chased by a Corgi (dog)
5	p. 92	Molly
6	p. 93	*"I am His Highness' dog at Kew, Pray tell me, whose dog are you?"*
7	p. 93	There is a special play Gillamon wants her to see that night.
8	p. 94-95	She wants to find a book for Patrick; *Plutarch's Lives,* Volume 2; yes, she finds it.
9	p. 97	*Cato*
10	p. 101	"It will have something to do with 'liberty or death.'"

FLEDGLING:

QUESTION	PAGE NUMBER
1	p. 91
2	pp. 91–92
3	pp. 92–93; AWORD FROM THE AUTHOR
4	pp. 93–95
5	p. 96
6	pp. 97–98
7	p. 99
8	p. 100
9	p. 100
10	p. 101

EAGLE:

QUESTION	PAGE NUMBER
1	p. 91
2	pp. 91–92
3	pp. 92–93, A WORD FROM THE AUTHOR
4	pp. 93–95
5	p. 96
6	pp. 97–98
7	p. 99, Opinion
8	p. 100; Opinion
9	p. 100
10	p. 101

ANSWER KEY

Chapter 13: Another Cato: Another Tragedy

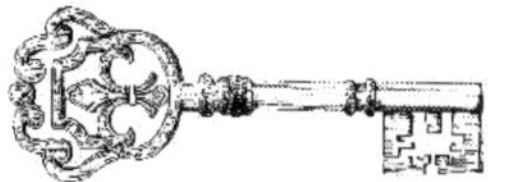

EAGLET:

QUESTION	PAGE NUMBER	ANSWER
1	p. 102	Because they were going to make a side trip
2	p. 103	1687
3	p. 103	To the Tower of London; William the Conqueror; after he invaded England
4	p. 104	Menagerie
5	p. 104	To free one creature
6	p. 105	A baby bald eagle; back to Virginia with Liz
7	p. 105	Clarie, driving the coach; the livery of a gentleman's coachman
8	p. 105	Back to Virginia, Gillamon
9	p. 107	A cat, Kakia
10	p. 108	A baby eagle, Cato

FLEDGLING:

QUESTION	PAGE NUMBER
1	p. 102
2	p. 103
3	p. 103
4	A WORD FROM THE AUTHOR
5	p. 104
6	p. 105
7	p. 105
8	p. 106
9	pp. 106–7
10	p. 108

EAGLE:

QUESTION	PAGE NUMBER
1	p. 102–3
2	p. 103
3	p. 104; A WORD FROM THE AUTHOR
4	p. 104
5	p. 105
6	p. 105
7	p. 106
8	pp. 106–7
9	p. 108
10	p. 108

ANSWER KEY

Chapter 14: Willing to Soar

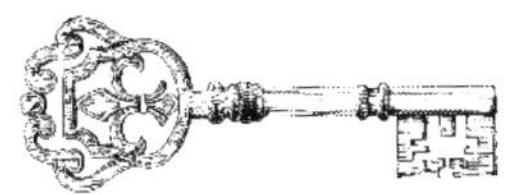

EAGLET:

QUESTION	PAGE NUMBER	ANSWER
1	p. 109	Two months old; he must learn to catch fish and to fly.
2	p. 110	Totopotomoy Creek in his woods
3	p. 110	He might have fallen out of his nest.
4	p. 111	By himself
5	p. 111	Check on him every day and help feed him some fish.
6	p. 112	A fish; yes
7	p. 112	Take care of Cato
8	p. 113	Earning an eagle feather; by doing something brave
9	p. 115	On a bald eagle; yes
10	p. 116	Yes

FLEDGLING:

QUESTION	PAGE NUMBER
1	p. 109-110
2	p. 110
3	p. 111
4	p. 111
5	p. 112
6	p. 112
7	p. 114
8	p. 115
9	p. 116
10	p. 116

EAGLE:

QUESTION	PAGE NUMBER
1	p. 109-110
2	p. 110
3	p. 111
4	p. 111-112
5	p. 112
6	p. 112
7	p. 114
8	p. 115
9	p. 116
10	p. 116

ANSWER KEY

Chapter 15: Teaching Cato

EAGLET:

QUESTION	PAGE NUMBER	ANSWER
1	p. 117	Mentally, from the ground
2	p. 117	"Like an eagle that stirs up its nest, that hovers over its young, He spread His wings and caught them, He carried them on His pinions.
3	p. 118	He will catch you when you fall.
4	p. 118	Cato could start out on some low branches.
5	p. 120	No
6	p. 121	Yes
7	p. 121	Mr. Gillamon's
8	p. 123	Max
9	p. 123	*"If I'm going to learn to fly, I have to learn to trust."*
10	p. 125	*"GET UP! TRY AGAIN!"*

FLEDGLING:

QUESTION	PAGE NUMBER
1	p. 117
2	p. 117
3	p. 118
4	pp. 118–19
5	p. 120
6	p. 121
7	p. 121
8	p. 123
9	p. 123
10	p. 125

EAGLE:

QUESTION	PAGE NUMBER
1	p. 117
2	p. 117
3	p. 118
4	pp. 118–19
5	p. 120
6	p. 121
7	pp. 121–22
8	p. 123
9	pp. 123–24
10	p. 124-125

ANSWER KEY

Chapter 16: Cato Teaching

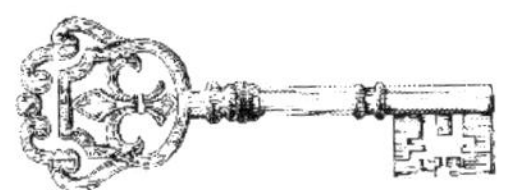

EAGLET:

QUESTION	PAGE NUMBER	ANSWER
1	p. 126	Frogs; outside playing with the frogs
2	p. 126	Help him figure out the future
3	p. 127	His tree of *libertas*
4	p. 127	"what we've had ta struggle with and then conquered"
5	p. 128	The account of Cato in *Plutarch's Lives*
6	p. 129	"and rise above his circumstances"
7	p. 129	Panther tracks
8	p. 130	Lifted off the ground and soared
9	p. 131	From the beginning
10	p. 132	Moral and political doctrine

FLEDGLING:

QUESTION	PAGE NUMBER
1	p. 126
2	p. 127
3	p. 128
4	p. 128
5	pp. 128–29
6	p. 129
7	p. 130
8	p. 130
9	p. 131
10	p. 132

EAGLE:

QUESTION	PAGE NUMBER
1	p. 126
2	p. 127
3	p. 128
4	p. 128
5	pp. 128–29
6	pp. 129–30
7	p. 130
8	p. 130
9	p. 131
10	p. 132

ANSWER KEY

Chapter 17: Peace, Peace, When There Is No Peace

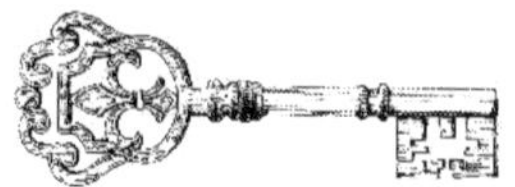

EAGLET:

QUESTION	PAGE NUMBER	ANSWER
1	p. 135	George Whitefield
2	pp. 135, 136	He started preaching in parks and fields, and on his own.
3	p. 136	Playing his fiddle
4	p. 609	Yes
5	p. 136	Jeremiah 6:14 "They have heeded also the hurt of the daughter of my people saying, 'Peace, peace when there is no peace.'"
6	p. 138	"Peace, peace, but there is no peace."
7	p. 138	Max and Kate; The Babylonians were coming.
8	p. 139	"They're daft ta be fightin'!"
9	p. 140	"A voice in the present wakes eternity *en masse*."
10	p. 141	Samuel Davies; he will impact Patrick's voice more than any other.

FLEDGLING:

QUESTION	PAGE NUMBER
1	pp. 135–36, 608
2	p. 136
3	pp. 136–37
4	p. 137
5	pp. 137–38
6	p. 138
7	p. 139
8	p. 140
9	p. 141
10	p. 141

EAGLE:

QUESTION	PAGE NUMBER
1	pp. 135–36, 608
2	p. 136
3	pp. 136–37
4	p. 137; Opinion
5	pp. 137–38; Opinion
6	p. 138
7	p. 139
8	p. 140
9	p. 141; Opinion
10	p. 141; Opinion

ANSWER KEY

Chapter 18: A Voice in the Present

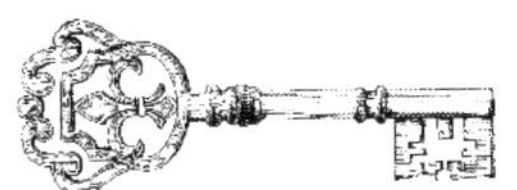

EAGLET:

QUESTION	PAGE NUMBER	ANSWER
1	p. 142	20 shillings; no jail time
2	p. 143	A license to preach; Polegreen Meeting House
3	p. 144	400
4	p. 145	Elizabeth Strong
5	p. 146	On a pigeon
6	p. 146	Psalm 97
7	p. 149	"Patrick has one of the most amazing memories I have ever seen."
8	p. 149	Samuel Davies; no
9	p. 151	Jeremiah 29:11
10	p. 152	"Jesus preached outside."

FLEDGLING:

QUESTION	PAGE NUMBER
1	p. 142
2	p. 143
3	p. 144
4	p. 145
5	p. 146
6	pp. 147–48
7	p. 149
8	p. 149
9	pp. 150–51
10	pp. 151–52

EAGLE:

QUESTION	PAGE NUMBER
1	p. 142
2	p. 143
3	p. 144
4	p. 145
5	p. 146
6	pp. 147–48
7	p. 149
8	p. 149, Opinion
9	pp. 150–51
10	pp. 151–52, Opinion

ANSWER KEY

Chapter 19: High and Mighty

EAGLET:

QUESTION	PAGE NUMBER	ANSWER
1	p. 153	1748; 12 years old; fall
2	p. 153	Jane, Sallie and Elizabeth, William and Samuel Meredith
3	p. 154	Edelweiss
4	p. 154	No
5	p. 155	Head to Cato's tree to climb it and get an eagle feather.
6	p. 155	A panther
7	p. 156	Climb down the tree
8	p. 157	"I think it's . . . broken."
9	p. 157	"That big cat wasn't jest sittin' there. It were *waitin'* for Patr-r-rick."
10	p. 158	He has broken his collarbone.

FLEDGLING:

QUESTION	PAGE NUMBER
1	p. 153
2	p. 154
3	p. 154
4	p. 155
5	p. 155
6	p. 156
7	p. 157
8	p. 157
9	p. 157
10	p. 158

EAGLE:

QUESTION	PAGE NUMBER
1	p. 153; Personal knowledge or research
2	p. 154; Opinion
3	p. 154; Opinion
4	p. 155
5	p. 155
6	p. 156
7	p. 157
8	p. 157
9	p. 157
10	p. 158

ANSWER KEY

Chapter 20: Honey to the Bones

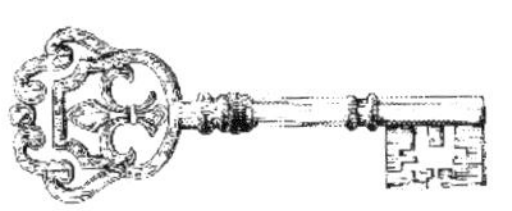

EAGLET:

QUESTION	PAGE NUMBER	ANSWER
1	p. 159	Max
2	p. 160	Max
3	p. 161	Samuel Davies
4	p. 161	It was poisoned.
5	p. 162	"She hasn't left my side since I got hurt."
6	p. 163	He was showing off.
7	p. 164	Pleasant words
8	p. 165	To God
9	p. 165	The Great Awakening
10	p. 166	A flute

FLEDGLING:

QUESTION	PAGE NUMBER
1	p. 159
2	pp. 160–61
3	p. 161
4	pp. 163–64
5	p. 164
6	p. 164
7	pp. 164–65
8	p. 165
9	p. 166
10	p. 166

EAGLE:

QUESTION	PAGE NUMBER
1	p. 159
2	pp. 160–61
3	p. 161; Reasoning
4	pp. 163–64
5	p. 164
6	p. 164
7	pp. 164–65
8	p. 165
9	p. 166
10	pp. 166–67

ANSWER KEY

Chapter 21: God's Riddle

EAGLET:

QUESTION	PAGE NUMBER	ANSWER
1	p. 168	Philadelphia, Pennsylvania; Christ Church; April 27, 1749
2	p. 168	Benjamin Franklin; 43; no
3	p. 168	*Pilgrim's Progress; Plutarch's Parallel Lives*
4	p. 169	His brother, James; write; no; he wrote fourteen letters posing as an old, widowed woman named "Silence Dogood."
5	p. 169	David Henry; Samuel Palmer
6	p. 169	1729 *Pennsylvania Gazette*; 1732 *Poor Richard's Almanack*
7	p. 169	David Henry's cousin, Patrick Henry
8	p. 171	Job 38; Gillamon
9	p. 172	"Can you make lightning appear and cause it to strike as you direct?"
10	p. 173	Steeples

FLEDGLING:

QUESTION	PAGE NUMBER
1	p. 168
2	pp. 168–69
3	p. 169
4	p. 170
5	p. 170
6	p. 171
7	Researching the story of the book of Job
8	p. 171
9	p. 172
10	pp. 172–73

EAGLE:

QUESTION	PAGE NUMBER
1	p. 168
2	pp. 168–69
3	p. 169
4	p. 170
5	p. 170
6	p. 171
7	Researching the story of the book of Job
8	p. 171; research
9	p. 172; *Wikipedia* "Message in a Bottle"
10	pp. 172–73

ANSWER KEY

Chapter 22: A Brilliant Move

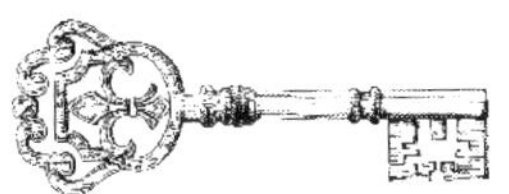

EAGLET:

QUESTION	PAGE NUMBER	ANSWER
1	p. 175	As a butterfly; John Syme, Jr. is of age, Studley is his; they will move twenty miles away to their new home.
2	p. 175	Max and Liz are immortal; leave; George Washington
3	p. 176	He will be preaching at Ground Squirrel Meeting House; three miles from the Henrys' new home; he will be on assignment with Benjamin Franklin in Philadelphia; Cato
4	p. 178	Mount Brilliant
5	p. 179	200 miles; two days
6	p. 179	A year, possibly more; settle into a new nest outside town
7	p. 181	Electrify a turkey for a barbeque
8	p. 182	Patrick Henry's cousins
9	p. 183	*Accidentally* tips the canoe; Patrick ends up in dry clothes while George and Charles are left sopping wet.
10	p. 185	"*This* is a declaration of independence."

FLEDGLING:

QUESTION	PAGE NUMBER
1	pp. 174–75
2	pp. 175–76
3	pp. 176–77
4	p. 178
5	p. 179
6	p. 180
7	pp. 180–81
8	p. 182
9	p. 183
10	pp. 184–85

EAGLE:

QUESTION	PAGE NUMBER
1	pp. 174–75
2	pp. 175–76
3	pp. 176–77
4	p. 178
5	p. 179
6	p. 180
7	pp. 180–81
8	p. 182
9	p. 183; Imagination
10	pp. 184–85

ANSWER KEY

Chapter 23: Keys to the Future

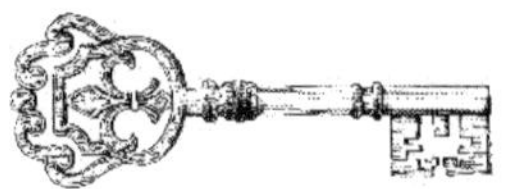

EAGLET:

QUESTION	PAGE NUMBER	ANSWER
1	p. 186	If ever there were a human version of Nigel, it would be Benjamin Franklin.
2	p. 187	As a blue butterfly
3	p. 187	His idea of putting a tall metal rod atop a tower or steeple to actually draw the electrical charge from a cloud
4	p. 187	A voice bold enough to say what others are thinking but are too afraid to speak
5	p. 189	Al; he crossed both pairs of his legs, and his eyes
6	p. 190	*Epic*
7	p. 190	King Louis XV of France
8	p. 191	"Let the experiment be made!"
9	p. 192	Yes
10	p. 192	It would prevent Franklin from becoming a hero in America.

FLEDGLING:

QUESTION	PAGE NUMBER
1	p. 186
2	p. 186
3	p. 187
4	p. 187
5	pp. 188–89
6	pp. 189–90
7	p. 190
8	pp. 190–91
9	p. 191
10	p. 192

EAGLE:

QUESTION	PAGE NUMBER
1	p. 186
2	p. 186
3	p. 187
4	p. 187-188
5	pp. 188–89
6	pp. 189–90
7	p. 190
8	pp. 190–91
9	p. 191
10	p. 192

ANSWER KEY

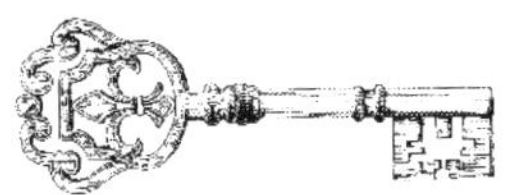

Chapter 24: The Key to our Shuccshessh

EAGLET:

QUESTION	PAGE NUMBER	ANSWER
1	p. 193	Philadelphia; June 4, 1752
2	p. 193	Locking the State House door; Pennsylvania Assemblyman; a key to the State House
3	p. 194	A green lizard; a flying squirrel
4	p. 194	Abraham Shamuel Penn; Ashpen
5	p. 195	Leonard
6	p. 195	Hide and seek with shtuff; a key
7	p. 195	In a field outside Philadelphia
8	p. 196	Land atop the roof
9	p. 196	Get inside the shed and put the Leyden jar on the floor
10	p. 197	Lightning was electricity.

FLEDGLING:

QUESTION	PAGE NUMBER
1	p. 193
2	p. 194
3	p. 195
4	p. 195
5	p. 195
6	p. 196
7	p. 196
8	p. 196
9	p. 197
10	p. 197

EAGLE:

QUESTION	PAGE NUMBER
1	p. 193
2	p. 194
3	p. 195
4	p. 195
5	p. 195
6	p. 196
7	p. 196
8	p. 196
9	p. 197
10	p. 197

ANSWER KEY

Chapter 25: The Art of Persuasion

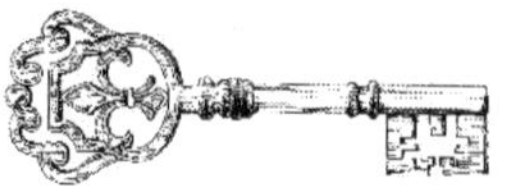

EAGLET:

QUESTION	PAGE NUMBER	ANSWER
1	p. 198	Hanover; June, 1752; sixteen
2	pp. 198–99	A small storefront; Hanover County by the Pamunkey River at the crossroads of Newcastle Rd. and Old Church Rd.; merchants
3	p. 199	Purchase items on store credit; tobacco
4	p. 199	Studley Plantation; John Syme, Jr., Samuel Davies
5	p. 200	Jack Poindexter; "If I were any bettah, I'd be you."
6	p. 201	A block of salt; a filly; "I'm always partial to girls."
7	p. 202	"It may lead to failure if he is not paid for all the goods he gives on credit."
8	p. 203	George Washington was about to lose his brother, Lawrence; Al's George just lost his father, Prince Frederick.
9	p. 204	Elizabeth Strong; fourteen; Patrick
10	p. 207	"The persuader has been persuaded into thinking it was his idea to attend the barbeque."

FLEDGLING:

QUESTION	PAGE NUMBER
1	pp. 198–99
2	p. 199
3	p. 200
4	p. 200
5	p. 201
6	pp. 201–2
7	pp. 203–4
8	p. 204
9	pp. 206–7
10	p. 207

EAGLE:

QUESTION	PAGE NUMBER
1	pp. 198–99
2	p. 199
3	p. 200
4	p. 200
5	p. 201
6	pp. 201–2
7	pp. 203–4
8	p. 204
9	pp. 206–7
10	p. 207

ANSWER KEY

Chapter 26: Puppy Love

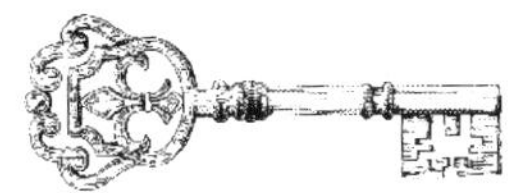

EAGLET:

QUESTION	PAGE NUMBER	ANSWER
1	p. 208	Shelton Plantation, Rural Plains, Hanover, Virginia; August, 1752; 30 years; 1609; King James I of England
2	p. 209	Warm apple pie topped with vanilla ice cream; "I'll fiddle for pie any day of the week."
3	p. 209	A puppy; Nelson
4	p. 210	He disappeared soon after Patrick left Mount Brilliant; she also disappeared.
5	p. 210	It was going to fail; another classroom and the key to open the next door on his life's journey
6	p. 211	"How to secure Houses, &c. from LIGHTNING"
7	p. 211	"A Pair of good Ears will drain dry an hundred Tongues."
8	p. 212	A beautiful brush and a looking glass; London
9	p. 213	Nelson
10	p. 213	Historical "The girl comes with the dog." "I'll gladly take both."

FLEDGLING:

QUESTION	PAGE NUMBER
1	pp. 208–9
2	p. 209
3	p. 210
4	p. 210
5	p. 211
6	p. 211
7	p. 212
8	p. 212
9	p. 213; p. 210
10	p. 213

EAGLE:

QUESTION	ANSWER
1	pp. 208–9
2	p. 209
3	p. 210
4	p. 210; Previous information
5	p. 211
6	p. 211
7	p. 212
8	p. 212
9	p. 213; p. 210
10	p. 213

ANSWER KEY

Chapter 27: Baptism by Ice

EAGLET:

QUESTION	PAGE NUMBER	ANSWER
1	p. 214	Williamsburg, Virginia; October 26, 1753; Robert Dinwiddie
2	p. 214	Augustine and Lawrence Washington
3	p. 215	Britain, France, and Spain
4	p. 216	George Washington; 21; volunteer to take the governor's letter to the French
5	p. 216	George Washington; the snow-covered land of the Ohio Valley
6	p. 218	"The French have no plans to leave the Ohio Valley." To the murdering town; he tried to run away crying, "Not alright. Not alright. Not alright."
7	p. 220	By jumping on their Indian guide and preventing him from shooting them
8	pp. 220, p. 222	A raft; Howard Beaver and his family
9	p. 224	Howard
10	p. 226	A pair of Scots

FLEDGLING:

QUESTION	PAGE NUMBER
1	p. 214
2	p. 215
3	pp. 215–16
4	p. 216
5	pp. 217–18
6	pp. 218–20
7	p. 220
8	pp. 220–22
9	pp. 222–24
10	pp. 225–26

EAGLE:

QUESTION	PAGE NUMBER
1	p. 214; Research
2	p. 215; Research
3	pp. 215–16
4	p. 216
5	pp. 217–18
6	pp. 218–20
7	p. 220
8	pp. 220–22
9	pp. 222–24
10	pp. 225–26

ANSWER KEY

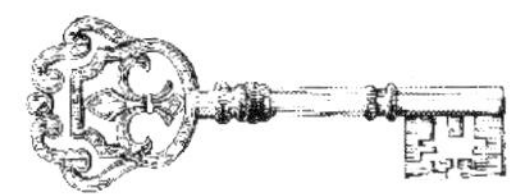

Chapter 28: Starting a War

1EAGLET:

QUESTION	PAGE NUMBER	ANSWER
1	p. 227	To take possession of the Ohio
2	p. 228	His journal
3	p. 228	Fort Necessity
4	p. 230	War
5	p. 231	Killed and scalped him; killed and scalped wounded French prisoners; "HALT! PUT DOWN YOUR WEAPONS!"; one
6	p. 232	No
7	p. 233	George Washington was made the commander of all the Virginia forces.
8	p. 234	That George Washington murdered Jumonville; start a war; The French and Indian War
9	p. 234	"JOIN, or DIE."; Georgia
10	p. 235	One government

FLEDGLING:

QUESTION	PAGE NUMBER
1	pp. 227–28
2	p. 228
3	p. 229
4	pp. 229–30
5	pp. 230–31
6	pp. 231–32
7	p. 232
8	p. 233
9	p. 234
10	p. 234–35

EAGLE:

QUESTION	PAGE NUMBER
1	pp. 227–28
2	p. 228
3	p. 229
4	pp. 229–30; Research
5	pp. 230–31
6	pp. 231–32
7	p. 232
8	p. 233
9	p. 234
10	pp. 234–35

ANSWER KEY

Chapter 29: Love and War

EAGLET:

QUESTION	PAGE NUMBER	ANSWER
1	p. 236	Harvard and Yale; a lightning rod
2	p. 237	A command with a lower rank; become a farmer
3	p. 237	A farmer
4	p. 237	That George Washington *"were poisoned with the virus."*
5	p. 238	Joseph; Egypt
6	p. 238	*Love*; Patrick is getting married to Sarah "Sallie" Shelton; eighteen and sixteen; Pine Slash Farm
7	p. 241	Uncle Patrick; Uncle Langloo; Benjamin and Samuel Crowley
8	p. 242	A half-mile down the road; he wanted to keep his girl close.
9	p. 243	"Are you going to be with us at Pine Slash?" "Oui, I plan to present myself to Patrick and Sallie there. It is time."
10	p. 244	Samuel Crowley; Elizabeth Strong

FLEDGLING:

QUESTION	PAGE NUMBER
1	pp. 236–37
2	p. 237
3	p. 238
4	p. 238; Bible research
5	p. 238; Bible research
6	p. 238; Research
7	p. 239
8	pp. 239–40; Research
9	pp. 241–42
10	pp. 243–44; Research; A WORD FROM THE AUTHOR; Opinion

EAGLE:

QUESTION	PAGE NUMBER
1	pp. 236–37
2	p. 237; Imagination
3	p. 238; Reasoning
4	p. 238; Bible research
5	p. 238; Bible research
6	p. 238; Research
7	p. 239
8	pp. 239–40; Research; Opinion
9	pp. 241–42
10	pp. 243–44; Research; A WORD FROM THE AUTHOR; Opinion

ANSWER KEY

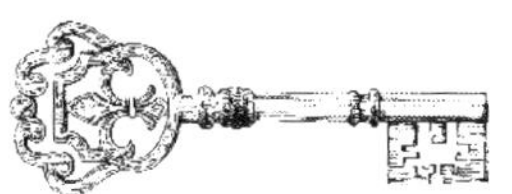

Chapter 30: Plowshares and Swords

EAGLET:

QUESTION	PAGE NUMBER	ANSWER
1	p. 245	Polegreen Meeting House; Hanover; March 5, 1755; a day of fasting and prayer
2	p. 246	The tobacco fields
3	p. 247	Rain to water it
4	p. 249	Spiritual poison
5	p. 250	A letter of suggestion; Nigel
6	p. 250	Dysentery; Fort Duquesne; ten miles; General Braddock; "all the way tomorrow"
7	p. 251	Unpaid volunteer aide-de-camp to General Braddock
8	p. 253	To sing and march right into Fort Duquesne tonight
9	p. 253	Open field formation; they used the trees for stealth and cover.
10	p. 256	"Who would have thought it!" "We shall know better how to deal with them another time." Opinion

FLEDGLING:

QUESTION	PAGE NUMBER
1	pp. 245–46
2	pp. 246–48
3	pp. 248–50
4	pp. 250–51
5	p. 251
6	pp. 251–52
7	p. 253
8	pp. 253–54; Opinion
9	pp. 254–55
10	pp. 255–56; Opinion

EAGLE:

QUESTION	PAGE NUMBER
1	pp. 245–46
2	pp. 246–48
3	pp. 248–50
4	pp. 250–51
5	p. 251; Opinion
6	pp. 251–52; Opinion
7	p. 253
8	pp. 253–54; Opinion
9	pp. 254–55
10	pp. 255–56; Opinion

ANSWER KEY

Chapter 31: Soldier On

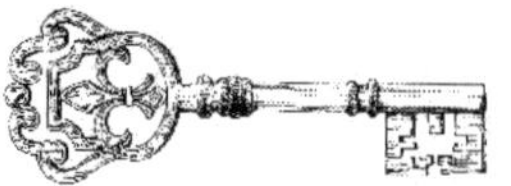

EAGLET:

QUESTION	PAGE NUMBER	ANSWER
1	p. 257	Six; hero of the Monongahela; Commander-in-Chief of all forces now raised in the defense of His Majesty's Colony; 23
2	p. 258	Two of the four concerns listed in the first paragraph of p. 258
3	p. 260	Liz; Liz
4	p. 260	Seventeen; Martha; Patsey
5	p. 261	Fifteen months; The College of New Jersey
6	p. 262	Things he could not learn any other way
7	p. 263	On his farm
8	p. 263	Their newly formed militia; Overton Plantation
9	p. 264	The colony's best recruiter
10	p. 265	*Godspeed; Soldier On*

FLEDGLING:

QUESTION	PAGE NUMBER
1	p. 257
2	p. 258
3	p. 260
4	p. 261; Bible research
5	p. 262; Bible research
6	pp. 262–263
7	pp. 263–264
8	p. 264
9	p. 264
10	pp. 264–265

EAGLE:

QUESTION	PAGE NUMBER
1	p. 257
2	p. 258-259
3	p. 260
4	p. 261; Bible Research
5	p. 262; Bible Research and analysis
6	pp. 262–263
7	pp. 263–264
8	p. 264; Dictionary research
9	p. 264
10	pp. 264–265

ANSWER KEY

Chapter 32: Fire to the Fiddle

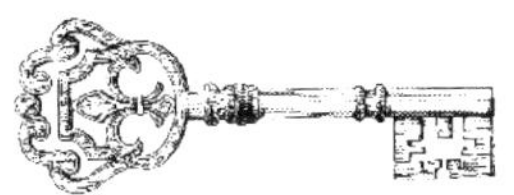

EAGLET:

QUESTION	PAGE NUMBER	ANSWER
1	p. 266	Pine Slash; April, 1757; two
2	p. 267	Flying with Cato; in the field watching Patrick and Patsey; a rat
3	p. 268	Fire at Patrick's house; swoop down to warn Liz and Patrick
4	p. 268	Yes
5	p. 268	Nelson
6	p. 268	Nelson; No; it's too dangerous
7	p. 270	Yes; yes; no
8	p. 272	Bitterness is poison.
9	p. 273	Leave Pine Slash.
10	p. 276	Hanover Tavern

FLEDGLING:

QUESTION	PAGE NUMBER
1	pp. 266–267
2	p. 267
3	p. 268
4	p. 268
5	p. 269
6	pp. 269–270; Dictionary; Bible Research
7	pp. 271–272
8	pp. 273–274
9	pp. 275
10	pp. 275–276

EAGLE:

QUESTION	PAGE NUMBER
1	pp. 266–267
2	p. 267
3	p. 268
4	p. 268; Opinion; Reasoning
5	p. 269; Opinion; Reasoning
6	pp. 269–270; Dictionary; Bible Research; Imagination
7	pp. 271–272 Reasoning; Opinion
8	pp. 273–274
9	p. 275
10	pp. 275–276

ANSWER KEY

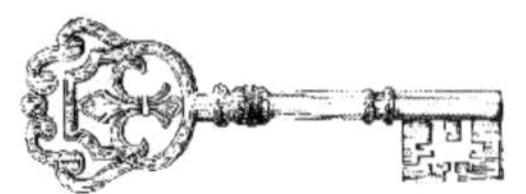

Chapter 33: The Little Marquis

EAGLET:

QUESTION	PAGE NUMBER	ANSWER
1	p. 279	The IAMISPHERE; August 1, 1759
2	p. 280	The Libertas statue
3	p. 280	Chateâu de Chavaniac; Auvergne region of Southern France
4	p. 280	September 6, 1757
5	p. 281	Gilbert or Lafayette
6	p. 281	No; he has been away at war since before Gilbert was born
7	p. 282	Drove the French out of Ohio and back to Canada; went home to Mt. Vernon and married Martha Dandridge Custis
8	pp. 282–83	Patrick Ferguson; Charles Cornwallis; William Phillips
9	p. 285	Red and curly; blue eyes and fair complexion
10	p. 286	The *Libertas* statue

FLEDGLING:

QUESTION	PAGE NUMBER
1	p. 279
2	p. 280
3	p. 280
4	p. 281
5	p. 281
6	Research
7	p. 282
8	pp. 282–83
9	p. 284
10	p. 285

EAGLE:

QUESTION	PAGE NUMBER
1	p. 279
2	p. 280
3	p. 280
4	p. 281
5	p. 281
6	Research
7	p. 282
8	pp. 282–83
9	p. 284
10	p. 285

ANSWER KEY

Chapter 34: A Voice in the Tavern

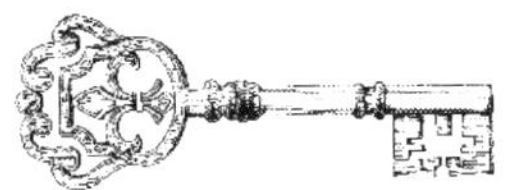

EAGLET:

QUSTION	PAGE NUMBER	ANSWER
1	p. 287	Hanover Tavern; December 5, 1759
2	p. 287	*Ohio*, *Quebec*, the *West Indies*, *India,* and on the *high seas*
3	p. 288	Barefoot and in an Ozna linen shirt and checked pants; playing a lively Scottish jig on his fiddle and dancing
4	p. 288	The first Thursday of each month; major cases held in the Quarter Sessions of March, June, September, and December
5	p. 289	No; no
6	p. 290	In the cabin attached to Hanover Tavern; helping his father-in-law run the tavern and farming Pine Slash Farm
7	p. 291	Have Patrick see Liz "catch him" and take him outside
8	p. 292	A lawyer
9	p. 293	Some law books and a horse; some law books
10	p. 296	Give Patrick one of his horses; *MizP*

FLEDGLING:

QUESTION	PAGE NUMBER
1	p. 287
2	pp. 287–88, Research
3	pp. 288–89
4	pp. 289–90
5	p. 291
6	p. 291
7	pp. 291–92
8	pp. 292–93
9	p. 295
10	p. 296

EAGLE:

QUESTION	PAGE NUMBER
1	p. 287
2	pp. 287–88, Research
3	pp. 288–89
4	pp. 289–90
5	p. 291
6	p. 291
7	pp. 291–92, Reasoning
8	pp. 292–93
9	p. 295, Reasoning
10	p. 296

ANSWER KEY

Chapter 35: Happy Christmas, Mr. Henry

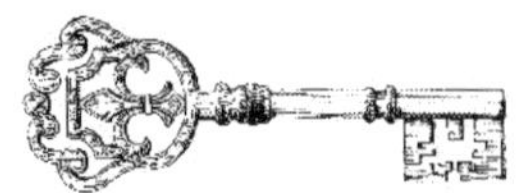

EAGLET:

QUESTION	PAGE NUMBER	ANSWER
1	p. 297	Dandridge home near Mount Brilliant; December 20, 1759; George Washington
2	p. 298	Silk gowns; satin breeches and coats; shiny gold-buckled shoes
3	pp. 298–99	Mr. Gillamon; Thomas Jefferson
4	p. 300	Play the fiddle; "No, I do not play the violin"
5	p. 300	Studying law under Mr. George Wythe
6	p. 301	Thomas Jefferson – Books; Patrick Henry – People
7	p. 302	Samuel Crowley
8	p. 302	Minister, teacher, or lawyer; minister and teacher; lawyer
9	p. 305	*Coke upon Littleton; Trials Per Pais*
10	p. 306	A lawyer; yes

FLEDGLING:

QUESTION	PAGE NUMBER
1	p. 297
2	pp. 298–99
3	p. 300
4	p. 301
5	p. 301
6	p. 302; Research
7	p. 302; Opinion
8	p. 303
9	pp. 303–4
10	pp. 304–6

EAGLE:

QUESTION	PAGE NUMBER
1	p. 297
2	pp. 298–99
3	p. 300
4	p. 301
5	p. 301; Opinion
6	p. 302; Research; Opinion based on reading Chapter 35
7	p. 302; Opinion
8	p. 303
9	pp. 303–4
10	pp. 304–6

ANSWER KEY

Chapter 36: Sweet on MizP

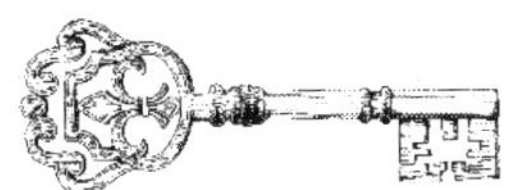

EAGLET:

QUESTION	PAGE NUMBER	ANSWER
1	p. 307	Studying his law books
2	p. 307	Liz
3	p. 308	A large brown stallion; Bill
4	p. 309	To become Patrick Henry's horse
5	p. 311	Max and Nigel
6	p. 312	Knit a cat a pair of britches
7	p. 312	Molasses
8	p. 313	MizP
9	p. 314	A certificate of recommendation signed by all the justices serving Hanover Courthouse
10	pp. 316–17	Give her to Patrick; *"Do goats stink?"*

FLEDGLING:

QUESTION	PAGE NUMBER
1	p. 307
2	pp. 307–8; Reasoning
3	p 308-309
4	p 309-310
5	p 310-311
6	p 311
7	p 312; Opinion
8	p 313
9	p 314-315
10	p 316-317; Opinion

EAGLE:

QUESTION	PAGE NUMBER
1	p. 307; Reasoning
2	pp. 307–8; Reasoning
3	pp. 308–9
4	p 309–10
5	pp. 310–11
6	p. 311
7	p. 312; Opinion
8	p. 313
9	pp. 314–15
10	pp. 316–17; Opinion

ANSWER KEY

Chapter 37: With a Wythe and a Prayer

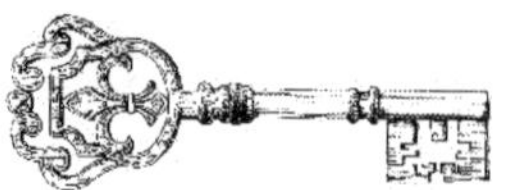

EAGLET:

QUESTION	PAGE NUMBER	ANSWER
1	p. 318	To Williamsburg; to get his law license; bread, cheese, and apples
2	p. 319	Bill
3	p. 319	William and Mary; 80
4	p. 320	The Raleigh Tavern
5	p. 321	That he will not impress the lawyers or be taken seriously as an aspiring lawyer
6	p. 321	George Wythe
7	p. 322	To perfection – a stark contrast to Patrick
8	p. 326	Yes, reluctantly
9	p. 326	Robert Carter Nicholas; no
10	p. 327	Peyton Randolph

FLEDGLING:

QUESTION	PAGE NUMBER
1	pp. 318–19
2	p. 319
3	p. 320
4	p. 321; Opinion
5	p. 321
6	p. 322
7	p. 323
8	pp. 324–25
9	pp. 325–26
10	pp. 326–27

EAGLE:

QUESTION	PAGE NUMBER
1	pp. 318–19
2	p. 319
3	p. 320
4	p. 321; Opinion
5	p. 321
6	p. 322
7	p. 323
8	pp. 324–25
9	pp. 325–26
10	pp. 326–27

ANSWER KEY

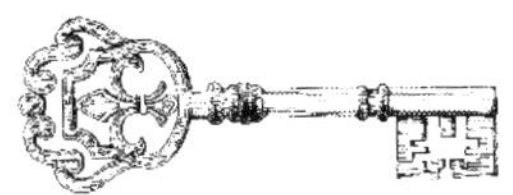

Chapter 38: Barely Passing the Bar

EAGLET:

QUESTION	PAGE NUMBER	ANSWER
1	p. 328	Peyton Randolph
2	p. 329	Clearly not
3	p. 329	No
4	p. 330	To go see his brother, John
5	p. 331	Clarie; as a servant
6	p. 331	That Peyton had signed the license, along with George Wythe
7	p. 332	His appearance
8	p. 333	Yes
9	p. 335	Yes
10	p. 335	Buy a new suit

FLEDGLING:

QUESTION	PAGE NUMBER
1	p. 328
2	p. 329
3	p. 330
4	p. 331
5	p. 332
6	pp. 332–33
7	p. 333
8	p. 333
9	p. 334
10	p. 335

EAGLE:

QUESTION	PAGE NUMBER
1	p. 328
2	p. 329
3	p. 330
4	p. 331
5	p. 332
6	pp. 332–33
7	p. 333
8	p. 333
9	p. 334
10	p. 335

ANSWER KEY

Chapter 39: The Power Behind the Throne

EAGLET:

QUESTION	PAGE NUMBER	ANSWER
1	p. 336	Hanover; April, 1761; "On the Death of King George;" Samuel Davies
2	p. 336	Thirty-seven
3	p. 337	". . . when your king is a child"
4	p. 338	Twenty-two
5	p. 338	He struck down the temporary Two Penny Acts
6	p. 339	Governor Fauquier and the lawmakers of Virginia
7	p. 340	Yes; the Parsons
8	p. 340	Made a move that infringes on the rights of her crown jewel, Virginia
9	p. 341	King George III and Queen Charlotte; Westminster Abbey; September 22, 1761
10	p. 342	A jewel fell out of it and landed on the blue rug behind the throne

FLEDGLING:

QUESTION	PAGE NUMBER
1	p. 336
2	p. 337; Reasoning
3	p. 337; Reasoning
4	p. 338
5	p. 338
6	pp. 338–39
7	pp. 339–40
8	p. 340
9	p. 341; Research
10	p. 342

EAGLE:

QUESTION	PAGE NUMBER
1	p. 336; Knowledge of previous chapters of VRK
2	p. 337; Reasoning
3	p. 337; Reasoning
4	p. 338
5	p. 338
6	pp. 338–39
7	pp. 339–40
8	p. 340
9	p. 341; Research
10	p. 342; Reasoning

ANSWER KEY

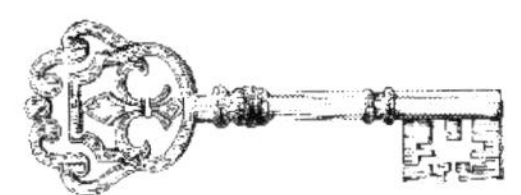

Chapter 40: Two Pennies for Your Thoughts

EAGLET:

QUESTION	PAGE NUMBER	ANSWER
1	p. 343	Hanover Tavern; November 5, 1763; Max, Liz, and MizP; in the barn behind Hanover Tavern
2	p. 344	1,185
3	p. 344	William
4	p. 344	The Two Penny Act
5	p. 345	The Two Penny Act is void from *inception!*
6	p. 345	John Lewis; he resigns from the case
7	p. 345	Patrick Henry
8	p. 347	Underestimate the power of the people when their liberties are threatened
9	p. 348	Patrick Henry; yes
10	p. 351; Dictionary	Rapacious; aggressively greedy or grasping

FLEDGLING:

QUESTION	PAGE NUMBER
1	pp. 343–44
2	p. 344; Math skills
3	p. 344
4	pp. 344–45
5	p. 345
6	p. 346
7	pp. 346–47
8	p. 347
9	p. 348
10	pp. 350–51; Reasoning; Dictionary

EAGLE:

QUESTION	PAGE NUMBER
1	pp. 343–44
2	p. 344; Math skills
3	p. 344
4	pp. 334–45
5	p. 345
6	p. 346
7	pp. 346–47
8	p. 347
9	p. 348
10	pp. 350–51; Reasoning; Opinion; Dictionary

ANSWER KEY

Chapter 41: Cause for the Parsons to Smile

EAGLET:

QUESTION	PAGE NUMBER	ANSWER
1	p. 352	December 1, 1763; Scottish Marigolds
2	p. 353	Patsey; made a laurel
3	p. 353	". . . doing the right thing."
4	p. 354	Reverend Maury
5	p. 355	Samuel Meredith; John Syme, Jr., Anthony Winston
6	p. 357	Attend court; leave the grounds; yes
7	p. 357	Samuel Morris and Roger Shackleford
8	p. 360	Peter Lyons; Reverend Maury
9	p. 362	". . . money supposedly due a group of wolves who profess to be shepherds."
10	p. 363	Uncle Patrick; his stomach lurched, and he instantly broke into a sweat

FLEDGLING:

QUESTION	PAGE NUMBER
1	pp. 352–53
2	p. 355
3	pp. 356–57
4	p. 357
5	pp. 358–59
6	pp. 359–60; Research and opinion
7	p. 360
8	pp. 360–61
9	pp. 361–62
10	pp. 362–63

EAGLE:

QUESTION	PAGE NUMBER
1	p. 352–53
2	pp. 355
3	pp. 356–57
4	p. 357
5	pp. 358–59; Reasoning
6	pp. 359–60; Research and opinion
7	p. 360; Reasoning
8	pp. 360–61
9	pp. 361–62
10	pp. 362–63; reasoning

ANSWER KEY

Chapter 42: A Voice in the Court

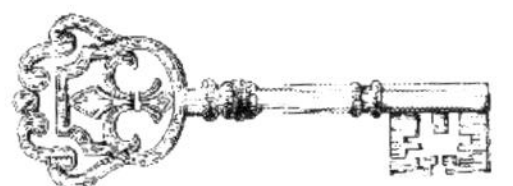

EAGLET:

QUESTION	PAGE NUMBER	ANSWER
1	p. 364	Disdain; "I simply cannot watch!" He buries his face in Liz's fur
2	pp. 364–65	The marigold laurel; images of bullies
3	p. 365	*"Now, mon Henry! It is time to find your voice in this court!"*
4	p. 366	The parsons
5	p. 367	One Protective King + His loyal subjects = Freedom
6	p. 368	Burgesses *represent* the House of Commons; Council *represents* the House of Lords; the Governor r*epresents* the King.
7	p. 368	Treason
8	p. 368	It puts both the king and the parsons on trial
9	p. 371	One penny
10	p. 374	France; wolves

FLEDGLING:

QUESTION	PAGE NUMBER
1	pp. 364–65
2	p. 366
3	p. 367
4	p. 367
5	pp. 367–68
6	p. 368
7	p. 369
8	p. 370
9	p. 371
10	pp. 372–74

EAGLE:

QUESTION	PAGE NUMBER
1	pp. 364–65
2	p. 366
3	p. 367
4	p. 367
5	pp. 367–68
6	pp. 368–69
7	p. 369
8	p. 370; Reasoning
9	p. 371
10	pp. 372–74

ANSWER KEY

Chapter 43: Soldiers, Smugglers, Sugar, and Stamps

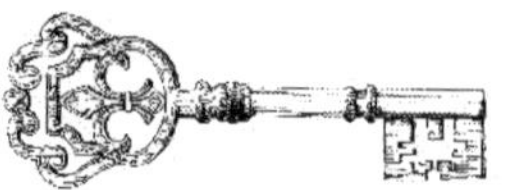

EAGLET:

QUESTION	PAGE NUMBER	ANSWER
1	p. 375	London; Leo; Lord Grenville
2	p. 376	"What, what?"
3	p. 377	£220, 000
4	p. 377	Molasses and sugar
5	p. 378	Sugar
6	p. 379	A Stamp Act
7	p. 380	*Fifty-five*; a half-penny to £10
8	p. 380	No taxation without representation
9	p. 382	The House of *Burgesses*
10	p. 389	Sons of Liberty

FLEDGLING:

QUESTION	PAGE NUMBER
1	pp. 375–77
2	pp. 377–78
3	p. 378
4	pp. 378–79
5	p. 380
6	pp. 380–81
7	pp. 381–82
8	pp. 382–84
9	pp. 385–86
10	pp. 386–89

EAGLE:

QUESTION	PAGE NUMBER
1	pp. 375–77
2	pp. 377–78
3	p. 378
4	pp. 378–79
5	p. 380; Reasoning
6	pp. 380–81
7	pp. 381–82
8	pp. 382–84
9	pp. 385–86
10	pp. 386–89

ANSWER KEY

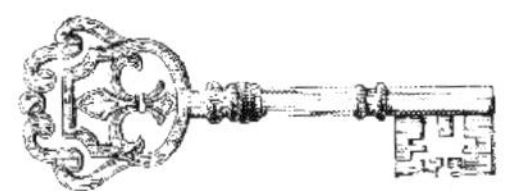

Chapter 44: A Voice in the House

EAGLET:

QUESTION	PAGE NUMBER	ANSWER
1	p. 390	Mount Brilliant; April 27, 1765; The House of Commons had passed the Stamp Act.
2	p. 390	In three days; the Johnson brothers
3	p. 391; Dictionary	"I relish the compliment my dear." To enjoy greatly
4	p. 392	Williamsburg; Clarie brought her; he is wearing new clothes; "Be still my heart! He looks so handsome in his new clothes."
5	p. 393	29; coroner; "It is a rather *dead-end* job."
6	p. 395	Challenge the most powerful man in Virginia; Speaker John Robinson
7	p. 396	The Stamp Act
8	p. 397	*"They are afraid to take a stand and let their voices heard."*
9	p. 397	"the voice of the people"
10	p. 398	Seven new resolves

FLEDGLING:

QUESTION	PAGE NUMBER
1	p. 390
2	pp. 390–91; Dictionary
3	p. 392
4	p. 393
5	pp. 393–94
6	pp. 394–95
7	p. 395
8	pp. 395–97
9	pp. 397
10	p. 398

EAGLE:

QUESTION	PAGE NUMBER
1	p. 390
2	pp. 390–91; Dictionary
3	p. 392
4	p. 393; Research
5	pp. 393–94
6	pp. 394–95
7	p. 395
8	pp. 395–97
9	p. 397
10	p. 398; Research

ANSWER KEY

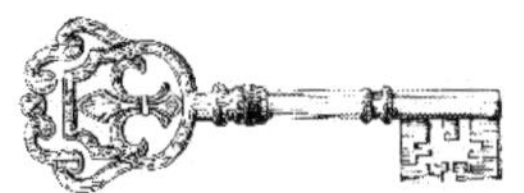

Chapter 45: If This Be Treason

EAGLET:

QUESTION	PAGE NUMBER	ANSWER
1	p. 399	Seven resolves mean the seven "words"; the meaning of "two short"
2	p. 400	Dampen the spark of the last two resolves
3	pp. 400–1	29; Patrick; liberty
4	p. 402	Richard Bland; Peyton Randolph
5	p. 403	Taxation by the people or their chosen representatives
6	p. 404	It erupted into a violent debate.
7	p. 405	If *this* be treason, make the most of it.
8	p. 406	Because it was the first time a colony declared independence from taxation by Parliament
9	p. 407	Patrick was gone, so the vote was a tie; Speaker Robinson voted "no"
10	pp. 408–9	"Copies of all *seven* of Patrick's resolutions, plus the preamble"

FLEDGLING:

QUESTION	PAGE NUMBER
1	p. 399
2	pp. 399–400
3	pp. 400–1
4	p. 402; Reasoning
5	p. 403
6	p. 404
7	p. 404
8	p. 406
9	p. 407
10	pp. 408–9

EAGLE:

QUESTION	PAGE NUMBER
1	p. 399
2	pp. 399–400; Research; Reasoning
3	pp. 400–1
4	p. 402; Reasoning
5	p. 403; Reasoning
6	p. 404; Research; reasoning
7	p. 404; Research
8	p. 406
9	p. 407
10	pp. 408–9; Literary analysis and reasoning

ANSWER KEY

Chapter 46: The Beast of the Gévaudan

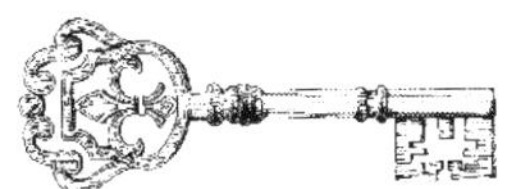

EAGLET:

QUESTION	PAGE NUMBER	ANSWER
1	p. 410	Les Hubacs, France; June 30, 1764; she is a shepherd girl
2	p. 411	His cousin; Marie; nine years old
3	p. 412	Stop howling like a wolf; she hates the sound of wolves, especially lately
4	p. 413	There has been another attack; thirty miles away
5	p. 414	Bibi
6	p. 414	More than sixty
7	p. 415	Jacques Portefaix; twelve years old
8	p. 416	A greasy looking village peasant; he smelled awful
9	p. 416	Those in the aristocracy
10	p. 418; Reasoning	He kicked Kate; no; the Enemy

FLEDGLING:

QUESTION	PAGE NUMBER
1	p. 410; Glossary
2	pp. 411–12
3	p. 413
4	p. 414
5	pp. 414–15
6	pp. 415–16
7	p. 416
8	pp. 416–17
9	pp. 417–18
10	p. 418; Reasoning

EAGLE:

QUESTION	PAGE NUMBER
1	p. 410; Glossary
2	pp. 411–12; Dictionary
3	p. 413
4	p. 414; Analysis
5	pp. 414–15; Hypothesizing
6	pp. 415–16
7	p. 416
8	pp. 416–17
9	pp. 417–18
10	pp. 418; Reasoning

ANSWER KEY

Chapter 47: Marquis and the Beast

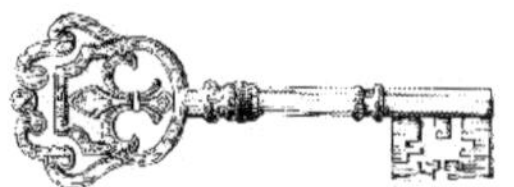

EAGLET:

QUESTION	PAGE NUMBER	ANSWER
1	p. 419	A reputation garnered through virtue, merit, great qualities, good actions, and beautiful works
2	p. 420	Lancelot; French
3	p. 420	*Cur Non*; Why Not?
4	p. 421	No
5	p. 422	Hot *chocolat*; baguette, jam, and boiled egg
6	p. 422	No
7	p. 423	Max; No
8	p. 424	A foul stench; a wolf; six feet long, three feet tall; at least 130 lbs.
9	p. 428	He had the beast chase him "ta the bog where he p-r-ro-ceeded ta get nice an' stuck."
10	p. 430	"A beast that needs ta be tamed first. Glory."

FLEDGLING:

QUESTION	PAGE NUMBER
1	p. 419
2	pp. 419–20
3	pp. 421–22
4	p. 422
5	pp. 422–23
6	p. 423
7	p. 424
8	pp. 424–25
9	pp. 427–29
10	pp. 429–30

EAGLE:

QUESTION	PAGE NUMBER
1	p. 419
2	pp. 419–20; Research
3	pp. 421–22; Research
4	p. 422; Research and cooking
5	pp. 422–23
6	p. 423; Reasoning
7	p. 424
8	pp. 424–25
9	pp. 427–29
10	pp. 429–30; Reasoning

ANSWER KEY

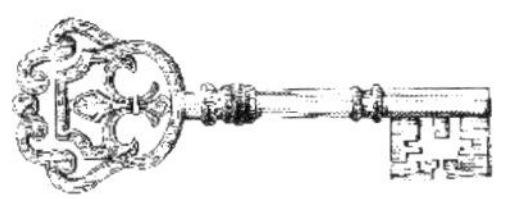

Chapter 48: Sons of Liberty

EAGLET:

QUESTION	PAGE NUMBER	ANSWER
1	p. 433	Patrick Henry
2	pp. 433–34	In the papers throughout the colonies
3	p. 434	Rhode Island; *The Newport Mercury*
4	p. 434	The Great Awakening
5	p. 435	Sons of Liberty
6	p. 435	Georgia
7	p. 436	Fired him; replaced him with Charles Watson-Wentworth, Marquis of Rockingham
8	p. 436	Set the colonists on a path from being Englishmen to Americans
9	p. 436	Revolution
10	pp. 436–37	The King's armor bearer had killed a massive wolf and had it stuffed and sent to Versailles.

FLEDGLING:

QUESTION	PAGE NUMBER
1	p. 433
2	pp. 433–34
3	p. 434
4	p. 434; Research and analysis
5	p. 435
6	p. 435
7	p. 436
8	p. 436
9	p. 436; Reasoning
10	pp. 436–37; Dictionary and analysis

EAGLE:

QUESTION	PAGE NUMBER
1	p. 433
2	pp. 433–34
3	p. 434
4	p. 434; Research and analysis
5	p. 435
6	p. 435
7	p. 436; Reasoning
8	p. 436
9	p. 436; Reasoning
10	pp. 436–37; Dictionary and analysis

ANSWER KEY

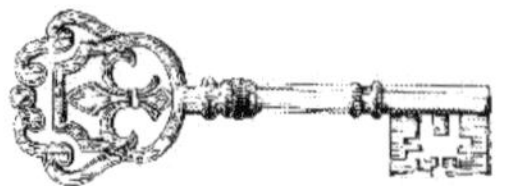

Chapter 49: Hard Acts to Follow

EAGLET:

QUESTION	PAGE NUMBER	ANSWER
1	p. 438	Roundabout Plantation; May, 1766; the *London Chronicle*
2	p. 438	One million British pounds; March; May
3	p. 439	Yes
4	p. 439	Declared that Britain had the right to tax and make decisions for the colonies "in all cases"
5	p. 440	William Pitt
6	p. 441	Hard acts
7	p. 442	Noble Ruler of the House
8	p. 442	House of Burgesses
9	p. 442	Boston; Clarie; Al in London to help with Benjamin Franklin
10	p. 443	A flying squirrel

FLEDGLING:

QUESTION	PAGE NUMBER
1	p. 438
2	p. 438
3	p. 439
4	p. 439
5	p. 440
6	pp. 440–41
7	pp. 441–42
8	p. 442
9	p. 442; Reasoning
10	pp. 442–43

EAGLE:

QUESTION	PAGE NUMBER
1	p. 438; Reasoning
2	p. 438
3	p. 439; Research and cartography
4	p. 439
5	p. 440; Research
6	pp. 440–41
7	pp. 441–42; name-meaning dictionary
8	p. 442
9	p. 442; Reasoning
10	pp. 442–43

ANSWER KEY

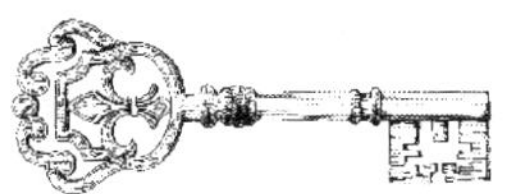

Chapter 50: Threatening Skies and Seizing Liberty

EAGLET:

QUESTION	PAGE NUMBER	ANSWER
1	p. 444	Williamsburg; November, 1766
2	p. 445	Called the burgesses back into session
3	p. 445	One-third
4	p. 446	Any three of: celebrity; inventor; postmaster; colonial agent
5	p. 446	"If people will not die or be free, it is of no consequence what sort of government they live under."
6	p. 447	A balcony for spectators
7	p. 447	Lifting a piece of fish to his mouth
8	p. 449	Boston; Clarie; setting fire to a boat in Boston Harbor
9	p. 450	Rocks; children
10	p. 451	British troops; Yes

FLEDGLING:

QUESTION	PAGE NUMBER
1	p. 444
2	p. 445
3	p. 446
4	pp. 446–47
5	p. 447
6	p. 448
7	p. 449
8	pp. 449–50
9	p. 450
10	p. 451

EAGLE:

QUESTION	PAGE NUMBER
1	p. 444; Reasoning
2	p. 445
3	p. 446
4	pp. 446–47; Reasoning
5	p. 447
6	p. 448
7	p. 449
8	pp. 449–50
9	p. 450
10	p. 451; Reasoning

ANSWER KEY

Chapter 51 Coach and Six or Ten-Shilling Jackets

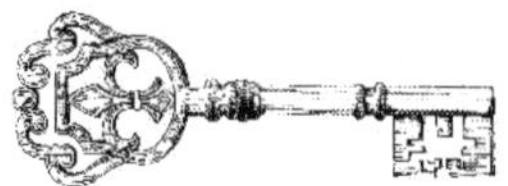

EAGLET:

QUESTION	PAGE NUMBER	ANSWER
1	p. 452	Williamsburg; May 8, 1769; white, cream; six
2	p. 453	Bachelors; he needs to settle a nest and have eaglets; no
3	p. 453	Tom Jefferson
4	p. 454	"…a flaming sword pointed at the people's liberties…"
5	p. 455	Nero was more revolting than a rat
6	p. 456	Four; unanimously
7	p. 456	"…put an end to this abominable business immediately; keep the door locked
8	p. 458	Dissolve the burgesses; continue their meeting elsewhere
9	p. 459	A Virginia Association for a Non-Importation Agreement
10	p. 460	"The fight with England will move beyond words. It will turn bloody."

FLEDGLING:

QUESTION	PAGE NUMBER
1	p. 452
2	p. 453
3	p. 453; Reasoning
4	p. 454
5	p. 455
6	pp. 455–56
7	pp. 456–57
8	pp. 457–58
9	p. 459
10	p. 460

EAGLE:

QUESTION	PAGE NUMBER
1	p. 452
2	p. 453
3	p. 453; Reasoning
4	p. 454
5	p. 455
6	pp. 455–56
7	pp. 456–57; Reasoning
8	pp. 457–58
9	p. 459
10	p. 460

ANSWER KEY

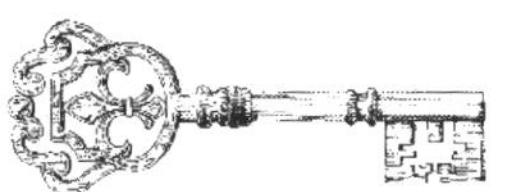

Chapter 52: Comfort and Joy

EAGLET:

QUESTION	PAGE NUMBER	ANSWER
1	p. 461	Roundabout Plantation; December 21, 1769; wassail
2	p. 461	NC, RI, and NY; MA and MD
3	p. 462	Called the House of Burgesses back into session
4	p. 462	Homespun gowns and breeches
5	p. 463	Two weeks in April and October for civil cases; two weeks in June and December for criminal cases
6	p. 463	Twice a year; May and November for weeks on end
7	p. 464	Isaac Coles and William Christian
8	p. 464	There is a heaviness in her eyes and a melancholy look.
9	p. 464	What if they find a larger place for the Henry family to live
10	p. 465	Scotchtown; Kate

FLEDGLING:

QUESTION	PAGE NUMBER
1	p. 461
2	p. 461
3	p. 462
4	p. 462
5	p. 463
6	p. 464
7	p. 464
8	pp. 464–65
9	p. 465
10	p. 465

EAGLE:

QUESTION	PAGE NUMBER
1	p. 461
2	p. 461
3	p. 462
4	pp. 462–63
5	p. 463
6	p. 464
7	p. 464; Reasoning
8	pp. 464–65
9	p. 465
10	p. 465; Reasoning

ANSWER KEY

Chapter 53: Innocent Blood

EAGLET:

QUESTION	PAGE NUMBER	ANSWER
1	p. 466	Boston; February 22, 1770
2	p. 466	Sons of Liberty
3	p. 466	They could be tarred and feathered
4	p. 467	Ebenezer Richardson; a Customs Informer
5	p. 467	Worse
6	p. 467	An egg; in the face
7	p. 468	Working men and sailors from the docks
8	p. 468	Fires it into the crowd; no; it is not loaded
9	p. 468	She gets hit on the arm with a rock.
10	p. 469	He is shot by Richardson.

FLEDGLING:

QUESTION	PAGE NUMBER
1	p. 466
2	p. 466
3	p. 466; Research
4	p. 467
5	p. 467
6	p. 467
7	p. 468
8	p. 468
9	pp. 468–69
10	p. 469

EAGLE:

QUESTION	PAGE NUMBER
1	p. 466
2	p. 466
3	p. 466; Research
4	p. 467
5	p. 467; Research
6	p. 467
7	P. 468
8	p. 468
9	pp. 468–69
10	p. 469; Research and reasoning

ANSWER KEY

Chapter 54: Bloody Boston

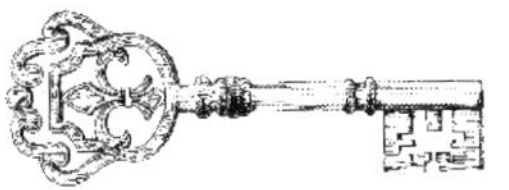

EAGLET/FLEDGLING/EAGLE:

QUESTION	PAGE NUMBER	ANSWER
1	p. 470	Henry Knox
2	p. 470	Captain John Preston; 29th Regiment of Foot; forty
3	p. 471	Jock Frost; Max
4	p. 471	2,000 people
5	p. 472	Having three hundred children dressed as angels in white walk behind the casket
6	p. 472	Their liberty
7	p. 472	"ta fire a cannon, much less a musket"
8	p. 480	Paul Revere
9	p. 480	"Stretching the truth to inspire others to join your cause"
10	p. 481	John Adams

ANSWER KEY

Nigel's Nuggets

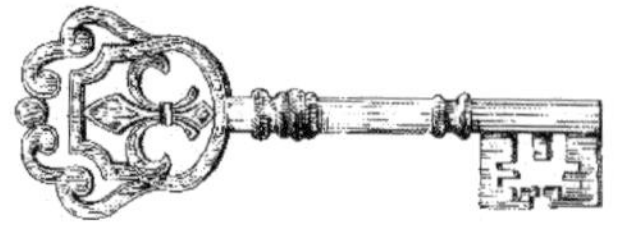

Chapter 54: Bloody Boston

____

Title

Captain John Goldfinch heads to Murray's Barracks to break up a brawl.

Edward Garrick falsely accuses Captain Goldfinch of not paying his wigmaker's bill.

Private Hugh White confronts Edward Garrick.

Edward Garrick and Bartholomew Broaders enter the Customs House to eat dinner.

Edward Garrick taunts Private White.

Private White hits Garrick on the side of his head with the butt of his musket.

Garrick and Broaders shout and rant about what has happened, drawing a crowd.

Private White loads his musket as a crowd gathers around him. Knox advises him not to fire.

The crowd surrounding Private White begins to throw snowballs.

Edward Langford, a town watchman, stands between White and the crowd telling them to stop throwing snowballs.

A group of sailors led by Crispus Attucks has just finished working at John Gray's Rope Walk when they hear about the brawl at Murray's Barracks and that there is trouble at the Customs House and head in that direction. They are armed with clubs.

The church bells begin ringing, and people rush outside thinking there is a fire. There is no fire.

The crowd swells to two hundred. They quickly learn about the events of the evening.

Private White sends for reinforcements. Captain Thomas Preston sends seven privates and follows shortly.

The soldiers form a semicircle around Private White. The crowd throws snowballs and oyster shells at the soldiers.

Captain Preston walks in front of his men and orders the crowd to disperse.

Local innkeeper, Richard Palmes, armed with a club, confronts Captain Preston demanding reassurance that the soldiers will not shoot.

Captain Preston responds that by no means will the soldiers fire and reminds Palmes that he is standing in front of his men.

The crowd continues to taunt the soldiers and throw things at them.

Crispus Attucks grabs the bayonet of one of the soldiers jerking it back and forth and yelling, "Have you come to finish what you started, Lobsterback?"

Private Montgomery is struck in the head by a club thrown from the crowd and is knocked to the ground.

People in the crowd yell at the soldiers to fire and also tell them they dare not do so, and issue shouts to kill the soldiers.

Montgomery gets to his feet, cocks his musket, yells FIRE, and fires into the crowd.

Palmes swings his club striking Montgomery on the arm. He swings again, aiming for Preston's head, but slips and strikes him on the arm knocking him to the ground.

The other soldiers fire on the crowd and eleven people are shot.

Preston gets to his feet and holds his sword under the men's muskets to keep them from firing and orders them to march back to the main guard.

The town constable, Burdick, orders the crowd to disperse.

Crispus Attucks, Samuel Gray, and James Caldwell are dead; Samuel Maverick and Patrick Carter lay mortally wounded.

ANSWER KEY

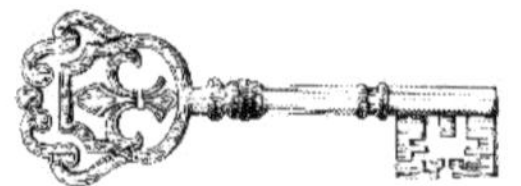

Chapter 55: A Darkness Begins

EAGLET:

QUESTION	PAGE NUMBER	ANSWER
1	p. 482	The IAMISPHERE; Gillamon and Clarie
2	p. 482	They stopped importing British goods; Lord North
3	p. 483	A tax on tea; repeal the rest
4	p. 483	Parliament was repealing the Townshend Acts
5	p. 483	With violence
6	p. 484	They *are stubborn things*; yes; two; manslaughter
7	p. 485	He has died; Scotchtown; a cloud of darkness; Kate
8	p. 486	His mother and grandmother; the king's musketeers
9	p. 486	John Murray, Lord Dunmore
10	p. 487	By trying to do the exact opposite

FLEDGLING:

QUESTION	PAGE NUMBER
1	p. 482
2	p. 483
3	p. 483
4	p. 484
5	Reasoning and research
6	pp. 484–85
7	p. 485; Reasoning
8	p. 486
9	p. 486
10	p. 487

EAGLE:

QUESTION	PAGE NUMBER
1	p. 482
2	p. 483
3	p. 483; Research
4	p. 484
5	Reasoning and research
6	pp. 484–85
7	p. 485; Reasoning
8	p. 486; Research
9	p. 486
10	p. 487

ANSWER KEY

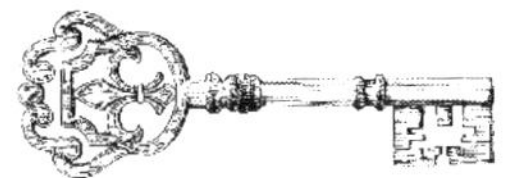

Chapter 56: Gasping for Liberty

EAGLET:

QUESTION	PAGE NUMBER	ANSWER
1	p. 488	Scotchtown Plantation, Virginia; January 18, 1773; She is slipping away from him.
2	p. 488	Violently; sadness and shame; as a curse
3	p. 489	Set it ablaze; yes
4	p. 490	To cease the slave trade
5	p. 492	Patrick's father, John Henry; Uncle Patrick
6	p. 493	That precious jewel of liberty; Kate
7	p. 493	His mother & unmarried sisters; Kate; London; Al; Franklin
8	p. 495	The Baptists
9	p. 497	Those who are gasping for liberty, whether they be slaves, preachers, or the Colonies themselves
10	p. 497	The Asylum; no

FLEDGLING:

QUESTION	PAGE NUMBER
1	p. 488
2	p. 489
3	p. 489
4	pp. 490–91
5	p. 492; Reasoning
6	p. 493
7	p. 493
8	pp. 494–95
9	pp. 496–97
10	p. 497; Research

EAGLE:

QUESTION	PAGE NUMBER
1	p. 488; Research
2	p. 489
3	p. 489; Research and reasoning
4	pp. 490–91
5	p. 492; Reasoning
6	p. 493
7	p. 493
8	pp. 494–95
9	pp. 496–97
10	p. 497; Research

ANSWER KEY

Chapter 57: Troubling Letters

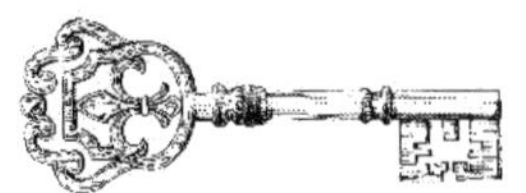

EAGLET:

QUESTION	PAGE NUMBER	ANSWER
1	p. 498	Cheese; Nigel; cranberries
2	p. 499	It will not last long.
3	p. 499	Acquire important letters, get them to Franklin; Wm. Whatley
4	p. 500	Lombard Street; it was one of the original Roman roads.
5	p. 501	"We'll be bank robbers!"
6	p. 502	Hutchinson; Cushing; the letters be read, but not made public
7	p. 504	A Committee of Correspondence; between all the Colonies; a *Continental Congress*
8	pp. 504–5	Public Hospital for Persons of Insane and Disordered Minds
9	p. 506	No
10	p. 507	Samuel Adams

FLEDGLING:

QUESTION	PAGE NUMBER
1	p. 498
2	p. 499
3	p. 500
4	p. 501
5	pp. 501–3
6	p. 503
7	p. 504
8	pp. 504–6
9	p. 506
10	p. 507; Knowledge of previous VRK chapters; Reasoning

EAGLE:

QUESTION	PAGE NUMBER
1	p. 498
2	p. 499
3	p. 500
4	p. 501; Reasoning
5	pp. 501–3; Reasoning
6	p. 503
7	p. 504
8	pp. 504–6
9	p. 506
10	p. 507; Knowledge of previous VRK chapters; Reasoning

ANSWER KEY

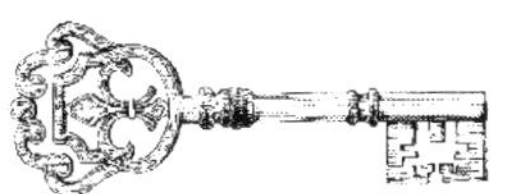

Chapter 58: Brewing Trouble with the Cat's-Paw

EAGLET:

QUESTION	PAGE NUMBER	ANSWER
1	p. 508	An old woman; Al; Clarie and Max; honor Franklin's request
2	p. 509	No
3	p. 510	*Cat's-paw*
4	p. 510	The cat's-paw to make the Colonies pay the tea tax
5	p. 514	Starting a revolution
6	p. 514	Samuel Adams; no
7	pp. 515–16	Dumped 340 chests of tea into the harbor; Benjamin Franklin
8	p. 517	No
9	p. 519	*Poor Richard's Almanack*; Isaiah 53:7
10	p. 521	"… he was an Englishman. When he walked out the door, he was an American."

FLEDGLING:

QUESTION	PAGE NUMBER
1	p. 508
2	p. 509
3	pp. 510–11
4	pp. 510–11
5	pp. 513–14
6	pp. 514–15
7	pp. 515–16
8	p. 517
9	p. 519; Reasoning
10	pp. 520–21

EAGLE:

QUESTION	PAGE NUMBER
1	p. 508
2	p. 509
3	pp. 510–11
4	pp. 510–11
5	pp. 513–14
6	pp. 514–15
7	pp. 515–16
8	p. 517
9	p. 519; Reasoning
10	pp. 520–21; Reasoning

ANSWER KEY

Chapter 59: A Voice That is Hungry

EAGLET:

QUESTION	PAGE NUMBER	ANSWER
1	p. 522	Scotchtown; April 28, 1774; the *Virginia Gazette*
2	p. 523	"…isn't jest ta' keep them gettin' out, but ta' keep harm from gettin' in."
3	p. 525	Talk to her; yes
4	p. 525	Close it
5	p. 526	John Hancock, Sam Adams, and two others
6	p. 527	A General Congress of all the colonies; no
7	p. 529	A day of fasting, humiliation, and prayer
8	p. 529	June 1; the closing of the port of Boston
9	p. 530	To halt the import of British goods
10	p. 530	His first Continental Congress

FLEDGLING:

QUESTION	PAGE NUMBER
1	p. 522
2	p. 523
3	pp. 524–25
4	pp. 525–26
5	pp. 526–27
6	pp. 527–28
7	pp. 528–29
8	p. 529
9	pp. 529–30
10	p. 530

EAGLE:

QUESTION	PAGE NUMBER
1	p. 522
2	p. 523
3	pp. 524–25
4	pp. 525–26
5	pp. 526–27
6	p 527–28
7	pp. 528–29; Dictionary
8	p. 529
9	pp. 529–30
10	p. 530; Reasoning

ANSWER KEY

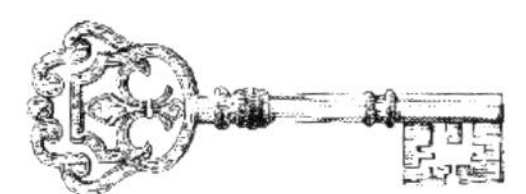

Chapter 60: To Philadelphia

EAGLET:

QUESTION	PAGE NUMBER	ANSWER
1	p. 531	August 6, 1774; food and supplies
2	p. 531	An extra-legal convention; no
3	p. 532	Inside the Capitol building
4	p. 532	. . . WE STAND, DIVIDED WE FALL
5	p. 532	The importation of slaves; the import of British goods; the consumption of British tea
6	p. 533	". . . a bridle for my mouth as well as for my horse. . ."
7	p. 534	Liz and Kate
8	p. 534	"Take care of my girl."
9	p. 534	The form of a militia soldier
10	p. 535	To Philadelphia; to a place called Point Pleasant

FLEDGLING:

QUESTION	PAGE NUMBER
1	p. 531
2	p. 532
3	p. 532; Reasoning
4	p. 532
5	pp. 532–33
6	p. 533
7	pp. 533–34
8	pp. 534–35
9	p. 535; Reasoning
10	p. 535

EAGLE:

QUESTION	PAGE NUMBER
1	p. 531
2	p. 532
3	p. 532; Reasoning
4	p. 532
5	pp. 532–33
6	p. 533; Research and reasoning
7	pp. 533–34; Reasoning
8	pp. 534–35
9	p. 535; Reasoning
10	p. 535; Map research

ANSWER KEY

Chapter 61: A Voice Unified

EAGLET:

QUESTION	PAGE NUMBER	ANSWER
1	p. 536	Philadelphia, September 4, 1774; settling down and starting a family
2	p. 537	By pigeon
3	p. 537	Gillamon and Max
4	p. 538	"But that precious jewel of liberty is worth fighting for."
5	p. 540	". . . one Colony. One nation. May God guide our steps."
6	p. 540	September 5, 1744
7	p. 541	Carpenter's Hall; The Pennsylvania State House
8	p. 542	How would they vote?
9	p. 544	Abigail
10	p. 544	Each colony will have one, singular vote

FLEDGLING, ***Option 1***:

QUESTION	PAGE NUMBER
1	Plutarch research
2	p. 536; Reasoning
3	pp. 536–37
4	p. 538; Reasoning
5	pp. 539–40
6	pp. 540–41
7	p. 541
8	p. 542
9	pp. 543–44
10	p. 544

EAGLE, ***Option 1***:

QUESTION	PAGE NUMBER
1	Plutarch research
2	p. 536; Reasoning
3	pp. 536–37
4	p. 538; Reasoning
5	pp. 539–40; Research and reasoning
6	pp. 540–41
7	p. 541
8	p. 542
9	pp. 543–44
10	p. 544; Reasoning

ANSWER KEY

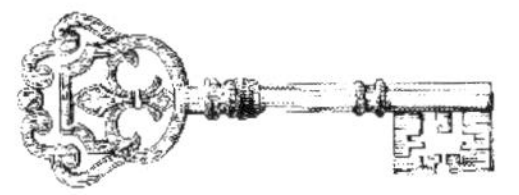

Chapter 62: God Bless America

EAGLET:

QUESTION	PAGE NUMBER	ANSWER
1	p. 545	Carpenter's Hall; Philadelphia; September 6, 1774; no
2	p. 545	R-r-root out any smelly minions
3	p. 546	No one to enter unless approved by Congress; the door to Carpenter's Hall will be bolted shut each day
4	p. 546	To open the next day's session with prayer; Reverend Duché; Christ Church
5	p. 547	Psalm 35
6	p. 547	They share approving glances; they are delightfully surprised
7	p. 547	His knees; no
8	p. 548	Drive the delegates to their knees in prayer
9	p. 549	Patrick; R H Lee; George Washington; John and Sam Adams
10	pp. 549–50	The Suffolk Resolves; yes

FLEDGLING:

QUESTION	PAGE NUMBER
1	p. 545
2	pp. 545–46
3	p. 546
4	p. 546
5	p. 547
6	p. 547
7	p. 548; Reasoning
8	pp. 548–49
9	p. 549
10	pp. 549–50

EAGLE:

QUESTION	PAGE NUMBER
1	p. 545
2	pp. 545–46
3	p. 546
4	p. 546
5	p. 547; Reasoning
6	p. 547
7	p. 548; Reasoning
8	pp. 548–49
9	p. 549
10	pp. 549–50

ANSWER KEY

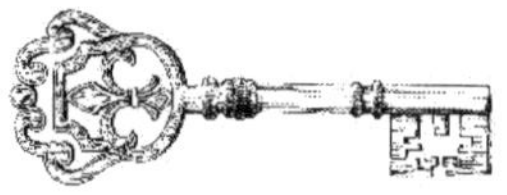

Chapter 63: Unjust Desserts and Passing the Mantle

EAGLET:

QUESTION	PAGE NUMBER	ANSWER
1	p. 551	Gillamon's home; Philadelphia; September 29, 1774; Max
2	p. 552	Rodents
3	p. 552	25,000; one million
4	p. 553	*Cato*; Betsy Ross
5	p. 554	Suddenly took ill; make sure everything is secure
6	pp. 554–55	Charlotte; something she ate; a vial; pours it into the batter of cream; no
7	pp. 555–56	Poison them; no
8	p. 556	May 1775; Plutarch, Veritas, and Alexander
9	pp. 556–57	With George Washington to Mt. Vernon; Nigel
10	p. 559	His magnificent red cloak; an ivory letter opener

FLEDGLING:

QUESTION	PAGE NUMBER
1	p. 551
2	pp. 551–52
3	pp. 553–54
4	p. 554
5	pp. 554–55
6	pp. 555–56
7	p. 556
8	p. 557
9	pp. 557–58; Reasoning
10	p. 559

EAGLE:

QUESTION	PAGE NUMBER
1	p. 551
2	pp. 551–52
3	pp. 553–54
4	p. 554
5	pp. 554–55; Reasoning
6	pp. 555–56; Reasoning
7	p. 556
8	p. 557
9	pp. 557–58; Reasoning
10	p. 559

ANSWER KEY

Chapter 64: Winds of War

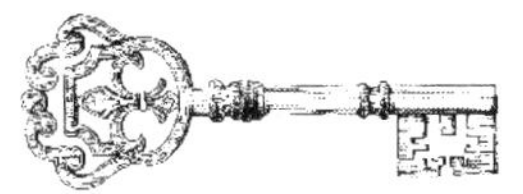

EAGLET:

QUESTION	PAGE NUMBER	ANSWER
1	p. 560	Point Pleasant, Virginia; October 10, 1774; Colonel Lewis
2	p. 560	In the side; Clarie; a frontiersman; Samuel; no
3	p. 561	If there is any hope of reconciling with England; no
4	p. 562	Colonel William Christian; Patrick's sister, Anne
5	p. 564	*British*
6	p. 566	Samuel Crowley; first patriot to die in the Revolutionary War
7	p. 567	A crucial role for the EO7 in the future; Littleberry
8	p. 567	". . . war have started to blow."
9	p. 567	Mount Vernon; Nigel
10	p. 568	". . . for every activity under heaven—a time for war and a time for peace, a time to be born, and a time to die."

FLEDGLING:

QUESTION	PAGE NUMBER
1	p. 560
2	p. 561
3	pp. 561–62
4	p. 562
5	p. 564
6	p. 564
7	p. 566
8	p. 567; reasoning
9	p. 567
10	pp. 567–68

EAGLE:

QUESTION	PAGE NUMBER
1	p. 560
2	p. 561
3	pp. 561–62
4	p. 562
5	p. 564
6	p. 564
7	p. 566
8	p. 567; Reasoning
9	p. 567
10	pp. 567–68; Reasoning

ANSWER KEY

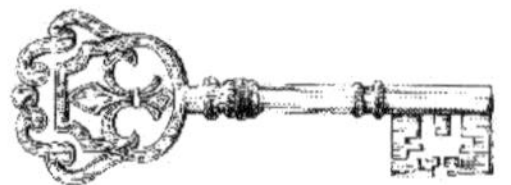

Chapter 65: Farewell, My Love

EAGLET:

QUESTION	PAGE NUMBER	ANSWER
1	p. 569	Scotchtown; December 15, 1774; twice the normal length
2	p. 570	Yes
3	p. 571	His sweetheart
4	p. 571	His newborn baby
5	p. 572	Seize all the gunpowder
6	p. 573	Get out of London soon.; there is nothing left for him there.
7	p. 573	Bloodshed with the Colonies; no; home–to America; their fight for liberty
8	p. 574	I wish to be free; to let her go
9	p. 574	"I am not afraid; how beautiful it is there."
10	p. 574	"Farewell, my love,"; death

FLEDGLING:

QUESTION	PAGE NUMBER
1	p. 569
2	pp. 570–71; Reasoning
3	p. 571
4	p. 571; Reasoning
5	p. 572
6	pp. 572–73
7	p. 573; Dictionary; Reasoning
8	p 574; Reasoning
9	p 574; Reasoning
10	p. 575

EAGLE:

QUESTION	PAGE NUMBER
1	p. 569
2	pp. 570–71; Reasoning
3	p. 571
4	p. 571; Reasoning
5	p. 572
6	pp. 572–73
7	p. 573; Dictionary; Reasoning
8	p. 574; Reasoning
9	p. 574; Reasoning
10	p. 575

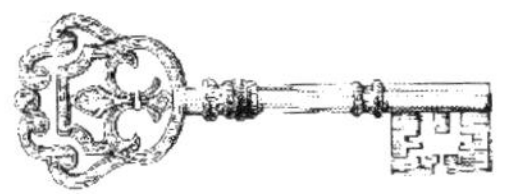

Chapter 66: Cloak and Dagger

PART ONE
EAGLET:

QUESTION	PAGE NUMBER	ANSWER
1	p. 576	Scotchtown; March 17, 1775; three weeks; Richmond
2	p. 578	*The Royal Governor*; treason; *the entire war*
3	p. 579	Max, Liz, Clarie, MizP, Nigel, and Cato; Kate
4	p. 580	"than just when breath leaves the body."
5	p. 581	His ivory letter opener
6	pp. 583–84	**See *Fill in the Blank* below**
7	p. 584	From the skies above
8	p. 585	It has been laced with poison; he will die.
9	p. 587	"Liberty or death;" he picks it up with his talons.
10	p. 588	". . . America's first legislature met in 1619.; . . . liberty itself was born on its altar of grace.

Fill in the Blank from pages 583–84:

The footprints on Plutarch's terrace were *hers*. She is not a mortal being. Kakia in the Greek means, evil, trouble, and desire to injure. Someone tried to poison young George Washington on Barbados with smallpox, and there was an attempt on George Washington and Patrick Henry in Philadelphia. The panther that failed to kill Patrick was poisoned. Kakia could be like Gillamon for the EO7. She might be able to change form as do Gillamon and Clarie.

PART TWO

FLEDGLING:

QUESTION	PAGE NUMBER
1	pp. 576–78
2	p. 578
3	p. 579
4	p. 580
5	pp. 581, 583–84; **See *Fill in the Blank* on PAGE ONE, Chapter 66 Answer Key**
6	p. 584
7	pp. 585–86
8	p. 586
9	p. 587
10	pp. 587–88

EAGLE:

QUESTION	PAGE NUMBER
1	pp. 576–78
2	p. 578
3	p. 579
4	p. 580; Reasoning
5	pp. 581, 583–84; **See *Fill in the Blank* on PAGE ONE, Chapter 66 Answer Key**
6	p. 584
7	p. 585–86
8	p. 586–87
9	p. 587
10	pp. 587–88; Reasoning

ANSWER KEY

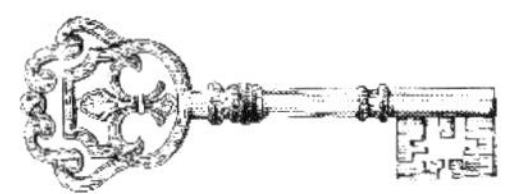

Chapter 67: Liberty or Death

EAGLET:

QUESTION	PAGE NUMBER	ANSWER
1	p. 590	Max; the ivory letter opener
2	p. 590	Cato; cleaned it off in the James River
3	p. 590	Max; a crate
4	p. 590	". . . take the letter opener and be ready for my signal. Go!"
5	p. 591	"Know that you are loved, and you are able."
6	p. 591	"A state of defense"
7	p. 592	Edmund Pendleton
8	p. 592	"Give me liberty or give me death."
9	p. 599	". . . declaring war against the king of England."
10	p. 600	To Cato; at the falls

FLEDGLING:

QUESTION	PAGE NUMBER
1	p. 590
2	p. 590
3	pp. 591–92
4	pp. 592–98; Reasoning
5	pp. 592–98; Reasoning
6	pp. 592–98; Reasoning
7	pp. 592–98; Reasoning
8	p. 599; Research
9	p. 599
10	p. 600

EAGLE:

QUESTION	PAGE NUMBER
1	p. 590
2	p. 590
3	pp. 591–92
4	pp. 592–98; Reasoning
5	pp. 592–98; Reasoning
6	pp. 592–98; Reasoning
7	pp. 592–98; Reasoning
8	p. 599; Research
9	p. 599
10	p. 600; Reasoning

ANSWER KEY

Chapter 68: On Eagle's Wings

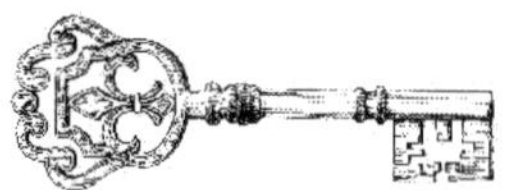

PART ONE
EAGLET:

QUESTION	PAGE NUMBER	ANSWER
1	p. 601	With Max
2	p. 601	On the ground
3	p. 601	"*Oui*, he used the letter opener, Cato."
4	p. 602	"I'm afraid it's too late. He's been poisoned. It won't be long now. Give them this moment."
5	p. 602	"Despair . . . not . . . the . . . tragic . . ."
6	p. 602	". . . that we can die but once . . . to serve our country."
7	p. 603	He grips his beak around a feather and pulls it out; Patrick
8	pp. 603–4	". . . having to tell those we love farewell while we remain behind."
9	p. 604	See ***Fill in the Blank*** below
10	p. 605	See ***Fill in the Blank*** below

Fill in the Blank from page 604:

"Extraordinary. While Cato was dying on the *outside* of the church, Patrick was 'dying' on the *inside* of the church." "My Henry" has also been dying on the *inside* from the weight of a grieving heart . . ." "Yet the Voice of the Revolution threw off his own chains of grief to exclaim Cato's words and rally a nation to Independence."

Fill in the Blank from page 605:

"Aye. Amazin' wha' this mission finally led ta." "Jest seven little words." "Give me liberty or give me death," "I do believe the power of those seven little words will forever soar through the air of freedom." "*Oui,*". . . on eagle's wings."

ANSWER KEY

Chapter 68: On Eagle's Wings

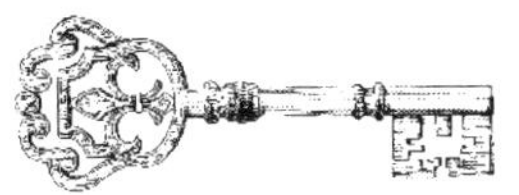

PART TWO

FLEDGLING:

QUESTION	PAGE NUMBER
1	p. 601
2	p. 601
3	p. 602
4	p. 602
5	p. 603
6	p. 603
7	p. 603
8	p. 604; Bible research
9	p. 604; **See *Fill in the Blank* on PAGE ONE, chapter 68 Answer Key**
10	p. 605; **See *Fill in the Blank* on PAGE ONE, chapter 68 Answer Key**

EAGLE:

QUESTION	PAGE NUMBER
1	p. 601
2	p. 601
3	p. 602
4	p. 602
5	p. 603; Opinion and reasoning
6	p. 603
7	p. 603
8	p. 604; Bible research; Reasoning
9	p 604; **See *Fill in the Blank* on PAGE ONE, chapter 68 Answer Key**
10	p 605; **See *Fill in the Blank* on PAGE ONE, chapter 68 Answer Key**

About the Epic Scribe . . .

Award-winning author and speaker Jenny L. Cote, who developed an early passion for God, history, and young people, beautifully blends these three passions in her two fantasy fiction series, *The Amazing Tales of Max and Liz®* and *Epic Order of the Seven®*. Likened to C. S. Lewis by readers and book reviewers alike, she speaks on creative writing to schools, universities and conferences around the world. Jenny has a passion for making history fun for kids of all ages, instilling in them a desire to discover their part in HIStory. Her love for research has taken her to most Revolutionary sites in the U.S., to London (with unprecedented access to Handel House Museum to write in Handel's composing room), Oxford (to stay in the home of C. S. Lewis, 'the Kilns', and interview Lewis' secretary, Walter Hooper at the Inklings' famed The Eagle and Child Pub), Paris, Normandy, Rome, Israel, and Egypt. She partnered with the National Park Service to produce Epic Patriot Camp, a summer writing camp at Revolutionary parks to excite kids about history, research and writing. Jenny's books are available online and in stores around the world, as well as in multiple e-book formats. Jenny has been featured by FOX NEWS on Fox & Friends and local Fox Affiliates, as well as numerous Op-Ed pieces on FoxNews.com. She has also been interviewed by nationally syndicated radio and print media, as well as international publications. Jenny holds two marketing degrees from the University of Georgia and Georgia State University. A Virginia native, Jenny now lives in Roswell, Georgia. To schedule Jenny to speak or for an interview, please visit her website: www.epicorderoftheseven.com.

. . . and her books.

BIBLICAL SAGA

FROM JENNY L. COTE

Available on audio

AMERICAN REVOLUTION SAGA

Available on audio

Coming 2022

VBS

PODCAST

WWW.EPICORDEROFTHESEVEN.COM

Upcoming books include two more American Revolution titles and a WWII Saga featuring C. S. Lewis. Jenny's books have been developed into VBS curriculum (*Heroes of HIStory*) with animation, and original music. Books one and seven are available in audio from Audible, with other books to follow. Tune in to the weekly Epic Order of the Seven: The Podcast hosted by Denny Brownlee, featuring Max, Liz, Nigel and Jenny. Future plans include Study Guides for all books, an animated TV/DVD series and feature film adaptation. Please visit: www.epicorderoftheseven.com and the Jenny L. Cote Facebook Page.

Eagle Feathers to Copy

The eagle feathers used throughout the VRK Study Guide for each level are presented here in different sizes, depending upon how you wish to use them for display. As you copy and cut them out, you may wish to label them to represent your accomplishment (ex: Chapter 7). Feel free to use any design you wish as your earned feather for each chapter, Nigel's Nuggets, or Cato's Eagle-Eye View, regardless of which level you complete. You may choose one design to be for your level (eaglet, fledgling, eagle), one design for Nigel's Nuggets, and one design for Cato's Eagle-Eye view. It's up to you!

Let your creativity soar with your earned eagle feathers and have fun decorating and displaying them with pride! Don't forget to share your creation with Jenny L. Cote by sending a picture to jenny@epicorderoftheseven.com and she'll post it on her website.

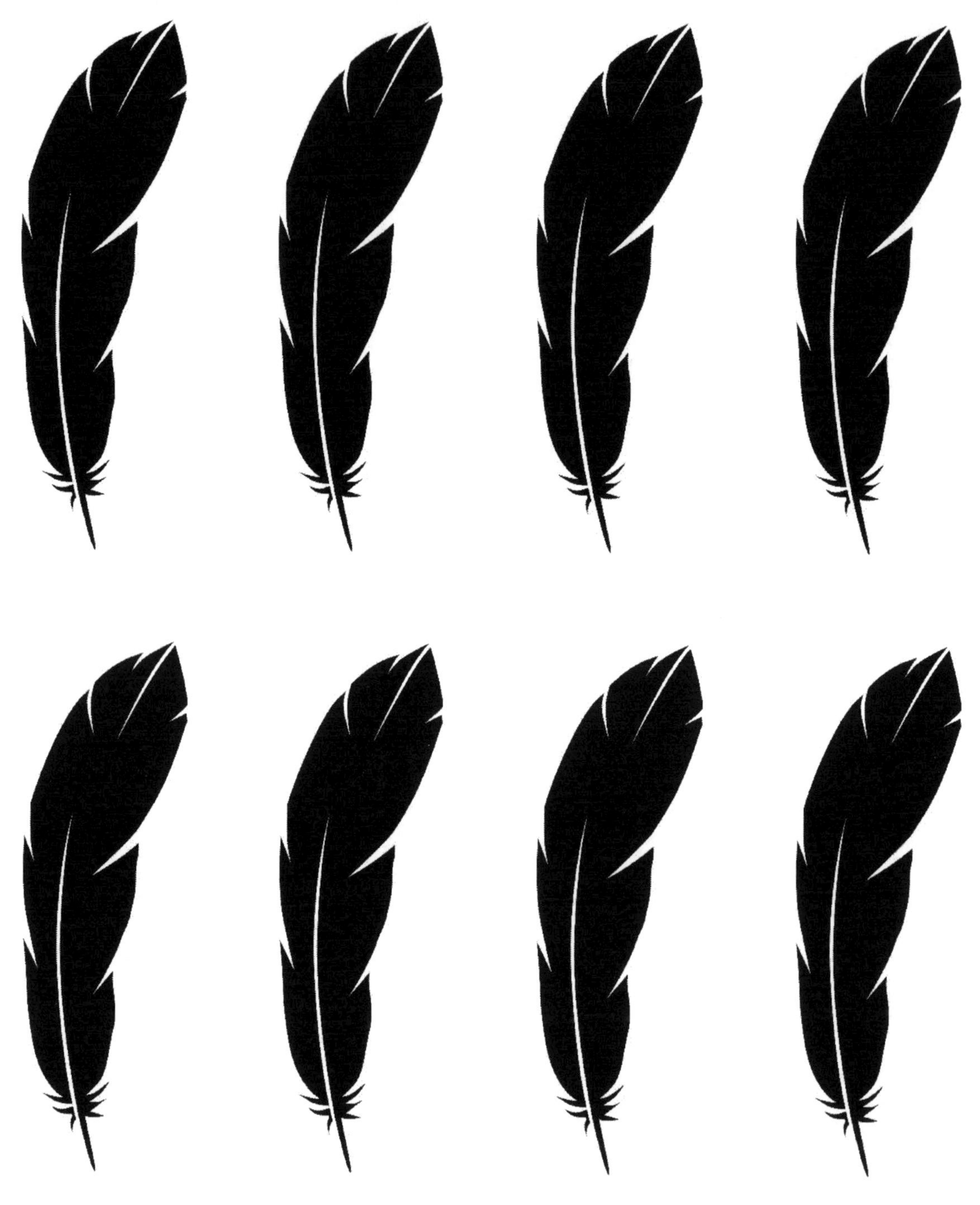

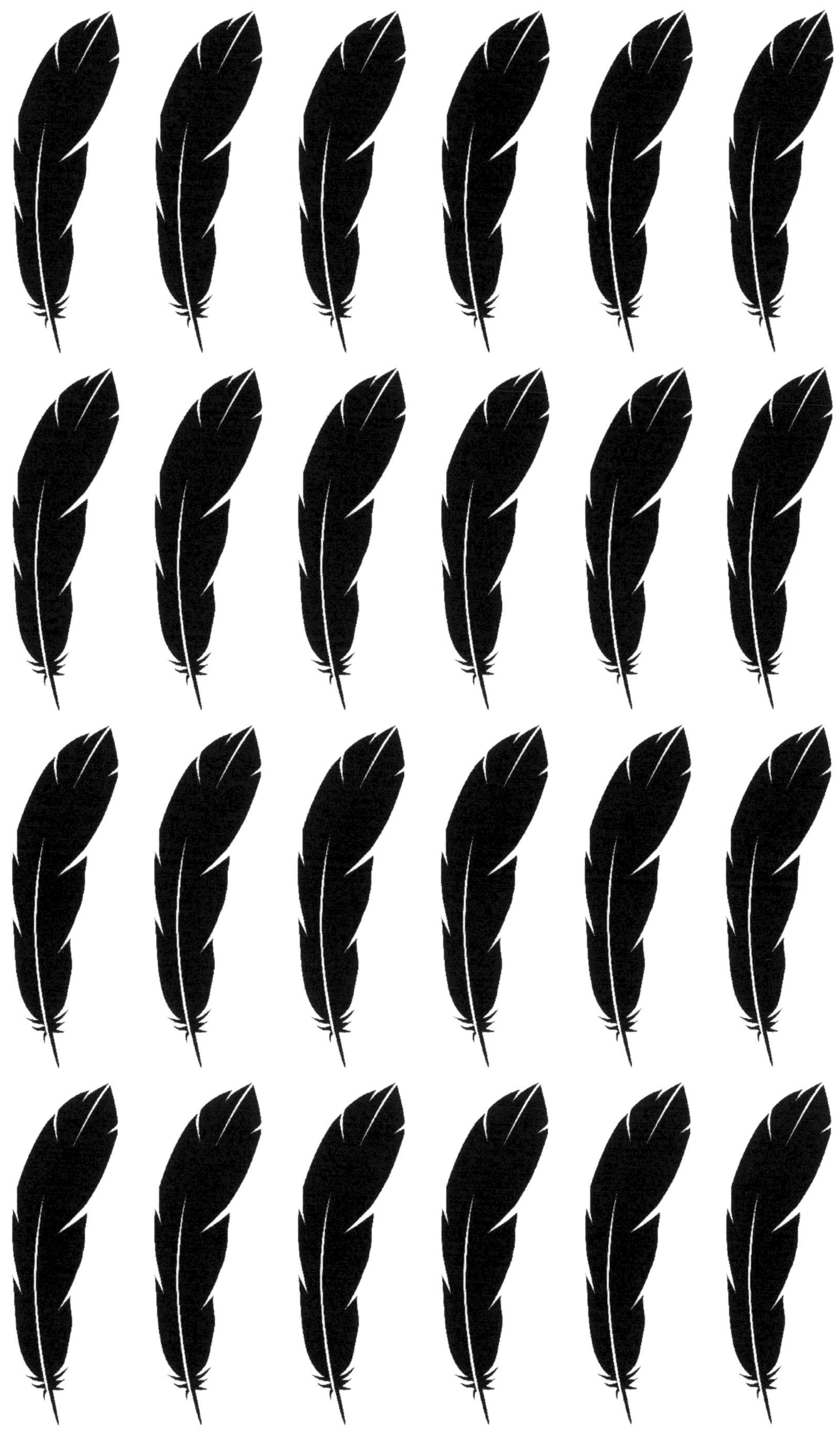

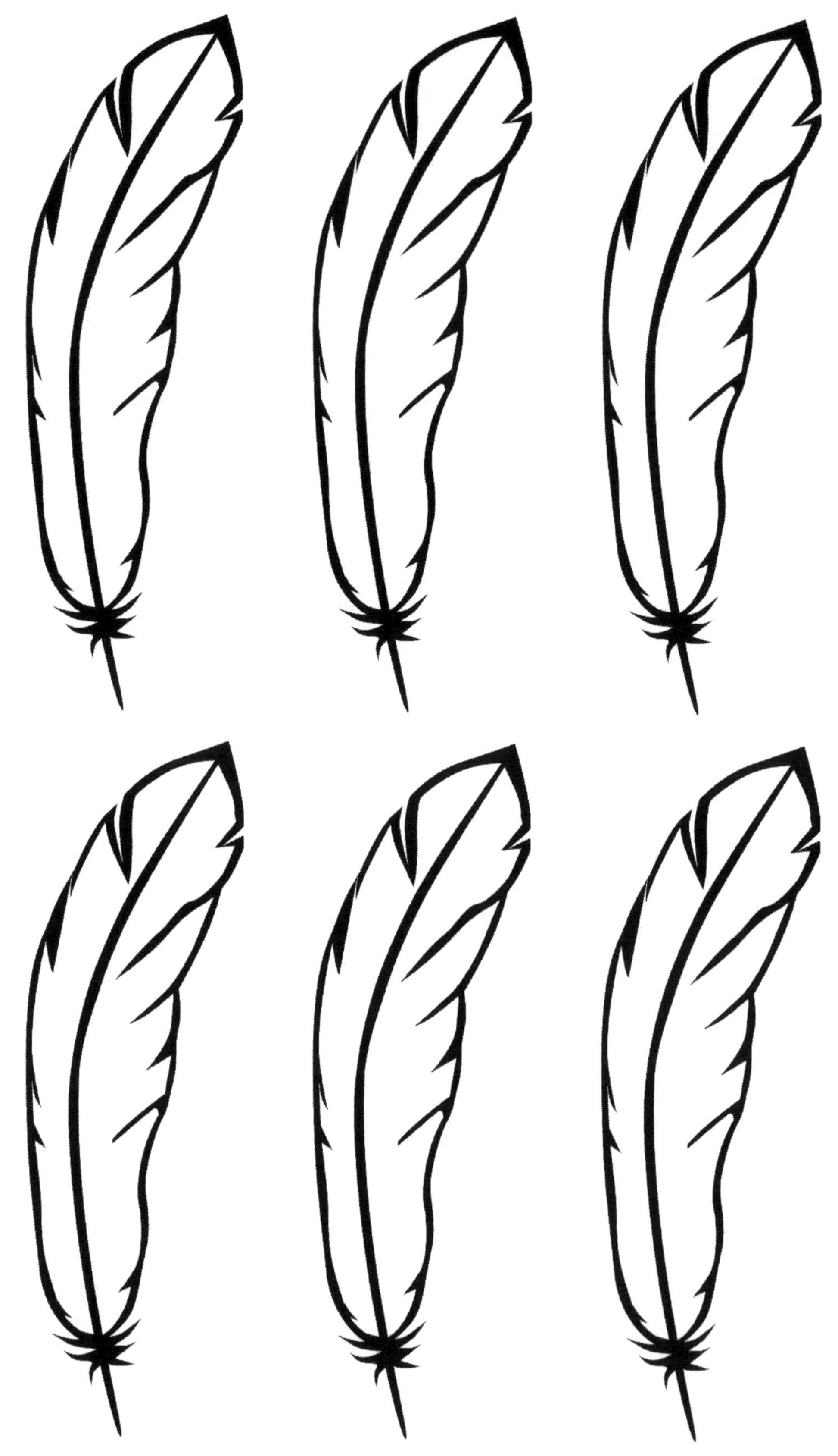

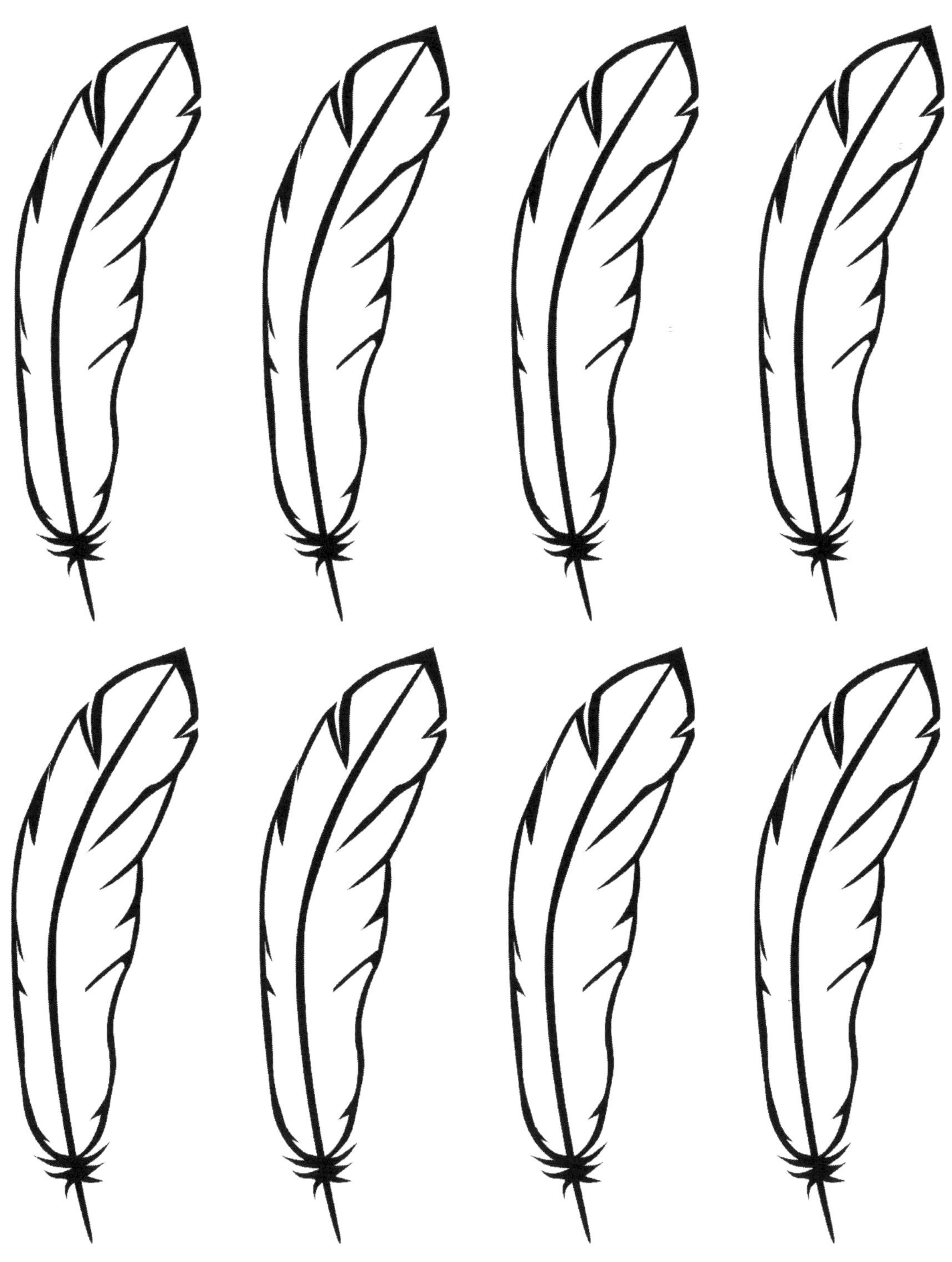

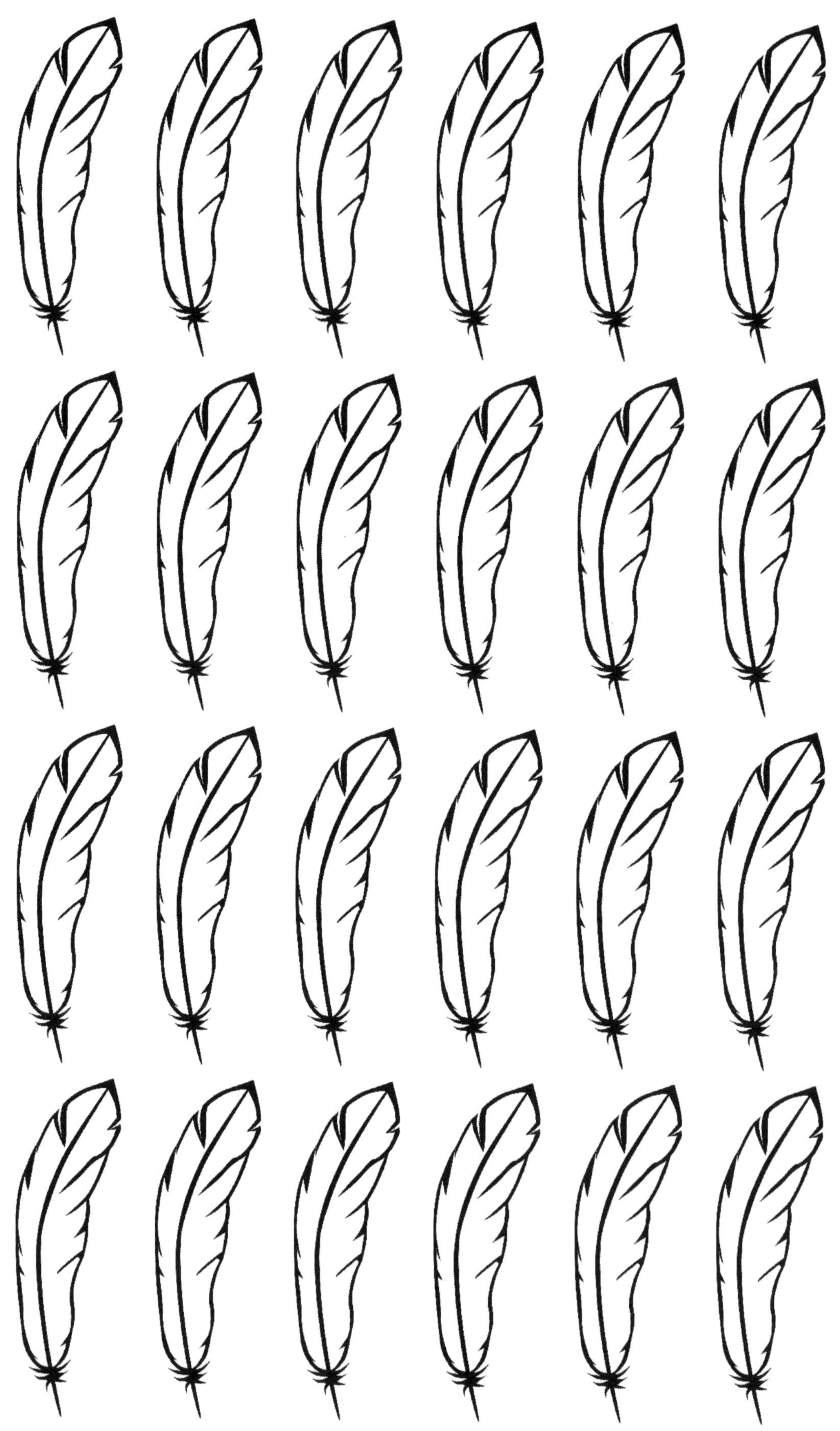

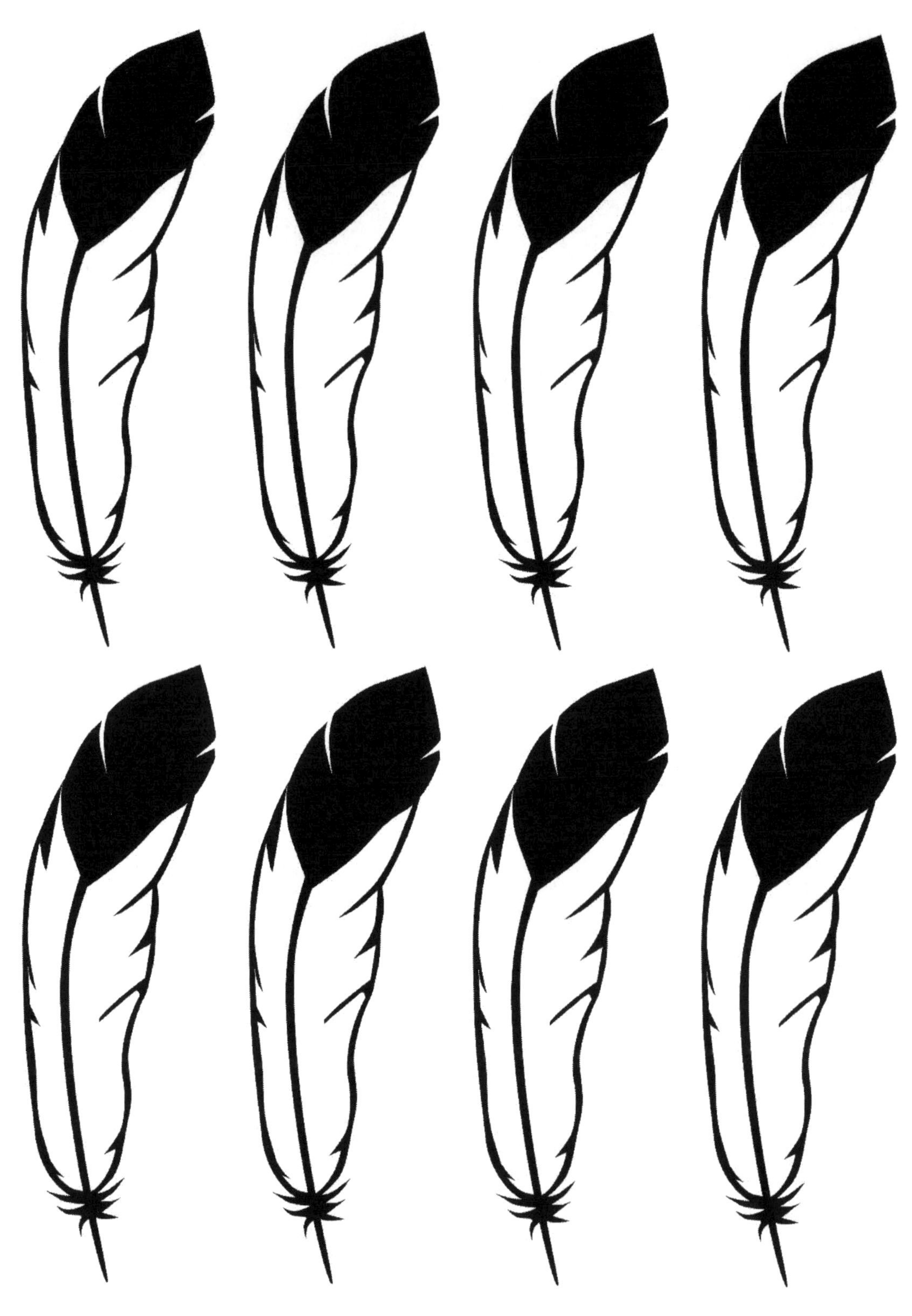

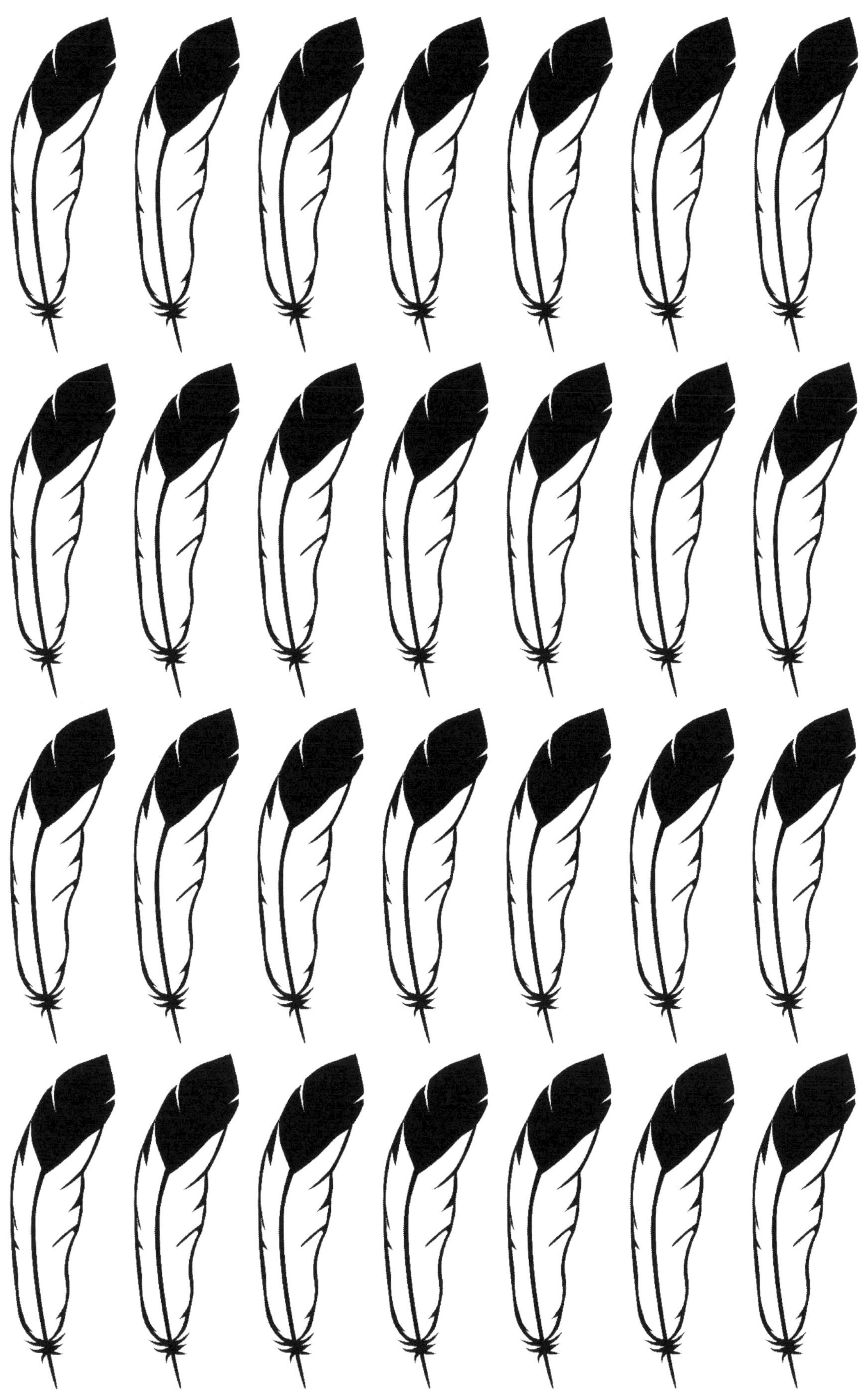

VRK BOOK PART TESTS & FINAL EXAMINATION

with Review Aid and Answer Keys

INTRODUCTION

This document contains four Book Part Tests and a Final Examination designed for families using the VRK Study Guide for a transcript credit. Please feel free to reformat or reduce the number of questions to best fit your family's needs. Also, do not hesitate to give a test orally. The test questions for the Book Part Tests and Final Examination are all taken from Eaglet Level questions from the VRK Study Guide. Questions will be in multiple choice, true/false, matching, or fill-in-the-blank format.

Each Book Part Test covers one of the four parts of the book. The Final Examination covers the entire book. Included with each Book Part Test and the Final Examination is a Review Aid with a list of specific Eaglet level question numbers with their corresponding VRK Study Guide chapters. This is the question bank to be used to study for the Book Part Tests and the Final Examination.

Please note, there are chapters not covered on the Book Part Tests. Readers should study the original Eaglet questions provided as a guide. Readers should not expect that the questions for the Book Part Tests or Final Examination will be worded in exactly the same manner as they appear in the VRK Study Guide.

The Book Part Tests consist primarily of history rather than literature questions. The Final Examination is heavily skewed toward history questions. An Answer Key is provided for each Book Part Test and the Final Examination. Book Part Tests are either 25 or 34 questions. The Final Examination is 100 questions.

Book Part One Test

The Voice, the Revolution, and the Key

PART ONE: FIDDLING AROUND (1743–45)

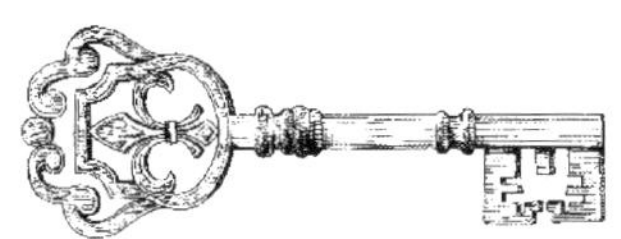

Review Aid

Book Part One Test

Chapter Number	**Questions**
Character Profiles	Pages xxv, xxvi
Prologue	7
1	5, 6, 7, 8
3	4
5	9
6	2
7	3
8	3, 10
10	7
12	3, 6
13	9, 10
15	8
16	6

Book Part One Test

The Voice, the Revolution, and the Key
PART ONE: FIDDLING AROUND (1743–45)

Questions 1–7: Matching

1) A well-fed orange Irish cat, scared of everything, lives to eat and sleep, immortal	A) Kate
2) A White West Highland Terrier, sweet, feisty, and always sticking up for the underdog, immortal	B) Clarie
3) A jolly intellectual British mouse, joined the team in Egypt, has impeccable manners, loves music, flies by carrier pigeon, immortal	C) Liz
4) A wise mountain goat, serves as a spiritual being, delivers mission assignments to the EO7, can take any form, immortal	D) Max
5) A sweet lamb from Judea, serves as a guide in the IAMISPHERE, can take any shape or form, immortal	E) Al
6) Curly-haired Black Scottish Terrier, faithful leader of the Team, brave, immortal	F) Nigel
7) Petite, brilliant black cat from Normandy, France, strategic leader of the team, immortal	G) Gillamon

Questions 8–12: Fill in the Blank

8) The seven words for which Patrick Henry is most famous are: ____________________

____ .

9) The unseen realm of how the Maker observes time—past, present, and future—all happening at once: ______________________________.

10) The first boy the EO7 sees in the IAMISPHERE is: ____________________________.

_______________ is assigned primarily to him.

11) The future _____________________________________ is the second boy the EO7 sees in the IAMISPHERE. ______________. Al is assigned to him.

12) _________________________________ will be Nigel's mission.

Questions 13–16: Multiple Choice

13) What kind of creatures does Patrick Henry identify by listening to their call?

A) Frog
B) Panther
C) Bird
E) Wolf

14) Where did the use of birthday candles originate?

A) Rome
B) London
C) Philadelphia
D) Athens

15) What are Gillamon and Clarie's natural forms?

A) A Scottie and a Westie
B) A Mouse and a Black Cat
C) An Orange Cat and a Lamb
D) A Mountain Goat and a Lamb

16) Who does not attend the St. Andrew's Day Festival, but might have gotten sick if he had?

A) Nigel
B) Al
C) Gillamon
D) Max

Questions 17–20: True/False

17) _________ Jane's friend is Sarah "Sallie" Shelton.

18) _________Uncle Patrick says a man needs a fiddle to woo a lass; a gun to provide for her and protect her with.

19) _________Paul was bitten by a snake.

20) _________Prince Frederick and Princess Augusta live at the White House.

Questions 21–25: Matching

21) Who has a collar that says, "I am His Highness's dog at Kew, Pray tell me, whose dog are you?"	A) Max
22) Whom does Liz set free without Gillamon knowing?	B) Cato
23) Liz and Gillamon leave the Tower of London with a creature in a bag. Who is it?	C) Molly
24) Whom does Patrick use to demonstrate flying?	D) Liz
25) Who said, "He has chosen to be an eagle and rise above his circumstances?"	E) Kakia

ANSWER KEY
Book Part One Test

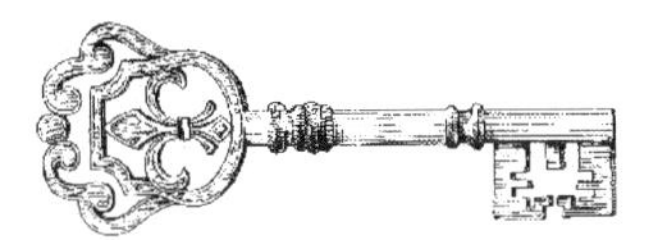

Questions 1–7: Matching

1) E
2) A
3) F
4) G
5) B
6) D
7) C

Questions 8–12: Fill in the Blank

8) "Give me liberty or give me death."
9) IAMISPHERE
10) Patrick Henry, Liz
11) King George III
12) Benjamin Franklin

Questions 13–16: Multiple Choice

13) C
14) A
15) D
16) B

ANSWER KEY

Book Part One Test

Questions 17–20: True/False

17) True

18) False

19) True

20) True

Questions 21–25: Matching

21) C

22) E

23) B

24) A

25) D

Book Part Two Test

The Voice, the Revolution, and the Key

PART TWO: RUMORS OF WARS (1745–59)

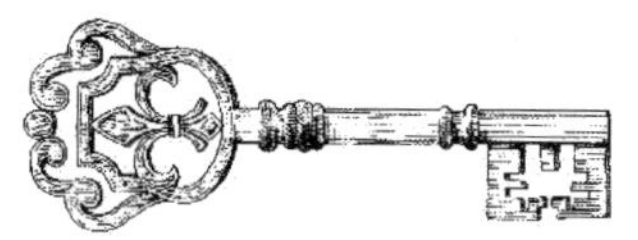

Review Aid

Book Part Two Test

Chapter Number	Questions
18	7
19	3, 10
20	4, 10
21	4, 6
22	4, 5, 10
23	9
24	4, 5
25	5, 9
26	2, 9
27	7, 8, 9
29	6, 10
30	9
32	2, 5, 9

Book Part Two Test

The Voice, the Revolution, and the Key
PART TWO: RUMORS OF WARS (1745–59)

Questions 1–5: True/False

1) __________John Henry says Samuel Davies has one of the most amazing memories he has ever seen.
2) __________Al brought Liz Glacier Lilies from the Alps.
3) __________Patrick broke his collarbone.
4) __________The panther that tried to hurt Patrick was later poisoned.
5) __________Samuel Davies gave Patrick a harmonica for a get-well gift.

Questions 6–11: Fill in the Blank

6) ______________________ wrote the Silence Dogood letters.

7) ______________________ began publishing *Poor Richard's Almanack* in 1732.

8) Liz named the new home of the Henry Family ___________________________.

9) Cato flew Nigel 200 miles from Virginia to _______________________, Pennsylvania.

10) Patrick called the ____

a declaration of independence.

11) Benjamin Franklin's proposed electricity experiment was successfully attempted in

______________________.

Questions 12–17: Matching

12) What is the name of the flying squirrel who barrels into Nigel and Cato?	A) Leonard
13) What is the name of the lizard with the flying squirrel?	B) Nelson
14) Who tells Patrick, "If I were any bettah, I'd be you?"	C) Elizabeth Strong
15) Who comes to Polegreen Church with Sarah Shelton?	D) Sarah "Sallie" Shelton
16) Who gives Patrick warm apple pie after he plays the fiddle at the Sheltons' barbeque?	E) Abraham Shamuel Penn
17) Who does Sallie give Patrick for Christmas?	F) Jack Poindexter

Questions 18–25: Multiple Choice

18) Who saves George Washington and Gist from being shot?

A) Howard
B) Al
C) Max
D) Gillamon

19) Who pushes against George Washington's foot and helps him back onto the raft when he falls in the river?

A) Howard
B) Al
C) Max
D) Gillamon

20) Whom does Patrick Henry marry?
A) Martha Custis
B) Elizabeth Strong
C) Beverly Lyons
D) Sarah "Sallie" Shelton

21) Whom does Cupid's arrow strike at Patrick's wedding?
A) Samuel Crowley
B) John Syme, Jr.
C) George Washington
D) Samuel Meredith

22) Who uses trees and stealth for cover in battle?
A) The Dutch
B) The Spanish
C) The British
D) The French

23) What kind of creature runs by Liz just before the EO7 realizes the Henry home is on fire?
A) A rat
B) A panther
C) A cat
D) A dog

24) Who goes back into the Henry home to save the fiddle from the fire?
A) Leonard
B) Nelson
C) Max
D) Howard

25) After the fire, Gillamon tells Liz and Nigel it is time for the Henry family to do something. What is it?
A) Rebuild Pine Slash
B) Leave Pine Slash
C) Move to Mount Brilliant
D) Move to Williamsburg

ANSWER KEY

Book Part Two Test

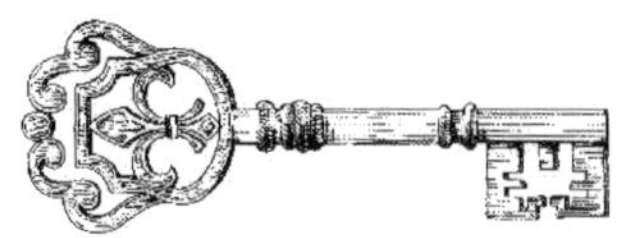

Questions 1–5: True/False

1) False
2) False
3) True
4) True
5) False

Questions 6–11: Fill in the Blank

6) Benjamin Franklin
7) Benjamin Franklin
8) Mount Brilliant
9) Philadelphia
10) Declaration of Arbroath
11) France

Questions 12–17: Matching

12) E
13) A
14) F
15) C
16) D
17) B

ANSWER KEY
Book Part Two Test

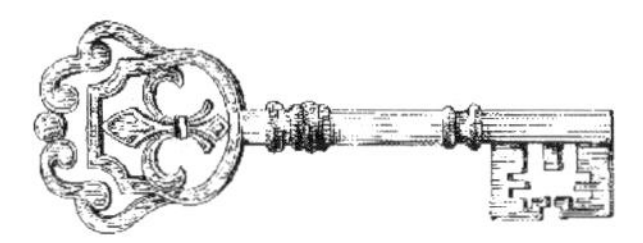

Questions 18–25: Multiple Choice

18) B

19) A

20) D

21) A

22) D

23) A

24) B

25) B

Book Part Three Test

The Voice, the Revolution, and the Key

PART THREE: DESPAIR NOT THE TRAGIC (1759-65)

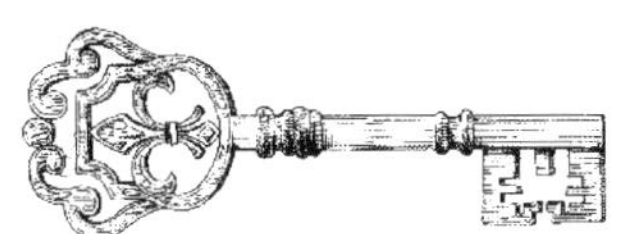

Review Aid

Book Part Three Test

Chapter Number	Questions
33	6
34	4
35	7, 8
36	6, 9
37	3, 6, 9
38	3, 7, 10
39	2
40	6, 9
41	2, 8, 10
42	4, 6, 9
43	3, 4
44	6, 7, 9
45	6, 7, 8, 9
46	6, 7
47	1, 3

Book Part Three Test

The Voice, the Revolution, and the Key
PART THREE: DESPAIR NOT THE TRAGIC (1759-65)

Questions 1–9: True/False

1) __________ Gilbert Lafayette, Kate's human, has not met his father because he is away at war.
2) __________ Court day in colonial Hanover County, Virginia, was held the first Thursday of the month.
3) __________ Elizabeth Strong became engaged to John Syme, Jr.
4) __________ Gillamon said the professions of minister, teacher, and lawyer called for the the gift of oratory.
5) __________ George Wythe prepared a certificate of recommendation signed by all the justices at Hanover Courthouse for Patrick Henry.
6) __________ Patrick Henry passed the College of William and Mary on the way into Williamsburg.
7) __________ George Wythe was the first examiner Patrick Henry saw in Chapter 37 of VRK.
8) __________ Robert Carter Nicholas declined to sign Patrick Henry's law license.
9) __________ Peyton Randolph examined Patrick Henry and signed his law license.

Questions 10–14: Multiple Choice:

10) What does John Randolph object to the moment he sees Patrick Henry?

A) He had showed up without an appointment.
B) He smelled badly.
C) He did not know Patrick Henry.
D) Patrick Henry's attire.

11) What did John Randolph advise Patrick Henry to purchase after he won his first few cases?

A) A new wig
B) A home in Williamsburg
C) A new set of clothing
D) A new horse

12) How old was Samuel Davies when he died?

A) 37
B) 24
C) 63
D) 49

13) Who is the lawyer who unsuccessfully argued for the people of Virginia in the Parson's Cause case?

A) John Randolph
B) John Lewis
C) George Wythe
D) Peyton Randolph

14) Who took over the Parson's Cause Case for the portion where damages were awarded?

A) John Lewis
B) Patrick Henry
C) Peyton Randolph
D) Robert Carter Nicholas

Questions 15–19: Matching

15) To whom does Patsey give a Marigold laurel?	A) The Parsons
16) This man objected to the jurors in the Parson's Cause Case.	B) Reverend (Uncle) Patrick Henry
17) Who walked into the courtroom before the defense attorney began his argument to the jury in the Parson's Cause Case?	C) Peter Lyons
18) Patrick Henry failed to speak highly of this group:	D) Patrick Henry
19) Patrick Henry said this group represented the British House of Commons.	E) The Burgesses

Questions 20–29: Fill in the Blank

20) Reverend Maury was awarded ____________________ in damages in the Parson's Cause Case.

21) It cost £____________________ pounds per year to maintain an army of ten thousand men in the North American Colonies in the 1760s.

22) ____________________ and ____________________ were being smuggled into the North American Colonies in the 1760s.

23) Patrick Henry's first word in the Virginia House of Burgesses challenged Speaker ________________________________.

24) Patrick Henry asked why the Burgesses would not even discuss ____________________ ____________________.

25) Patrick Henry said the Stamp Act Resolves did not represent the ____________________ ________________________________.

26) After ____________________________ read his seven proposed Stamp Act Resolves the chamber erupted into violent debate.

27) Patrick responded to accusations of treason by saying: ________________________ ____________________________________.

28) Patrick Henry's fifth proposed resolve was the first instance of a colony declaring independence from ____________________ by the British Parliament.

29) Patrick Henry's ____________________ Stamp Act Resolve was struck down after he left Williamsburg.

Questions 30–33: Multiple Choice

30) At the start of Chapter 46, over sixty young women and children had been attacked by:

A) Panthers
B) Snakes
C) Wolves
D) Rats

31) Who spurred a group of children on to surround a wolf until it let its victim go?

A) Gilbert Lafayette
B) Jeanne Boulet
C) Marie Lafayette
D) Jacques Portefaix

32) A reputation garnered through virtue, merit, great qualities, good actions, and Beautiful works:

A) Glory
B) Honor
C) Valor
D) Courage

33) What is the Lafayette Family motto?

A) Ab Initio
B) Cur Non
C) Sic Semper Tyrannis
D) Carpe Diem

Question 34: Fill in the Blank **(One Point)**

34) ______________________ says: "There's enough blue sky to knit a cat a pair of britches."

ANSWER KEY
Book Part Three Test

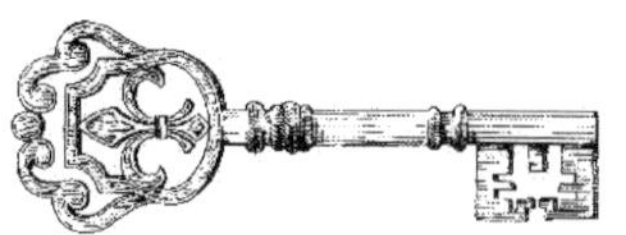

Questions 1–9: True/False

1) True
2) True
3) False
4) True
5) False
6) True
7) True
8) True
9) False

Questions 10–14: Multiple Choice

10) D
11) C
12) A
13) B
14) B

Questions 15–19: Matching

15) D
16) C
17) B
18) A
19) E

ANSWER KEY
Book Part Three Test

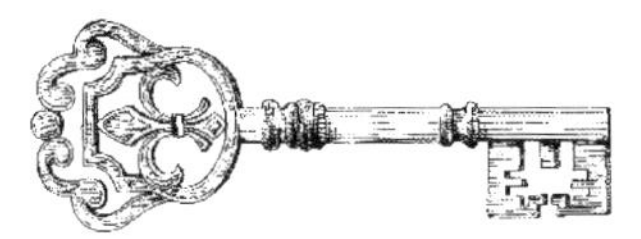

Questions 20–29: Fill in the Blank

20) One penny

21) £ 220,000

22) Molasses; sugar

23) John Robinson

24) The Stamp Act

25) The voice of the people

26) Patrick Henry

27) If this be treason, make the most of it.

28) Taxation

29) Fifth

Questions 30–33: Multiple Choice

30) C

31) D

32) A

33) B

Questions 34: Fill in the Blank **(One Point)**

34) MizP

Book Part Four Test

The Voice, the Revolution, and the Key
PART FOUR: LIBERTY OR DEATH (1765–75)

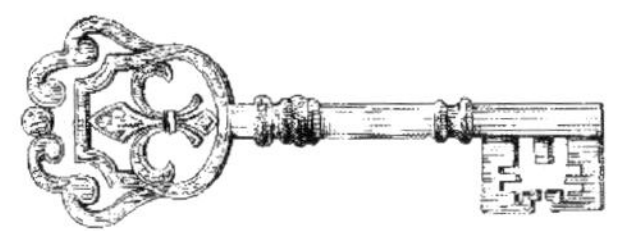

Review Aid

Book Part Four Test

Chapter Number	Questions
48	3, 5
49	7
50	2
51	2, 4
52	7
53	8
54	1, 5, 10
55	6, 8, 10
56	2, 6
57	7
58	1, 3, 7
59	4
60	2
61	8
62	4
63	8, 10
64	6
66	5, 6, 9
67	5
68	7, 8

Book Part Four Test

The Voice, the Revolution, and the Key
PART FOUR: LIBERTY OR DEATH (1765–75)

Questions 1–7: Multiple Choice

1) What paper first published the Stamp Act Resolves?

   A) *Newport News*
   B) *Pennsylvania Gazette*
   C) *Virginia Gazette*
   D) *Boston Gazette*

2) Boston's "Loyal Nine" became the:

   A) Boston Liberty League
   B) Massachusetts Free Press
   C) Sons of Liberty
   D) Patriots of America

3) What does Patrick Henry's name mean?

   A) Noble ruler of the house
   B) Loyal king of the land
   C) Royal son of the kingdom
   D) Wise ruler of the people

4) Which governor dissolved the Virginia House of Burgesses in response to the Stamp Act Resolves?

   A) Dinwiddie
   B) Fauquier
   C) Botetourt
   D) Dunmore

5) What did Cato, Nigel, and Botetourt have in common?

   A) They wore glasses.
   B) They had been bitten by a snake.
   C) They were born in London.
   D) They were bachelors.

6) Who described the Townshend Acts as: ". . . a flaming sword pointed at the people's liberties?

A) George Washington
B) Peyton Randolph
C) Patrick Henry
D) Richard Henry Lee

7) What is the name of the home Liz finds for the Henrys in Chapter 52?

A) Scotchtown
B) Pine Slash
C) Studley
D) Rural Plains

Questions 8–13: Matching

8) Who fired into an angry mob killing Christopher Seider?	A) Gilbert Lafayette
9) Who was the nineteen-year-old working at Wharton and Bowe Booksellers?	B) Ebenezer Richardson
10) Who had three hundred children dressed in white walk behind Christopher Seider's casket?	C) John Adams
11) The defense lawyer for Captain Preston and his men	D) Henry Knox
12) He trained to be a musketeer.	E) Lord Dunmore
13) He helped the cause of American Independence by trying to do the opposite.	F) Sam Adams

Questions 14–20: Fill in the Blank

14) John Adams said, "Facts are ______________________________."

15) Sallie Henry acted ______________________________ toward her children.

16) John Henry asked Patrick to hold on ta' ______________________________ ______________________________.

17) ______________________________ proposed a committee of correspondence throughout Massachusetts.

18) ______________________ delivered Benjamin Franklin's letter to Sam Adams at the beginning of Chapter 58.

19) ______________________________ is a figure of speech meaning that someone is used unknowingly by another to accomplish the other's own purposes.

20) The _________________________ dumped 340 chests of tea into the harbor to protest The Tea Act.

Questions 21–28: True/False

21) _________ England closed the New York harbor in response to the Tea Party.

22) _________ An extra-legal convention met in Richmond on August 1, 1774.

23) _________ The first question to spark a debate at the First Continental Congress was the way the colonies would vote.

24) _________ Benjamin Franklin proposed opening the sessions of the First Continental Congress with prayer.

25) _________ Cato named his eaglets Plutarch, Veritas, and Alexander.

26) _________ Gillamon left his magnificent red cloak for Patrick.

27) _________ In Chapter 64, Patrick says he counts Colonel Lewis as the first patriot to die in the Revolutionary War.

28) _________ Liz figures out that the fragment from Plutarch's "Winged Victory" has become Patrick's ivory letter opener.

Questions 29–33: Fill in the Blank

29) Liz and Nigel realized that the footprints on Plutarch's terrace were ______________.

She is not a ________________ being.

30) Liz and Nigel realize that Kakia could be like ___________________, for the EO7.

She might be able to change _______________.

31) Kakia gives Cato two choices regarding picking up the letter opener, liberty or death.

Cato chooses _______________.

32) Cato uses all his remaining strength to grip his beak around a feather and pull it out for

____________________.

33) Nigel says, "The price of _____________________________ is having to tell those we love farewell while we remain behind."

Question 34: Fill in the Blank **(One Point)**

34) Gillamon always says: "____

__________________________."

ANSWER KEY
Book Part Four Test

Questions 1–7: Multiple Choice

1) A

2) C

3) A

4) B

5) D

6) D

7) A

Questions 8–13: Matching

8) B

9) D

10) F

11) C

12) A

13) E

Questions 14–20: Fill in the Blank

14) Stubborn things

15) Violently

16) That precious jewel of liberty

17) Samuel Adams

18) Clarie

19) Cat's-paw

20) Bostonians

ANSWER KEY
Book Part Four Test

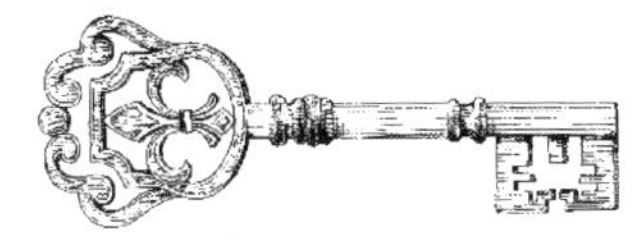

Questions 21–28: True/False

21) False

22) False

23) True

24) False

25) True

26) True

27) False

28) True

Questions 29–33: Fill in the Blank

29) Kakia, mortal

30) Gillamon, form

31) Death

32) Patrick

33) Being immortal

Question 34: Fill in the Blank **(One Point)**

34) Know that you are loved and you are able.

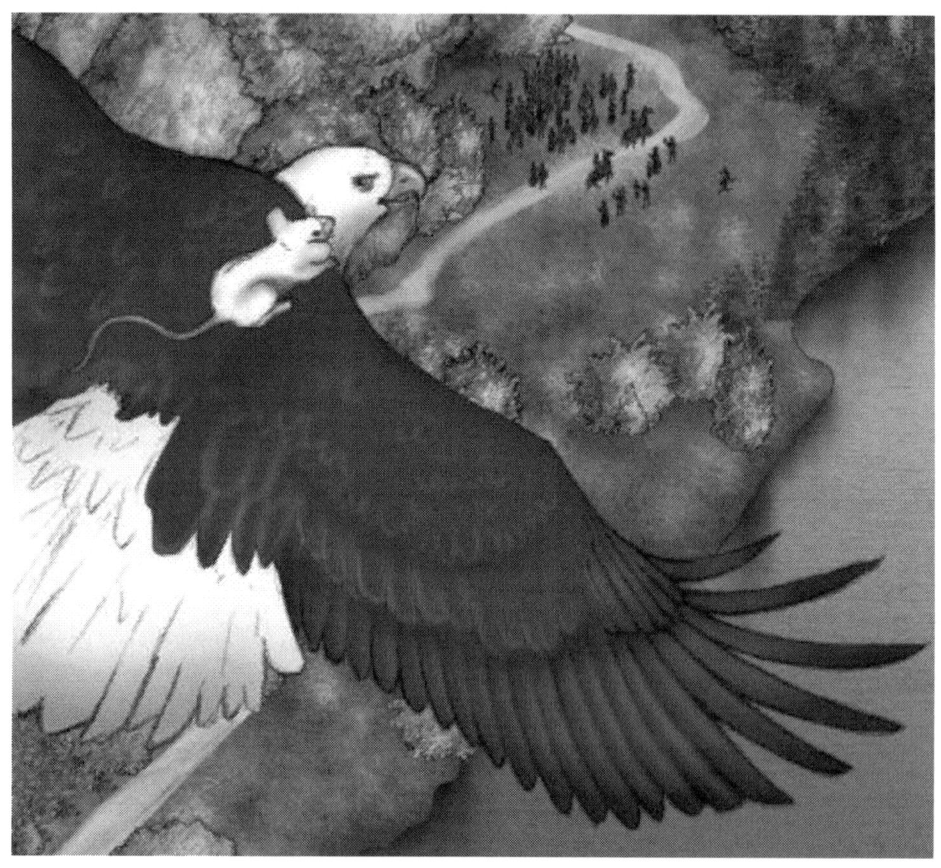

Final Examination

The Voice, the Revolution, and the Key

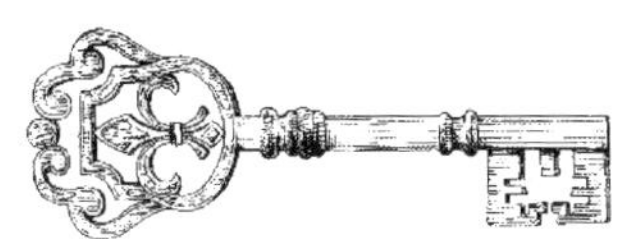

Review Aid

Final Examination

Chapter Number	Questions
Prologue	3, 5, 6
1	4
2	2, 6
3	2
5	1, 2, 9
6	7
9	2, 9
10	3
11	2, 3, 4, 7
12	2
13	2, 9
15	8
16	10
17	1, 2, 4
18	2
19	3
20	9
21	3
22	7

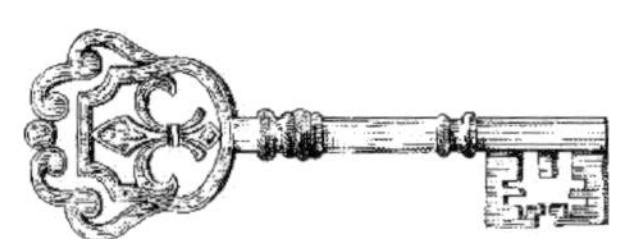

Review Aid

Final Examination

Chapter Number	Questions
23	3
24	10
25	2
26	8
27	3
28	1, 5, 8, 9
29	6
30	1, 6, 10
31	1, 9
32	3, 10
33	3, 7
34	2, 5
35	5
36	6
37	8
38	7, 9
39	5, 8
40	5, 10
41	9
42	5, 6, 9

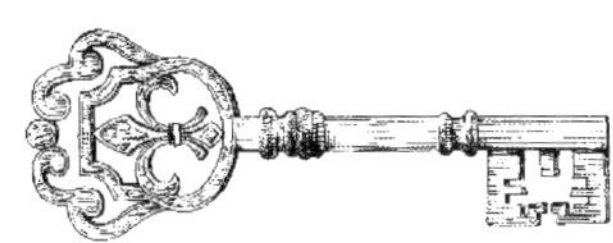 *Review Aid*

Final Examination

Chapter Number	Questions
43	2, 7, 8, 10
44	10
45	5, 7
46	9
49	2, 7
51	6
52	1
53	2, 10
54	8, 9
55	6
57	6
58	7, 10
59	7
61	7, 10
62	3
64	5, 6
65	1, 7
66	2, 10
67	5, 9
68	6

Final Examination

The Voice, the Revolution, and the Key

Questions 1–5: Matching

1) What was happening all over the world in 1943?	A) The Revolutionary War
2) What major war happened during Patrick Henry's life?	B) Thomas Jefferson
3) Sword of the Revolution	C) Patrick Henry
4) Voice of the Revolution	D) World War II
5) Pen of the Revolution	E) George Washington

Questions 6–10: True/False

6) _________ The King of England stood during the *Hallelujah Chorus*.

7) _________ It took the EO7 members about eight weeks to cross the Atlantic.

8) _________ Patrick Henry's family lived in Philadelphia, Pennsylvania.

9) _________ Hanover, Virginia, is closer to Williamsburg than to Richmond.

10)_________ Patrick's uncle, Patrick Henry, was the pastor of St. Paul's Parish, Hanover, VA.

Questions 11–20: Fill in the Blank

11) ____________________ was the first colony founded in America.

12) The use of birthday candles originated in _________________.

13) ____________________ was crucified on an "X" shaped cross.

14) The ______________________ determines whether you call it a violin or a fiddle.

15) "With all thy _________ love God above, and as thyself thy _____________ love."

16) _________ tracks are sharp and pointed.

17) Cato had two choices, ______________ or ______________.

18) Winged Victory was the name of the statue on __________________ desk.

19) Plutarch started the _________________ genre.

20) _______________ was Plutarch's ninth life.

Questions 21–30: Multiple Choice

21) Which city was the center of power for the entire world in the mid-eighteenth century?

A) Jerusalem
B) Rome
C) London
D) Athens

22) Who wrote the play *Cato?*

A) Demosthenes
B) Addison
C) Plutarch
D) Cicero

23) Liz sets a cat free from the menagerie in London. Who is it?

A) Kakia
B) Al
C) Charlatan
D) Cato

24) Whom does Patrick use to demonstrate flying to Cato?

A) Nigel
B) Max
C) Liz
D) Clarie

25) What did Cato devote himself to the study above everything of?

A) Ethics
B) The Law
C) Religious Studies
D) Moral and political doctrine

26) Where did George Whitefield preach when he was not assigned a pulpit?

A) On the grounds of St. James's Palace
B) At stagecoach stops
C) On the banks of the Thames
D) In parks and fields

27) Which Great Awakening preacher preached at St. Paul's Parish in Hanover in 1745?

A) Jonathan Edwards
B) Samuel Davies
C) Charles Wesley
D) George Whitefield

28) What was Samuel Davies' first posting (congregation)?

A) Polegreen Meetinghouse
B) St. John's Parish
C) St. Paul's Parish
D) Pine Slash Meetinghouse

29) What did Al bring Liz from the Alps?

A) Marigolds
B) Edelweiss
C) Alpine Aster
D) Erigeron

30) What caused the colonies to come together for the first time?

A) The Parson's Cause
B) The Boston Tea Party
C) The Great Awakening
D) The First Continental Congress

Questions 31–40 True/False

31) _________ *Pilgrim's Progress* and *Plutarch's Parallel Lives* became numbered among Benjamin Franklin's favorite books at age eleven.

32) _________ Benjamin Franklin attempted to electrify a turkey for a barbeque.

33) _________ Benjamin Franklin had an idea to put a metal rod atop a tower or steeple to draw the electrical charge from a cloud.

34) _________ Thomas Jefferson discovered that lightning is electricity.

35) _________ John Henry rented a small storefront for his sons.

36) _________ Patrick Henry gave Sallie Shelton a shawl of finest Brussels lace for Christmas.

37) _________ England, Holland, and Spain controlled most of North America in the mid-eighteenth century.

38) _________ George Washington informed Governor Dinwiddie of France's absolute intention to take possession of the Ohio.

39) _________ None of the wounded French prisoners survived the attack by Chief Half-King and other warriors.

40) _________ General Braddock mistakenly admitted to murdering Jumonville.

Questions 41–46: Fill in the Blank

41) Benjamin Franklin's 1754 cartoon said ______________ or ________________.

42) Patrick and Sallie Shelton moved into ________ ____________ farm when they got married.

43) Governor Dinwiddie asked _________________ to support a day of fasting and prayer.

44) _____________________ was George Washington's commander in the summer of 1755.

45) George Washington suggested that the British fight like the _______________.

46) _____________________ was killed in battle after declining George Washington's advice.

Questions 47–55: Multiple Choice

47) How many near misses does George Washington tell his brother, Augustine, he has had?

A) Two
B) Eight
C) Four
D) Six

48) Whom did Governor Dinwiddie call the colony's best recruiter?

A) Samuel Davies
B) John Henry
C) George Washington
D) George Whitefield

49) What happens to the house at Pine Slash Farm?

A) It is destroyed in a flood.
B) It is destroyed in a fire.
C) It is sold to the Shelton family.
D) It undergoes major renovations and additions.

50) Where do Patrick and Sallie move after they leave Pine Slash Farm?

A) Roundabout Plantation
B) Mount Brilliant
C) Hanover Tavern
D) Red Hill

51) What was the fourteenth-century home of the Lafayette family?

A) Versailles
B) Château d'Amboise
C) Cimetière de Picpus
D) Château de Chavaniac

52) Who was George Washington's wife?

A) Sarah Shelton Peyton
B) Martha Dandridge Custis
C) Abagail Lee Beverly
D) Elizabeth Isham Lyons

53) England triumphed over France in the following locations in 1758:

A) Vancouver and Indiana
B) Quebec and Ohio
C) Toronto and Pennsylvania
D) Nova Scotia and Vermont

54) How were the Justices of the Peace in colonial Hanover County, Virginia, paid?

A) Only their lodging expenses were reimbursed
B) All their travel expenses were reimbursed
C) They were paid a salary and their expenses were reimbursed
D) None of the above

55) What was Thomas Jefferson's course of study?

A) Political Science
B) Classical Literature
C) The Law
D) Natural Sciences and Engineering

Questions 56–60: True/False

56) _________ MizP is known for saying there is enough blue sky to knit a cat a pair of britches.

57) _________ George Wythe declined to sign Patrick Henry's law license.

58) _________ John Randolph agreed to see Patrick Henry with no reservations.

59) _________ John Randolph signed Patrick Henry's law license.

60) _________ King George II upheld the Two Penny Act shortly before his death.

Questions 61–70: Matching

61) First time England infringed on VA's rights	A) Void from its inception
62) John Henry's ruling on the Two Penny Act	B) James Otis
63) Patrick Henry called this group "rapacious harpies"	C) One penny
64) One of Thomas Jefferson's tutors	D) Repeal of the Two Penny Act
65) One protective king + his loyal subjects =	E) King George III
66) Damages awarded in Parsons' Cause Case	F) £ 10
67) Patrick Henry said the burgesses represent	G) Reverend Maury
68) Known for saying "What, what?"	H) The House of Commons
69) Amount of top range of Stamp Act tax	I) Freedom
70) Coined "No taxation without representation"	J) The Parsons

Questions 71–75: Fill in the Blank

71) ____________________________ coined the term Sons of Liberty.

72) Patrick Henry wrote seven Stamp Act Resolves on a leaf of paper from __________________ ______________________.

73) Patrick Henry said the true mark of _____________________________ is taxation by the People or their chosen representatives.

74) Patrick Henry said, "If *this* be _____________________, make the most of it."

75) Only _________________ had the right to bear arms in mid-eighteenth-century France.

Questions 76–80: Multiple Choice

76) What was the cost in trade due to the boycott of British goods in response to the Stamp Act?

A) £ 100,000
B) £ 750,000
C) £ 1,000,000
D) £ 5,000,000

77) What does Patrick Henry's name mean?

A) Noble ruler of the house
B) Loyal king of the land
C) Royal son of the kingdom
D) Wise ruler of the people

78) How many resolves opposing the Townshend Acts are passed by the Virginia Burgesses?

A) Four
B) Seven
C) Five
D) Six

79) What does Nigel drink from a thimble at Christmas?

A) Eggnog
B) Hot Buttered Rum
C) Mulled Wine
D) Wassail

80) Who recruited young boys as apprentices to stir up trouble with merchants?

A) The Carpenter's Guild of Boston
B) The Sons of Liberty
C) The Dissenters
D) The East India Tea Company

Questions 81–90: True/False

81) _________ Christopher Seider was killed by Ebenezer Richardson.

82) _________ Paul Revere published an etching entitled *The Bloody Massacre*.

83) _________ Intimidation is stretching the truth to inspire others to join your cause.

84) _________ John Adams said, "Facts are stubborn things."

85) _________ Lord Dunmore ordered troops to Boston.

86) _________ William Pitt stood trial in the Cockpit on behalf of the Bostonians for their actions during the Boston Tea Party.

87) _________ When Benjamin Franklin set foot in the Cockpit he was an Englishman. When he walked out the door, he was an American.

88) _________ King George III, Lord North, and Governor Hutchinson passed a resolution calling for a day of fasting, humiliation, and prayer.

89) _________ The First Continental Congress met in New York.

90) _________ Each colony got one, singular vote in the First Continental Congress.

Questions 91–95: Matching

91) The meetings of this assembly were secret	A) The First Continental Congress
92) The Indians were armed with these kinds of muskets and rifles at the Battle of Point Pleasant	B) William Pitt
93) The First scout killed at the Battle of Point Pleasant	C) Samuel Crowley
94) Who had restraining clothes made for them?	D) Sallie Henry
95) Who tried to convince Parliament to avoid war with the colonies?	E) British

Questions 96–100: Fill in the Blank

96) ____________________ thought the Second Virginia Convention should act as the government of Virginia.

97) America's first legislature met in a ________________ in Jamestown, Virginia, in 1619.

98) ____________________________ admonished those voting 'Aye' after Patrick Henry's Liberty or Death speech they were potentially declaring war against the King of England.

99) _______________ said, "What a pity that we can die but once to serve our country."

100) Gillamon always says: ____.

ANSWER KEY
Final Examination

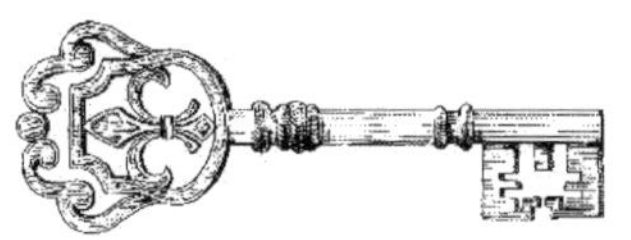

Questions 1–5: Matching

1) D
2) A
3) E
4) C
5) B

Questions 6–10: True/False

6) True
7) True
8) False
9) False
10) True

Questions 11–20: Fill in the Blank

11) Virginia
12) Rome
13) Andrew
14) Type of music played
15) Soul, neighbor
16) Deer
17) Liberty, death
18) Plutarch's
19) Biography
20) Cato

ANSWER KEY
Final Examination

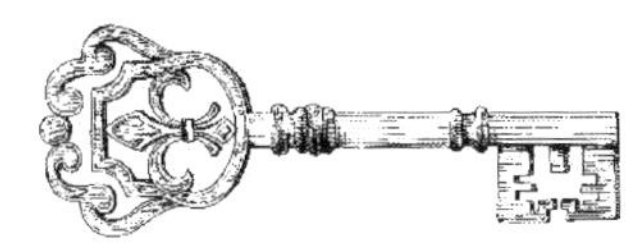

Questions 21–30: Multiple Choice

21) C

22) B

23) A

24) B

25) D

26) D

27) D

28) A

29) B

30) C

Questions 31–40: True/False

31) True

32) True

33) True

34) False

35) True

36) False

37) False

38) True

39) False

40) False

ANSWER KEY
Final Examination

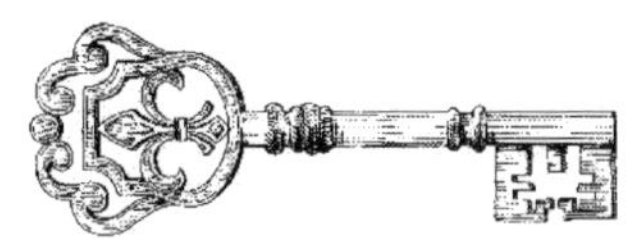

Questions 41–46: Fill in the Blank

41) JOIN, DIE

42) Pine Slash

43) Samuel Davies

44) General Braddock

45) French

46) General Braddock

Questions 47–55: Multiple Choice

47) D

48) A

49) B

50) C

51) D

52) B

53) B

54) D

55) C

Questions 56–60: True/False

56) True

57) False

58) False

59) True

60) False

ANSWER KEY
Final Examination

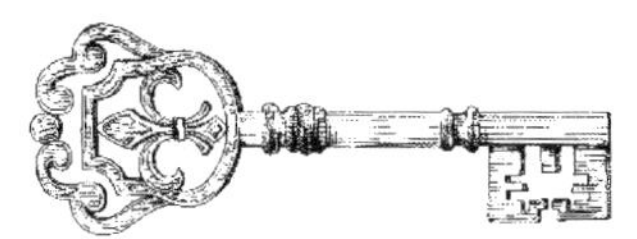

Questions 61–70: Matching

61) D

62) A

63) J

64) G

65) I

66) C

67) H

68) E

69) F

70) B

Questions 71–75: Fill in the Blank

71) Colonel Isaac Barré

72) *Coke Upon Littleton*

73) British freedom

74) Treason

75) Aristocracy

Questions 76–80: Multiple Choice

76) C

77) A

78) A

79) D

80) B

ANSWER KEY
Final Examination

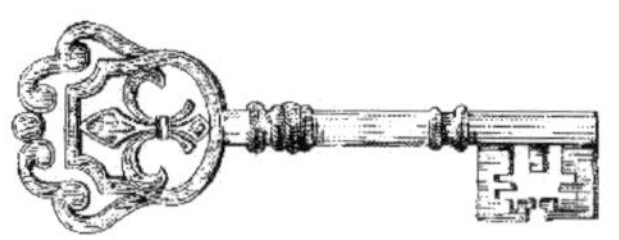

Questions 81–90: True/False

81) True

82) True

83) False

84) True

85) False

86) False

87) True

88) False

89) False

90) True

Questions 91–95: Matching

91) A

92) E

93) C

94) D

95) B

Questions 96–100: Fill in the Blank

96) Patrick Henry

97) Church

98) Peyton Randolph

99) Cato

100) Know that you are loved, and you are able.

Made in the USA
Columbia, SC
05 July 2021